The Devil in the New World

VITZILIPVTZILI
OV
VIZTLIPVZTLI

The Devil in the New World

The Impact of Diabolism in New Spain

Fernando Cervantes

Yale University Press

New Haven and London · 1994

Parentibus meis
Prioribus eorumque
Ex antiquis

Copyright © 1994 by Fernando Cervantes

Set in Monotype Columbus
Printed and bound in Great Britain by The Bath Press, Avon

Library of Congress Catalog Card Number: 94–60191

ISBN 0–300–05975–2

A catalogue record for this book is available from the British Library.

Contents

List of Illustrations

Acknowledgements

THE NUMBER OF debts I have incurred while preparing this book is far larger than I can justly repay in a short note, but it is a pleasure to begin by thanking David Brading who guided my research from its vague beginnings and for whose advice and perceptive criticisms I am deeply grateful. I am hardly less indebted to Anthony Pagden whose guidance and support at various stages has been invaluable, and to John Elliott who kindly read the complete manuscript and made a number of very helpful observations and suggestions. I am also grateful for the views of many friends and colleagues at Cambridge, many of whom read earlier drafts; in particular I wish to thank Susan Bayly, Eamon Duffy, Julius Lipner and Bob Scribner. A further word of gratitude is due to John Bossy, Stuart Clark, Christopher Martin and Heiko Oberman, who read and commented on a research paper dealing with much of what is now chapter 1, and to Herbert McCabe for his perceptive comments on what I thought was the final version of the chapter. I have also profited from conversations with James Alison, Francisco Arce, Gavin D'Costa, José Ignacio Echeagaray, Harman Grisewood, Serge Gruzinski, Andrew Hegarty, John Lynch, Alfonso Martínez, James McConica, Ken Mills, Hugo Nutini, Bob Ombres, Andrew Pyle, Dominic Scott, Dorothy Tanck, Elías Trabulse, Simon Tugwell, Daniel Ulloa and my father. At Yale I am especially grateful to Robert Baldock, Candida Brazil and Patty Rennie for the care with which they prepared the manuscript for publication, and to Malcolm Gerratt who was the most tactful and erudite of copy editors.

A year of research in Mexico would have been impossible without the hospitality of Rosa María Cervantes, Lolita and Gonzalo Robles, and my parents. I am also grateful to Leonor Ortiz Monasterio and the staff of the Archivo General de la Nación, and to Manuel Ramos and José Gutiérrez of the Centro de Estudios de Historia de México, Condumex, for their invaluable help with the illustrations.

It is also a pleasure to thank Leslie Bethell, Tony Bell and the staff of the Institute of Latin American Studies in London where, with the help of a Research Fellowship in 1989/90, I completed most of the research. During the last two years I have been given much free time to prepare the book for publication and for this I am grateful to Michael Costeloe, Gordon Minter and my colleagues at Bristol.

I also wish to express my gratitude to the British Academy for its generous funding of a research trip to Mexico in 1991, to the Arts Faculty Research Fund at Bristol for help with a further trip to Mexico in 1993, and to the various individuals who have lent me their support during the past few years: Manuel Arango, George Eccles, Miko and Dorothée Giedroyc, Fernando Ortiz Monasterio, Fr Manuel Ignacio Pérez Alonso and Fr John Tracy. Needless to say, my wife Annabelle has helped me most of all.

Finally, I thank the editors of *Past and Present* for allowing me to use material in chapters 4 and 5 which first appeared in my article 'The Devils of Querétaro: Scepticism and Credulity in Late Seventeenth-Century Mexico', no. 130 (February 1991), pp. 51–69 (World Copyright: The Past and Present Society, 175 Banbury Road, Oxford, England), and the editor of *Historical Research* for permission to reproduce a large part of my article 'Missionaries and Indians in Early Modern Mexico: The Native Response to the Devil', no. 160 (June 1993), pp. 177–96, in chapter 2.

Bristol, February 1994

Introduction

THE SUBJECT OF this book is as intriguing as it is neglected. Central though diabolism was in the early modern period to the so-called 'popular' cultural expressions that have become increasingly dominant in recent historiography, the subject of the devil is still one which is seldom addressed.[1]

This apparent incongruity is symptomatic of an approach to cultural history that has made diabolism both interesting and difficult to study. The interest is largely linked to the trend in recent historiography to move away from methods of studying the past that take little account of the culture of ordinary people. Cultural expressions that had traditionally been considered unworthy of scientific study have been brought to the forefront of historical investigations. The importance and widespread influence of diabolism and related beliefs and practices, formerly considered superstitious or irrational, can thus no longer be so easily dismissed by modern scholarship.

The difficulty, on the other hand, stems from an inescapable problem facing the historian of popular cultures. The fact that in the early modern period such cultures were primarily oral means that they are perceivable only through the 'filter' of literate sources where, for the most part, popular cultural expressions have been preserved in a somewhat deformed manner. It is true that this limitation should not necessarily lead to the conclusion that historians must content themselves simply with the views of the educated, without ever being able to reach the lost heritage of the illiterate.[2] Many justly famous studies have shown how the suitably critical

1   Apart from the studies by J. B. Russell – *The Devil: Perceptions of Evil from Late Antiquity to Primitive Christianity* (Ithaca and London, 1977); *Satan: The Early Christian Tradition* (Ithaca and London, 1981); *Lucifer: The Devil in the Middle Ages* (Ithaca and London, 1984); and *Mephistopheles: The Devil in the Modern World* (Ithaca and London, 1986) – it is difficult to think of any recent studies that deal seriously with the subject of diabolism.
2   This radical view is implicit in the work of Michel Foucault. See especially *Moi, Pierre Rivière, ayant égorgé ma mère, ma soeur et mon frère* (Paris, 1973).

use of certain types of archival sources can bring to light many peculiarities of marginal and forgotten cultures.[3] Yet it is undeniable that the success of such investigations largely depends upon the way in which they handle case histories and subject them to detailed analyses that cannot deal adequately with the wider cultural context.

Now it is clear that the idea of the devil cannot be subjected to such analyses without gross distortion. For if it is true that diabolism formed an integral part of popular cultures in the early modern period, it is no less clear that demonic beliefs and practices formed as much part of the culture of the 'educated élites'. It follows that if diabolism is to be properly understood, it needs to be studied at least as much from the perspective of intellectual history as from that of local cultural and social history.

It is small wonder, therefore, that the subject should have been largely avoided; for intellectual historians as a rule prefer to deal with subjects which are more readily understandable from a modern standpoint. A recurrent criticism levelled against them is that they tend to deal with the concepts of extremely circumscribed circles of intellectuals and that they have failed to take on board one of the most obvious lessons of social anthropology: that culture includes not just the ideas of the educated, but also the body of beliefs and practices experienced by the bulk of the population.

The generalized indifference that intellectual historians have shown towards the question of diabolism does indeed go some way towards justifying such criticisms. Yet it is curious that the critics of intellectual history fare no better than their adversaries when it comes to the devil. Despite the undeniable 'presence' of diabolism in the bulk of early modern popular cultural expressions, historians have been loath to see the subject as an integral part of such cultures. At best, the devil appears as a quaint appropriation of a dominant idea that provides good material for anecdote. At worst the concept is seen as an imposition of a hegemonic idea, masterfully deployed by the élites to keep the 'subordinate' groups under their grip.[4] It is a sharp irony that the note of embarrassment that underlies such interpretations is in many ways reminiscent of the aloofness that provides the target for the critics of intellectual history.

What we are faced with, therefore, is not so much the clash of two contrasting interpretations of the past, but the presence of two competing

3   Among others I have in mind the work of P. Burke, J. Caro Baroja, N. Z. Davis, J. Delumeau, C. Ginzburg, S. Gruzinski, K. Thomas, Y. Verdier. A good critical survey is J. Le Goff, 'Les mentalités: une histoire ambiguë', in J. Le Goff, ed., *Faire de l'histoire*, 1974, vol. 3, pp. 76–94.
4   The first tendency can be seen in, for example, E. Le Roi Ladurie, *Montaillou* (Harmondsworth, 1980), pp. 342–3, and K. Thomas, *Religion and the Decline of Magic* (Harmondsworth, 1978 edn), pp. 559–69. The most able example of the second tendency is C. Ginzburg, *I Benandanti*, Eng. trans. *The Night Battles: Witchcraft and Agrarian Cults in the Sixteenth and Seventeenth Centuries* (London, 1983).

schools presenting both sides of the same coin and basing their arguments on very much the same premise. On the one hand there are the intellectual historians whose sensitivity to the thought processes and needs that led to the rise and expansion of diabolism appears to have been blunted by a prejudice similar to that observed by Peter Brown in the traditional attitude towards the development of the cult of the saints; that is, the old supposition that a potentially 'enlightened' few, whose theism was identified with the 'elevated' message of Christianity, were being subjected to a continual upward pressure from the credulous and totally distinct superstitions of the 'vulgar'.[5] On the other hand there are the historians of popular cultures who, in converse fashion, tend to see those groups once classed as 'vulgar' as the bearers of a genuine and authentic culture.

Both schools are based on the same bipartite model. Yet there is no question that the idea of the devil belongs equally to both cultures and that it cannot be forced exclusively into either of them without gross simplification and impoverishment. Consequently, the subject of diabolism emphatically requires an approach that transcends the common division into 'popular' and 'élite' groups. Only thus will it be possible to understand early modern diabolism as part of a single culture in which both the popular and the educated had a share.

In an attempt to provide such an approach I have tried to place the bulk of the material analysed in the following pages (a high proportion of which originates from the 'popular' classes) in the context of the intellectual developments that dominate the period stretching from the discovery and settlement of the New World in the late fifteenth and early sixteenth centuries to the expulsion of the Jesuits in 1767; in other words, the period between the Reformation and the Enlightenment, during which the traditional belief in the devil underwent the most dramatic transformations in its history.

The obvious objection that arises from this is that, given that the devil is essentially a European construct, my choice of analysing its function and development in a non-European environment seems misplaced. My answer to this is twofold: in the first place New Spain cannot be understood without reference to Europe, since in many ways it was a land of the ancien régime, like Andalusia or Sicily; secondly, although its obvious differences with regard to Europe (especially the presence of Indians and blacks, with the consequent complications of race mixture and its effects on social organization and cultural interaction) in some ways complicate and obscure the analysis, in many others they make it more fruitful, and this *even* from the point of view of European history. For, as Serge Gruzinski has pointed out, it was precisely the sense of being confronted with cultures quite different

5   Peter Brown, *The Cult of the Saints: Its Rise and Function in Latin Christianity* (London, 1981), pp. 12–22.

from their own that led Europeans to take note of and to try to understand
what in Europe would have seemed too insignificant to be recorded.[6]

In choosing New Spain as my area of study, therefore, I have not merely
sought to understand the way in which a peculiarly European notion
adapted to an alien environment, I have also sought to explore the effects
that such new challenges had on the European notion itself. It is not merely that in the New World Europeans were confronted, as they never had
been before, with something quite dramatically 'other'. Perhaps more
significant is the way in which this European encounter with America
coincided with some of the most dramatic changes in European thought.[7]
How could we not wonder whether such coincidence was not linked to the
encounter itself?

The way in which these changes, seen in connection with the American
experience, affected the European notion of the devil constitutes a central
theme of this book. It has been my attempt to understand these changes
from the inside, as well as to bring to light the way in which they were
applied in the new continent. Thus, one of my central concerns has been
the conviction that the role of the historian is to attempt to understand the
past, as far as it is possible, on its own terms. This is not to claim that historians can at any time get away from the present. But it would be a very
impoverished present that did not show sympathy and understanding for
beliefs and convictions that now seem discredited to us. If readers of this
book come away with the realization that belief in the devil could have
appeared as rational and reasonable to the early modern mind as, say, belief
in the existence of viruses appears to us, it will have served its purpose.

6   Serge Gruzinski, *Man-Gods in the Mexican Highlands: Indian Power and Colonial Society
1520–1800* (Stanford, Calif., 1989), p. 6.
7   Anthony Pagden, *European Encounters with the New World: From Renaissance to Romanticism*
(New Haven and London, 1993), p. 12.

1

The Devil and the Amerindian

He that giveth his mind to the law of the Most High...will travel through strange countries.

Ecclesiasticus 39: 1–4

IT IS NOWADAYS difficult to appreciate the enormous significance that Columbus's voyage of discovery in 1492 had for contemporaries. From the vantage-point of the widespread negative reactions to the recent quincentenary celebrations of the event, the optimistic triumphalism of the early Castilian chroniclers – many of whom, in the famous phrase of Francisco López de Gómara, regarded the discovery as 'the greatest event since the creation of the world (excluding the incarnation and death of him who created it)'[1] – smacks of the blind and arrogant imperialism so forcefully denounced by the famous Dominican friar Bartolomé de las Casas, whose *Brevísima relación de la destrucción de las Indias* (1542) would eventually provide the cornerstone of the anti-Spanish 'Black Legend'. The influence of Las Casas, however, scarcely belittled the significance of the discovery of America. Nearly three hundred years after Columbus's first voyage the bulk of European opinion concerning the event could still echo López de Gómara. 'No event', wrote the Abbé Raynal in 1770, 'has been so interesting'; 'the most important event' wrote Adam Smith six years later, 'recorded in the history of mankind'.[2] The idea that these remarks were merely concerned with the discovery's effects upon commerce and material prosperity is belied by the little-known opinion of Father Pedro Alonso O'Crovley who, in 1774, wrote that America had 'filled all the vague diffusion of the imaginary spaces of man'.[3]

At the time of the discovery, however, O'Crovley's 'spaces' still had their roots in a long tradition of fantasy and legend which in part was the result of distorted interpretations of Herodotus – whose work was not translated into Latin until 1474, by Lorenzo Valla, in Venice – by travel writers and

---

1 *Historia General de las Indias*, Biblioteca de Autores Españoles, vol. 22 (Madrid, 1852), p.156.
2 Both cited in John Elliott, *The Old World and the New* (Cambridge, 1970), p. 1.
3 Cited in Anthony Pagden, *The Fall of Natural Man: The American Indian and the Origins of Comaparative Ethnology* (Cambridge, 1982), p. 10.

scientists throughout the middle ages. From the writings of Pliny, Mela, Solinus, Isidore, Vincent of Beauvais and Mandeville, among many others, Europeans had grown accustomed to expect the unusual and the fantastic to be the norm in remote corners of the world. Pliny's descriptions of garamantes, augiles, gamphastes, blemmyae, satyrs, scythians, arimaspi, thibii, and so on, were fittingly complemented by Isidore's giants, pygmies, cyclops, hermaphrodites and dog-faced men. The repetition of stale descriptions of fabulous peoples became almost compulsive in the late middle ages. Four out of the twelve 'best-sellers' of the fourteenth and fifteenth centuries dealt with marvels, and the hold of classical monsters upon the European mind made itself felt in poetry and drama as well as in sermons and in works of science.[4]

It is perhaps understandable that such a deep-rooted tradition should have remained apparently unshaken by the discovery of a new and remote continent, patently populated by beings who did not fit into its ancient and confident classifications. It is no great surprise, for instance, that Columbus's observations of the New World should have been so elaborately distorted by Peter Martyr, whose memorable transformation of the Caribbean into the abode of Amazons, green and yellow popinjays, golden pebbles, nightingales and lions, foreshadowed the vision of Rabelais, the chief exponent of a fabulous and nightmarish image of America, brilliantly captured in the art of Theodore de Bry[5] (see Plates 1 and 2).

Perhaps more surprising is the way in which traditional fables and legends were confirmed by many of the early explorers and discoverers. The power of myth over the imagination was compelling enough to make Europeans see exactly those very things they had gone out to find: giants and wild men, pygmies, cannibals and Amazons, women whose bodies never aged and cities paved with gold.[6] Yet, underneath all this, the medieval preconceptions of savagery began to lose their hold on the European mind. It was not so much that once savagery was seen face to face it could be described with the calm and surprisingly modern realism that characterize the Columbian accounts; for this attitude was short-lived, and later descriptions by explorers like André Thevet and Sir Walter Raleigh still hark back to the medieval imagination. The change took place at a more fundamental and inescapable level. It entailed the inevitable dissipation of the medieval indifference to the customs and behaviour of remote

4   Margaret Hodgen, *Early Anthropology in the Sixteenth and Seventeenth Centuries* (Philadelphia, 1964), pp. 20, 36–40, 57–8, 67.
5   On the sloth with which Europeans assimilated the significance of the new continent see Elliott, *Old World*, especially pp. 1–53. On Peter Martyr and Rabelais see Hodgen, *Early Anthropology*, pp. 31–3.
6   Antonello Gerbi, *La natura delle Inde nuove* (Milan and Naples, 1975), pp. 45–58; Angelo Maria Bandini, *Vita e lettere di Amerigo Vespucci* (Florence, 1745), p. 68. And see Pagden, *Fall of Natural Man*, p. 10.

Plates 1 and 2. Scenes by Theodore de Bry depicting the contrasting European perceptions of the New World as a place inhabited by either noble savages or degenerate cannibals.

.15.

heathen peoples. Indeed, from the earliest days of the discovery a clearly
ethical preoccupation with the nature and behaviour of the inhabitants
of America began to emerge. The theme of the primeval innocence and
nobility of the natives was constantly challenged by the no less arresting
insistence on their bestiality and the demonic character of their culture and
religion. Where Columbus and Vespucci could refer to the abundance and
fertility of the New World in a way that led Peter Martyr to contrast the
simplicity of the natives with the barbarism of their European invaders,
others, like Dr Chanca and Francisco de Aguilar, had no qualms about
writing of their 'bestiality...which [is] greater than that of any beast in the
world', or about the unlikelihood of the existence of 'another kingdom in
the world where the devil was honoured with such reverence'.[7]

Before about 1530 it would have been difficult to predict which one of
these views would emerge as dominant, for they can both be seen as equally characteristic of the time. The confident humanism at the heart of
Burckhardt's classic account of the Renaissance was just as pervasive as the
sense of disillusionment so finely portrayed by Huizinga in his *The Waning
of the Middle Ages*, and it is likely that moral judgements on the customs and
behaviour of the Indians were more influenced by the background and
interests of those who came into contact with them than by any overriding preconceptions they might have had. By the middle of the sixteenth
century, however, the picture looked very different. A negative, demonic
view of Amerindian cultures had triumphed and its influence was seen to
descend like a thick fog upon every statement officially and unofficially
made on the subject. The reasons for this enigmatic development are confused and contradictory; but I want to suggest that they should not necessarily be so.

*

From a modern perspective, it is tempting to see the eventual triumph of
the negative view of Amerindian cultures in the context of the irksome
issue of legitimation. It is well known that the Castilian crown's principal
claim to dominion in America rested on the bulls of donation made by
Pope Alexander VI in 1493. These bulls were grounded on the papal
assumption of 'plenitude of power', meaning temporal authority over both
Christians and pagans, an assumption that had no basis in natural law and
about which the lawyers and the theologians were known to be uneasy.
Once the Caesaro-papal claims of the bulls were questioned, the Castilian
crown would be deprived of any rights and would only be left with the

---

7   *Select Documents illustrating the Four Voyages of Columbus*, ed. Cecil Jane (London, 1930), i,
p.71; Francisco de Aguilar, *Relación breve de la conquista de Nueva España*, ed. F. Gómez de
Orozco (Mexico City, 1954), p. 163. On humanist writers see Elliott, *Old World*, pp. 1–27.

duty to evangelize.[8] In this context it would soon become clear that the more the natives were perceived to be under the power of Satan the more urgent the European presence became. It is no accident that the bulk of the sermons, both lay and ecclesiastic, that were preached to the American Indians in these early years sought to provide syntheses of Christian doctrine centred on the themes of liberation from sin and from the power of the devil, where the Spanish appear as bearers of the gospel's message, sent 'to give light to those who sit in darkness and in the shadow of death'.[9]

The obvious danger of this interpretation is that it tends to reduce the figure of the devil to a mere instrument of political expediency, and to underestimate the genuine belief of most contemporaries in the reality of diabolism. Yet attempts to counteract this tendency are apt to lead to the opposite, and perhaps more misleading, danger of giving the subject of diabolism too much importance too early. To place the devil of the discoverers in the context of the developments that would subsequently lead to the European witch-hunts is not only misleading but fundamentally erroneous. In the early years of the discovery, the figure of the devil makes more sense when set in the context of a confident quest for marvels than if seen as the expression of a pessimistic distrust of alien cultures. As Inga Clendinnen has written, the early discoverers

> were not vexed by Indian perfidy, nor deeply perturbed by grotesque idols, nor even by the possibility, suggested by some strange sculpted figures, that these people lacked a proper abhorrence of sodomy. For in those places they also found gold; and with gold, much more than a mere means to personal material advancement, they could transform the world....[10]

'Gold is most excellent', Columbus wrote in a famous passage. With it 'treasure is made, and he who possesses it can do as he wishes...and even drive souls into Paradise'.[11] The famous assertion of Bernal Díaz del Castillo that the Spaniards had gone to the New World 'to serve God and the King, and also to get rich' has, in the words of John Elliott, a 'disarming frankness'[12] that cannot be appreciated without reference to a positive view of the created world, a world much closer to the humanist vision of

8   Anthony Pagden, *Spanish Imperialism and the Political Imagination* (New Haven and London, 1990), p. 14.

9   Joaquín Antonio Peñalosa, *El Diablo en México* (Mexico City, 1970), p. 15. See the accounts of Bernal Díaz del Castillo (*Historia verdadera de la conquista de la Nueva España*) and Hernán Cortés (*Cartas de relación*). The Gospel passage is from Luke 1:79.

10   Inga Clendinnen, *Ambivalent Conquests: Maya and Spaniard in Yucatán (1517–1570)* (Cambridge, 1987), pp. 13–14.

11   Cristóbal Colón, *Textos y documentos completos*, ed. Consuelo Varela (Madrid, 1982), p. 327.

12   J.H. Elliott, *Imperial Spain* (Harmondsworth, 1970), p. 65.

Plate 3. The Knight, Death and the Devil by Albrecht Dürer

Erasmus's *Enchiridion Militis Christiani*, so memorably captured by Dürer in his famous engraving of the knight who advanced with open visor undeterred by death and the devil, than to the insecurities and accusations of the witch-hunts[13] (see plate 3). If it is true that the world of the conquistadores was regarded as the battleground of the conflict of good and evil, of the armies of God with his angels and his saints against Satan and his demons, it had nonetheless been redeemed. If the battle was extended in history, on the plane of eternity it had been won inexorably by the death and resurrection of Christ. No matter how formidable he might appear, the devil had no chance against the inevitable advance of Christ's Church.

This confident outlook pervaded the attitudes of the first explorers. According to Gonzalo Fernández de Oviedo, for instance, Columbus

13   On this see Hugh Trevor-Roper, *Princes and Artists: Patronage and Ideology at Four Habsburg Courts 1517–1633* (London, 1991 edn), pp. 20, 25, 35–6.

noticed with admiration the devotion that the Indians of Cibao had to
their deities and he even persuaded his companions to follow their example; for 'there was even more reason for Christians to cease from sin and to
confess their errors' so that, 'being in a state of grace with God Our
Saviour, he would give them more freely the temporal and spiritual goods
they sought', just as he rewarded the Indians with gold.[14] This tendency
received perhaps its best illustration in the conquest of Mexico, and particularly in Hernán Cortés's perception of the religious practices of the
Mexican Indians, described with surprising level-headedness in one of his
letters to Charles V. In a well-known passage Cortés explains how he made
it clear to Moctezuma and his companions that their man-made idols were
not worthy of the worship due to the one true God of the Christians. 'And
everyone', he writes

> especially the said Moctezuma, replied that…owing to the very long
> time that had passed since the arrival of their ancestors to these lands, it
> was perfectly possible that they could be mistaken in their beliefs…and
> that I, as a recent arrival, should know better the things that they
> should hold and believe.[15]

The significance of this passage resides in Cortés's apparent conviction
that the Indians were normal human beings, whose level of civilization was
'almost the same as the Spanish',[16] and whose 'errors', far from being the
result of direct demonic intervention, were more due to human weakness
and susceptible to instruction and correction. Accordingly, whenever
Cortés ordered the destruction of Indian 'idols' he invariably replaced them
with crosses and images of the Virgin, often entrusting the very same
Indians who had been responsible for the care and propitiation of the
defeated idols with the care of the new Christian images.[17] This initiative
reflects Cortés's hope that as soon as the Christian message was preached
to the Indians they would readily acknowledge the errors of their ways
and set their house in order. Implicit in this was a positive view of human
nature, almost reminiscent of St Thomas Aquinas's dictum that grace does
not destroy nature but perfects it.

It would, of course, be a mistake to push this connection too far.
Cortés's letters were carefully angled to win the approval of the emperor

14   Gonzalo Fernández de Oviedo, *Historia general y natural de las Indias*, ed. Juan Pérez de
Tudela Bueso, Biblioteca de Autores Españoles, 5 vols (Madrid, 1959), i, pp. 120–1.
15   Hernán Cortés, *Cartas de relación*, ed. M. Alcalá, 10th ed. (Mexico City,1978), p. 65.
Unless otherwise specified, all translations are my own.
16   Ibid., p. 66.
17   Díaz del Castillo, *Historia verdadera*, various editions, passim, especially chapters lxxvi-
lxxvii. The practice was opposed by the Mercedarian chaplain Bartolomé de Olmedo who
favoured a more thorough instruction in the basic principles of the Christian faith.

and the Council of the Indies, and there can be little doubt about the imaginary nature of the above passage, 'more of a story, a means of inventing a fable to serve his purpose by an astute, wise and artful captain', as Fernández de Oviedo would later remark.[18] Moreover, his sympathetic portrayal of the religious attitudes of the Indians is at variance with other accounts, notably Bernal Díaz's, where the conqueror's conduct is at times more reminiscent of the medieval tendency to see non-Christians as heathen devils. Nevertheless, the attitude of Cortés towards the Indians could hardly be compared to the portrayals of infidels that characterize the *chansons de geste*, where the Muslims appear as physical monsters or as horned demons who rushed into battle barking like mad dogs. In the late middle ages such views had been tempered by more favourable perceptions of non-Christians, especially after the Mongol mission in the thirteenth century, reflected in the new proposals to study Arabic in the University of Paris and in Raymond Lull's foundation of the college of Miramar in Majorca in 1276.[19] By the late fifteenth century the attitude seemed firmly entrenched. In Spain it achieved its most characteristic embodiment in the career of Hernando de Talavera, the first archbishop of Granada, whose interest in Arabic culture did much to reconcile the Muslims to the new Christian government of Ferdinand and Isabella after the conquest of Granada in 1492. It is true, as is well known, that Talavera's ideal of a process of gentle assimilation, from which both Muslims and Christians would gain, was soon challenged by the zealous intolerance of the archbishop of Toledo, Francisco Jiménez de Cisneros, who in 1499 introduced a policy of forcible conversion and mass baptisms. But Cisneros's attitude must not be interpreted as a reactionary hankering after the old medieval ideals of the Reconquista. The emphasis was on conversion, and the policy of mass baptisms without any previous preaching or instruction belied a triumphalist optimism and a somewhat naive confidence in the power of the sacraments against heresy and error.

The parallel with Cortés's approach is immediately evident. It is no great surprise that shortly after the conquest of Mexico Cortés asked Charles V to send a contingent of Franciscan friars (not secular priests or bishops, who 'would not abandon the custom...of squandering the assets of the Church in pomps and other vices') with the specific mission of converting the Indians of New Spain to the Christian faith.[20] Recruited from the newly founded, reformed province of San Gabriel de Extremadura, the twelve Franciscans who arrived in Mexico in 1524 were animated by a fervent millenarian hope in the rebirth of the Church in the New World.

---

18   Quoted in D. A. Brading, *The First America: The Spanish Monarchy, Creole Patriots and the Liberal State, 1492–1867* (Cambridge, 1991), p. 35.
19   Hodgen, *Early Anthropology*, pp. 87–9. On the Mongol mission see *The Mission to Asia*, ed. Christopher Dawson (London, 1980).
20   *Cartas*, pp. 203–4.

Their first experiences soon turned this hope into a positive certainty, for the conversion of the Indians appears to have been carried out in the midst of an enthusiasm submerged in ritual euphoria. The way in which thousands of Indians flocked to hear the Christian message and submitted readily to baptism soon confirmed the missionaries' belief that the millennium and the ultimate defeat of the devil were close at hand. In early Franciscan plays, the Indian leaders are made to recognize the Spaniards as the 'children of the Sun' and to acknowledge that they have been under Satan's rule. Through vivid representations of the battle between St Michael and Lucifer the Indians are persuaded that the demons are the erstwhile leaders of their doomed way of life, and the plays end with the humiliation and defeat of the devil to mark the beginning of the millenarian reign of true charity.[21] The same attitude can be seen in some early Franciscan representations of the triumph of the cross over hordes of helpless-looking demons. In Diego Muñoz Camargo's *Descripción de Tlaxcala* the devils appear in unmistakably medieval fashion, with the standard claws, bat wings, horns and tail.[22]

But this optimistic millenarianism never went unchallenged. The Dominicans, in particular, were critical of the Franciscan approach to baptisms *en masse*, and insisted upon the need for careful instruction in the basic principles of the faith before the administration of baptism and the other sacraments. Nor was it very long before their observations began to ring true, for despite the destruction and confiscation of idols it was soon discovered that clandestine native practices had anything but disappeared. Idolatry was deemed so widespread that in the early 1530s the Franciscan Archbishop of Mexico, Fray Juan de Zumarrága, in sharp contrast with the policies of his coreligionists, saw fit to implement the first inquisitorial practices against idolatrous and superstitious Indians.

Few moments in history are filled with more bitter irony. The thought of a Franciscan friar, who was also a humanist, conversant with the writings of Erasmus and author of a treatise which spelled out Christian doctrine in simple language, acting out the role of inquisitor general, engaged in a ruthless and frantic persecution of unfaithful Indian apostates which culminated in the burning at the stake of a charismatic Indian leader, would have seemed like a very bad kind of nightmare to the early missionaries.[23] And yet it is difficult to imagine an alternative course of action

21 M. Ekdahl Ravicz, *Early Colonial Religious Drama in Mexico: From Tzompantli to Golgotha* (Washington, D.C., 1970), p. 73; Richard C. Trextler, 'We think, They Act: Clerical Readings of Missionary Theater in Sixteenth-Century New Spain', in Steven L. Kaplan *Understanding Popular Culture: Europe from the Middle Ages to the Nineteenth Century* (Berlin, 1984) pp. 192, 203–5.
22 It is interesting to note that some also have the head-dresses and paint of pre-Columbian deities. Muñoz Camargo's was writing in the mid-1580s and by that time the association of devils with pagan deities (discussed below) had become firmly entrenched.
23 Archivo General de la Nación, Mexico City, Ramo Inquisición (hereafter A.G.N., Inq.),

Plate 4. Demons falling by virtue of the cross after the arrival of the Franciscans.

open to the archbishop. After all, the Indians were no longer innocent pagans awaiting Christian enlightenment, but proper Christians, baptized and allegedly instructed, and therefore subject to the same disciplinary treatment that was used in Europe against the sins of idolatry, heresy and apostasy. It seemed evident that all these crimes were widespread and thriving among the Indians. Idols were constantly being hidden in caves. Human sacrifice, although less frequent, lingered on, and it was very common to find young men with their legs cut open or with wounds in their ears and tongues inflicted with the purpose of providing human blood for the idols.[24] More alarming were a number of similarities that could be detected between Christian practices and native rites. Fasting, for instance, was an indispensable prelude to the sacrifices which, as a rule, ended in a communal banquet, often accompanied by the ingestion of hallucinogenic mushrooms, *teunanacatl* in Nahuatl. As Fray Toribio de Motolinía explained to the Count of Benavente, this term, translated literally into Spanish, meant 'the flesh of god', 'or of the devil whom they adore'.[25]

tomo 2, exp. 10 (hereafter 2.10); printed as *Proceso inquisitorial del Cacique de Texcoco*, Publicaciones del A.G.N., vol. 1 (Mexico City, 1910). A good summary is Richard E. Greenleaf, *Zumárraga and the Mexican Inquisition 1536–1543* (Washington, D.C., 1961), pp. 68–74.
24   A.G.N., Inq., 37.1; 40.7; 30.9; 40.8.
25   Fray Toribio de Motolinía, *Historia de los indios de la Nueva España* (Mexico City, 1973 edn), p. 20. A.G.N., Inq. 38(I).7. The ambivalent use of the words 'god' and 'devil' is not fortuitous: it corresponds to the ambivalent nature of Mesoamerican deities; see below, pp. 40–41.

Plate 5. The burning of idols.

How was it possible for the Christian sacraments to find such striking parallels in the idolatrous rites of remote pagans? At best the phenomenon could be explained as the result of a mysterious initiative on the part of God to prepare the Indians for the reception of the gospel. This indeed had been Motolinía's hope when confronted with some infant-bathing ceremonies which seemed to him to resemble baptism.[26] But such hopes were not easy to hold in face of the more frequent orgiastic ceremonies that were encountered and which seemed to the friars to represent a form of pseudo-sacramentalism imbued with Satanic inversion.

The crumbling optimism of the second decade of Franciscan evangelization was a reflection of the growing conviction among the missionaries that Satanic intervention was at the heart of Indian cultures. It had become clear to the friars that the deities of the Indians were not merely false idols but, in the words of Fray Bernardino de Sahagún, 'lying and deceitful devils', whom he was careful to represent as such. In the illustrations of the Templo Mayor, for instance, he gave Tlaloc a bearded goat-like visage, while Huitzilopochtli appears as an open-mouthed devil (see plate 6). 'And', he continued in the introduction to one of the sections of his monumental ethnographic compilation,

> if it be thought that these things are so forgotten and lost, and that faith in one God is so well planted and firmly rooted among these natives

26 Motolinía, *Historia*, p. 85.

that there is no need to speak about them,...I am also certain that the Devil neither sleeps nor has forgotten the cult that these Indian natives offered him in the past, and that he is awaiting a suitable conjuncture to return to his lost lordship.[27]

Such anxieties reached a dramatic climax in 1562, when the discovery of widespread idolatry at Mani, the centre of the missionary enterprise in Yucatán, led to the most extreme and ruthless interrogations and tortures in the history of conversion in Mexico. An official inquiry established that 158 Indians had died during or as a direct result of the interrogations. At least thirteen committed suicide rather than face the inquisitors. Eighteen disappeared; and many were crippled for life, their shoulder muscles irreparably torn, their hands paralysed 'like hooks'. Although Fray Diego de Landa, the Franciscan provincial responsible for the campaign, was summoned to Spain to answer charges, it is symptomatic of the new preoccupation with diabolism that, in the event, he was exonerated and indeed subsequently appointed bishop of Yucatán. There was, after all, no question as to his honesty and zeal. 'Being idolaters', he had explained, '...it was not possible to proceed strictly juridically against them...because...in the meantime they would all become idolaters and go to hell.'[28]

Attempts to account for this dramatic change of attitude on the part of the missionaries have led historians into a plethora of conflicting explanations. It could be said that 'the violence of the missionaries sprang in large measure from the shock of betrayal'.[29] Equally, it could be argued that the effects of the Reformation in Europe had tended to deprive the New World of some of the best elements of the Spanish missionary orders, now more concerned with the Protestant heretics than with those 'sad priests of the devil' with their 'obscene and bloody devotions and lacerations', as Diego de Landa would write.[30] Or again, one could say that as the colonization of the new territories became the increasing concern of the state, evangelization tended to become more a matter of acquiescence based on faith, authority and tradition than a matter of assent based on reason and argument.[31] My aim here is not to add a further explanation to the list but,

27 Bernardino de Sahagún, *Historia general de las cosas de Nueva España*, 6th edn. (Mexico City, 1985), pp. 704–5.
28 Inga Clendinnen, *Ambivalent Conquests*, pp. 76–7. See also her article, 'Disciplining the Indians: Franciscan Ideology and Missionary Violence in Sixteenth-Century Yucatán', *Past and Present*, no. 94 (Feb. 1982), pp. 27–48.
29 D. A. Brading, 'Images and Prophets: Indian Religion and the Spanish Conquest', in Arij Ouweneel and Simon Miller, eds, *The Indian Community of Colonial Mexico* (Amsterdam, 1990), p.185.
30 Clendinnen, *Ambivalent Conquests*, pp. 50–1, 119–20.
31 See, for example, Sabine MacCormack, "The Heart has its Reasons": Predicaments of Missionary Christianity in Early Colonial Peru', *Hispanic American Historical Review*, 65 (3) (Aug. 1985), pp. 443–5.

Plate 6. The demonization of Tlaloc
and Huitzilopochtli.

rather, to attempt to shed some light on such explanations by concentrating on the concept of the devil, a theme central to them all. My contention
is that a better appreciation of the philosophical intricacies of the idea of,
and the belief in, the devil can provide for a clearer appreciation not just of
the change of attitude we have detected, but also of the wider context of
the early modern European preoccupation with diabolism.

*

By the middle of the sixteenth century, the chief characteristics that would
go into the making of the early modern witch-hunts had been known for
many centuries. Already in the New Testament the devil can be seen as the
personification of evil: a being who did physical harm to people by attacking or possessing their bodies, who tempted them and who accused and
punished sinners. In contrast to the limits posed on the concept of the
devil by the rabbinic tradition, the early Christians seem to have expanded

and strengthened it by identifying Satan and his demons with the fallen angels. Origen of Alexandria was one of the first Christian thinkers to identify Satan with Isaiah's Daystar, Ezekiel's Prince of Tyre and Job's Leviathan,[32] thereby removing him decidedly from his previous divine origin and making it possible to clarify the nature and the ranks of good and evil angels and the extent of their power over nature and over men. This in turn prepared the ground for the teachings of the monks of the desert, for whom demonic temptations came to represent an ideal opportunity to participate in the cosmic struggle between Christ and Satan, and whose copious and vivid hagiographies imbued the personifications of evil with the chilling realism that has haunted the western imagination ever since.[33]

Yet a marked confidence in the power of the Church against the devil and his works was always effectively preserved. Indeed, a central and essential feature of the devil in Christian thought is his complete subordination to the will of God. From the earliest days Christian theologians repeatedly emphasized this point. Hermas, Polycarp and Plutarch taught that the devil had no power over the human soul; Justin Martyr, that the devil was a creature of God, with an essentially good nature which he had merely deformed through his own free will;[34] and Irenaeus and Tertullian, that the devil's powers over men were limited, since he could not force them to sin against their will. The view that evil was not an independent principle was to be reinforced by the Alexandrians, especially Clement and Origen, who were among the first to assert that evil does not exist in itself[35] and whose teachings would in turn prepare the ground for St Augustine's classic definition which denied evil all ontological existence.[36]

32   Isaiah, 14: 12–15 ('You who used to think to yourself, "I will climb up to the heavens and higher than the stars of God I will set my throne....I will rival the Most High."...Now you have fallen to Sheol, to the very bottom of the abyss!'); Ezekiel 28: 12–19 ('You were once an exemplar of perfection, full of wisdom, perfect in beauty....[But] your heart has grown swollen with pride....You have corrupted your wisdom owing to your splendour....You are an object of terror'); Job 40–41 ('From his mouth come fiery torches....His nostrils belch smoke....His breath could kindle coals...fear leaps before him as he goes...of all the sons of pride he is the king'). (Trans. Jerusalem Bible.) On Origen's demonology see J. B. Russell, *Satan: The Early Christian Tradition* (Ithaca & London, 1981), pp. 129–48.

33   Russell, *Satan*, pp. 166–85; Peter Brown, *The Body and Society: Men, Women and Sexual Renunciation in Early Christianity* (London, 1990), pp. 228–30.

34   J.B. Russell, *Satan*, pp. 42–50, 60–72.

35   Ibid., pp. 80–148.

36   St Augustine, *City of God*, xi.22, xii.3. Augustine's thesis was further expanded by St Thomas Aquinas in the thirteenth century. 'The perfection of a thing', he explained, 'depends on how far it has achieved actuality. It is clear, then, that a thing is good inasmuch as it exists....For everything, inasmuch as it exists, is actual and therefore in some way perfect. It follows then that, inasmuch as they exist, all things are good' (*Summa Theologiae*, Ia. 5. 1–3.); it follows also that 'nothing can be essentially evil, since evil must always have as its foundation some subject, distinct from it, that is good'; thus, 'there cannot be a being which is supremely evil, in a way that there is a being that is supremely good because it is essentially good' (*Compendium Theologiae*, ch. xvii).

If evil had no substance, no actual existence, no intrinsic reality, if nothing was by nature evil, then a principle of evil – an evil being independent of God – was an absurdity. The persuasive power of this philosophical principle in medieval Christian thought is difficult to overestimate. It can be seen at work even in those areas furthest removed from philosophy. Outside the monastery, for instance, the vivid and frightening devil of monastic spirituality was often toned down to the point of impotence. Thus the stories of Gregory of Tours in sixth-century Gaul follow the guidelines of Evagrius Ponticus and John Cassian in aiming to be amusing and light and in invariably leading to happy endings in which the saints triumphed over their demonic adversaries, often in a humorous way.[37] Even the more strictly juridical or canonical expressions of the Christian struggle against Satan, such as the exorcisms of the possessed, were set in a context of unshakable confidence. As Peter Brown has explained, exorcism was held to be the one irrefutable sign of *praesentia*: the physical presence of the holy. It was 'the one demonstration of the power of God that carried unanswerable authority'.[38]

It would seem that this conviction about the impotence of Satan against God and his Church was badly shaken in the early modern period. The reasons for this are complex and well beyond my scope, but some significant developments that can be traced back to the middle ages are in need of some emphasis.

One of these is the transposition of monastic spirituality from the cloister onto the secular world that the Gregorian reformers and their successors encouraged from the late eleventh century onwards. As Edward Peters has suggested, given that the secular world lacked the liturgical defences of the monastery, the motives and ideals that had led to the development of the monastic devil associated with sermons, *exempla* and hagiographies assumed a very different character in the untrained minds of the secular clergy and lay people.[39] As a result, quite independently of the rise in manifestations of dissent at this time, notably the Cathar movement, which indeed helped to sharpen the sense of the world's vulnerability to demonic influence, a feeling of helplessness against demonic instigations began to be felt in more personal and direct ways. Already in the writings of the Cistercian mystic and historian Caesarius of Heisterbach (*c.*1180–1240), it is clear that demons had become no mere external enemies doomed to be defeated by the bearers of a militant faith, but had penetrated into every corner of life and into the souls of individual Christians. Much more than the causes of droughts or epidemics, demons had begun to be seen, outside

---

37 J. B. Russell, *Lucifer: The Devil In the Middle Ages* (Ithaca and London, 1984), pp. 154–7.
38 *The Cult of the Saints: Its Rise and Function in Latin Christianity* (London, 1981), pp. 106–7.
39 *The Magician, the Witch and the Law* (Sussex, 1978), pp. 92–3.

as well as inside the cloister, as the instigators of interior desires that individuals could not acknowledge as belonging to themselves.[40]

This development is symptomatic of the more widespread trend towards spiritual introspection that gathered momentum during the late medieval period and which was marked by an emphasis on domestic lay piety and by an urge to achieve a closer identification of individual religious experiences with the sufferings of Christ. But the trend is also linked to a change of emphasis in late medieval perceptions of sin and penance. As John Bossy has explained, the traditional moral system taught throughout the medieval period was based on the seven 'deadly' or 'capital' sins, which could be viewed as a negative exposition of Jesus's twofold commandment to love God and one's neighbour. The system had the advantage of fitting into a whole string of septenary classifications and of providing a set of categories under which people could identify passions of hostility as un-Christian. Yet it had the disadvantage of making little of obligations to God and, more worrying still, of having no scriptural authority. This is one of the preoccupations behind the decision of most thirteenth-century scholastic theologians to build their treatment of Christian ethics around the Decalogue. The new perceptions of morality that this change of emphasis brought to the fore had effects that, in Bossy's words, 'may fairly be described as revolutionary'.

One of these effects was a notable enhancement of the status of the devil. By treating idolatry as the primary offence that a Christian could commit, the Decalogue led to a change from the traditional role of the devil as the antitype of Christ – the 'Fiend' who taught men to hate rather than to love – to his new role as the antitype of God the Father, and so the source and object of idolatry and false worship. By analogy, whereas traditionally witchcraft had been seen as the offence of causing malicious harm to others – it is interesting to note, for instance, that in Chaucer's exposition it had been dealt with, rather loosely, under wrath – in the new context it became a clear offence against the First Commandment. So too, just as the phenomenon of carnival could in the old context be explained as an inverted image of the traditional machinery of penance derived from a moral system based on the seven sins, in the new context the phenomenon of the witch could be explained as an inverted image of a moral system founded on the Ten Commandments, particularly the first. It is thus no accident, according to Bossy, that in proportion as the Ten Commandments became established as the accepted system of Christian ethics, witchcraft and diabolism should have become increasingly persuasive.[41]

40   Norman Cohn, *Europe's Inner Demons: An Enquiry inspired by the Great Witch Hunt* (London, 1975), p. 73.
41   *Christianity in the West 1400–1700* (Oxford, 1985), pp. 35–8, 138–9; John Bossy 'Moral Arithmetic: Seven Sins into Ten Commandments', in Edmund Leites, ed. *Conscience and Casuistry in Early Modern Europe* (Cambridge, 1988), pp. 215–30.

It is true that Bossy's argument can easily be made to backfire. If we consider the case of Thomism, for example, it is well known that Aquinas maintained not only that the Decalogue was a compendium of the natural law, but also that the natural law was valid independently of it.[42] Aquinas's treatment of the Commandments was thus an affirmation of the intrinsic goodness of nature independently of the effects of grace. If this was the case, any influence that the devil might have over nature would be strictly limited and circumscribed. Acceptance of the Decalogue, therefore, could also go hand in hand with a rejection of diabolism. Certainly the Aristotelian naturalism espoused by Aquinas would, in different contexts, show a marked penchant for scepticism with regard to devils, as is clear from the opinions of Ulrich Müller, Agostino Nifo and Pietro Pompo-nazzi.[43]

It is true, of course, that this scepticism never spread to strictly Thomist circles. The *Malleus Maleficarum*, for instance, a work widely regarded as central to early modern demonology, is unmistakably Thomist in inspiration. It is important, however, not to overlook the marked differences that exist between the assumptions that inspired the authors of the *Malleus* and those that came to characterize subsequent demonological works. Whereas the authors of the *Malleus* see witchcraft as primarily a social crime centring on malefice, particularly malefice in relation to the sexual act and marriage, the bulk of sixteenth- and seventeenth-century demonologists, by contrast, see witchcraft as a crime of idolatry and devil-worship. In other words, in the *Malleus* the crime of witchcraft is first and foremost an offence against nature, charity and the human race, whereas in subsequent works it becomes much more an an offence against God and his Church.

Now in a climate where the Thomistic understanding of natural law and the consequent concordance between nature and grace was accepted, this latter conclusion would have been difficult to reach. It is now generally

42 Aquinas's notion of natural law derives from the belief that, by using their reason and reflecting upon their nature, humans can formulate general principles of action. Natural law, in other words, is what reason tells humans to do or to avoid in order to function well as humans. To the question whether there is a law which is superior to natural law, Aquinas stated that if one is thinking in terms of a list of precepts, the answer is No; see Brian Davies, *The Thought of Thomas Aquinas* (Oxford, 1993), p. 247. This, of course, should not be understood, as it often was in late medieval theology, to mean that Aquinas wanted to deny that natural law ultimately derived from divine law. 'The eternal law', he wrote, 'is nothing other than the exemplar of divine wisdom as directing the motions and acts of everything' (ibid.). Yet the possibility of constructing a Thomistic account of natural law without reference to God became a central worry of late medieval thought. Even nowadays the debate continues: see, for example, John Finnis, *Natural Law and Natural Rights* (Oxford, 1980) and Alasdair MacIntyre's criticism in *Whose Justice? Which Rationality?* (London, 1988), pp. 188–95.
43 On this see H.R. Trevor-Roper, 'The European Witch-Craze of the Sixteenth and Seventeenth Centuries', in idem, *Religion, the Reformation and Social Change*, 3rd edn (London, 1984), pp. 130–1; and H. C. Lea, *Materials towards a History of Witchcraft* (Philadelphia, 1939), pp. 374, 377, 435, 366.

recognized, however, that the old assumption that Thomism dominated European intellectual life until the fourteenth century – 'the end of the journey' as Etienne Gilson once called it – is not only exaggerated but fundamentally erroneous. As Heiko Oberman insists, one only needs to remember Robert Kilwardby, Durandus de St Porciano, Robert Holcot and William Crathorn to realize that such compliance with Aquinas was not even a feature of the Dominican order.[44] Moreover, the circumstances for the development of Thomism in the fourteenth century were particularly inauspicious, for the defenders of Aquinas had to cope with the legacy of the Parisian condemnation of Averroism of the 1270s and with the consequent, urgent need to clear their master of the charge of Averroist tendencies. Since most of the charges addressed metaphysical issues, the consequence of the defence was the transmission of an over-metaphysical Aquinas which did not pay adequate attention to him as an interpreter of scripture and patristic theology. In this way there developed the caricature of an Aristotelian, anti-Augustinian and semi-Pelagian Aquinas which was offensive to mainstream theology and which explains why Thomism failed to appeal to philosophers and theologians well into the fifteenth century.[45]

As Oberman explains, the main effect of the concern with Averroism was the widespread Franciscan reaction against a 'metaphysically foolproof causal system which embraces the whole chain of being, including God as first and final cause'. Although the chain of being itself was not called into question, the resulting association of God and necessity was.[46] Scholastics thus tended to reject Aquinas's moral system, seeing it as a threat to the freedom and omnipotence of God, or as an attempt to bind God's moral decisions within a normative system which could be conceived as separate or distinct from God. The Franciscan alternative, as represented by Duns Scotus and William of Ockham, invoked faith in God as person and free agent, rather than as 'first cause' or 'unmoved mover'. Their insistence that God was not tied to creation by causation but, rather, related to it by volition seemed to make all metaphysical arguments based on necessary causal links lose their relevance in theological thought. To cite Oberman again, whereas in Aquinas's metaphysical ontology 'the natural and supernatural realms are organically joined by the being of God' in whom human beings participate by reason and faith, the Franciscan alternative 'retraces nature and supernature...to the *Person* of God, and points to God's will as...the "ceiling" of theology'. Little room was left here for the possibility of a natural knowledge of God or for the demonstrability of a natural religion. God's eternal decree of self-commitment had 'established

44   Heiko A. Oberman, 'The Reorientation of the Fourteenth Century', in *Studi sul XIV secolo in memoria di Anneliese Maier*, ed. A. Maieru and A. Paravicini Bagliani (Rome, 1981), p. 515.
45   Ibid., pp. 517–18.
46   Ibid., pp. 518–19.

the limits of theology which to surpass is to trespass, yielding sheer specu-
lation'.[47]

This Franciscan school of thought dominated medieval intellectual history from the time of Duns Scotus to the Great Schism and beyond. In fact,
it did not lose much of its impetus until the Erasmians and the Reformers
began to evoke a renewed longing for a comprehensive system of thought,
which in part inspired the Catholic neo-Thomist revival of the sixteenth
century. But even after the Council of Trent's catechism confirmed
Aquinas's view of the Commandments as a compendium of natural law, the
increasingly fragmented and eclectic theological debates characteristic of
the time proved fundamentally inimical to the Thomist conception of
inquiry as a long-term, cooperative pursuit of systematic understanding.[48]
The most authoritative philosopher of the period, the Jesuit Francisco
Suárez, for instance, formulated a philosophy that tended to an eclectic
synthesis of the thought of Aquinas, Scotus and Ockham which was irreconcilable with the Thomist theory of matter and form (hylomorphism).
Where Aquinas had applied the principles of Aristotelian physics to the
nature of man, teaching that matter was the principle of human individua-
tion and that the soul was the form of the body, Suárez insisted on a tran-
sition from apprehensions of essence to judgements of particular existence
that necessarily implied a separation of matter and spirit.[49]

The effects that this nominalist persistence in post-Tridentine thought
would have on subsequent demonological investigations would be difficult
to exaggerate; for the position was irreconcilable with Aquinas's theory of
the human intelligence, which was in turn the keystone of his formulation
of the concordance between nature and grace. Against the Platonists
Aquinas had argued that man was not primarily a spiritual being confined
in the 'prison' of the body, but a part of nature. Likewise, human intelligence was not that of a pure spirit; it was 'consubstantial' with matter, subject to the conditions of space and time, and only capable of *knowing* – i.e.
constructing an intelligible order – through the data of sensible experience
systematized by reason.[50] As Christopher Dawson put it,

> the intellectualism of St Thomas is equally remote from an absolute
> idealism and a rational empiricism, from the metaphysical mysticism of

47   Ibid., p. 519. See also, Heiko A. Oberman, '*Via Antiqua* and *Via Moderna*: Late Medieval
Prolegomena to Early Reformation Thought', *Journal of the History of Ideas*, 1987, pp. 23–40.
48   On this point see Alasdair MacIntyre, *Three Rival Versions of Moral Enquiry* (London,
1990), p. 150.
49   Francisco Suárez, *Disputationes Metaphysicae*, V, 6, nn. 15–17; and see F. C. Copleston, *A
History of Philosophy. Volume III: Ockham to Suárez* (New York 1953), pp. 360–1.
50   St Thomas Aquinas, *Summa contra Gentiles*, ii, 76; *Summa Theologiae*, Ia, 19. 4; 79. 3; 84.
6; *De veritate*, 2. 2; and see Davies, *The Thought of Thomas Aquinas*, pp. 43–4, 125–8, 214–15,
233–4.

the ancient east and from the scientific materialism of the modern west. It recognized the autonomous rights of the human reason and its scientific activity against the absolutism of a purely theological ideal of knowledge, and the rights of human nature and natural morality against the exclusive domination of the ascetic ideal.[51]

As we have seen, by concentrating their attacks on the early metaphysical writings of Aquinas rather than on his mature synthesis in the *Summa Theologiae*, the Franciscan nominalist school failed to see the significance of this balance. It is, to my mind, in this anti-Thomist tendency, and in the way in which it coincided with the current trend in favour of a moral system based more on the Ten Commandments than on the seven sins, that the foundations of early modern demonology are to be sought. It was precisely in the context of the twofold acceptance of nominalism as a philosophical system and of the Decalogue as a moral system that Jean Gerson influenced the famous conclusion of the University of Paris in 1398. Henceforth, all strictly maleficent witchcraft as well as all seemingly beneficent counter-witchcraft would tend to be regarded as idolatrous and as necessarily involving apostasy and submission to the devil. Malefice ceased to be the centre of the problem and gave way to idolatry and devil-worship as the main objects of concern. Once the nominalist inspiration behind this trend is accepted, Bossy's Ten Commandments come back with a vengeance: early modern demonology can be traced back to the Franciscan rejection of Aristotelian naturalism and to the growing acceptance of a moral system based on the Decalogue.

This does not mean, of course, that the witch-hunts of the sixteenth and seventeenth centuries are to be blamed on Franciscan nominalism. In fact, as Stuart Clark has explained, the 'interiorization' of the crime of witch-craft encouraged by the nominalists in effect played *against* witch prosecutions. By focusing on sin, and especially on the sin of idolatry, rather than on sorcery and malefice, misfortune came to be seen in a more Jobian light and the devil came to be perceived increasingly in the context of the mystery of redemption: a completely subservient being used by God for the spiritual improvement of the pious.[52] Nevertheless, this incipient scepticism about the reality of witchcraft was nowhere accompanied by a decline of diabolism itself. Indeed, the implications of diabolism in relation to the individual soul became much more immediate and compelling. The nominalist tendency to separate nature and grace made the realm of 'the supernatural' much less accessible to reason, thereby enhancing the attributes of

---

51 *Mediaeval Essays* (London and New York, 1953), p. 151.
52 Stuart Clark, 'Protestant Demonology: Sin, Superstition and Society (c1520–c1630)', in B. Ankarloo and G. Henningsen, eds, *Early Modern Witchcraft* (Oxford, 1990), pp. 45–81. Although Clark focuses on Protestant demonology, very much the same argument could be applied to the Catholic case.

both the divine and the demonic in relation to the individual. If in the long run this tendency contributed to the decline of witch prosecution, there can be little doubt that it would also become a central element in the seventeenth-century proliferation of cases of diabolical obsession and possession on both sides of the confessional front.

*

When we turn back to the events taking place in the New World, the influence of Franciscan nominalism becomes especially significant. It is revealing, for example, that the first work written in Mexico dealing strictly with diabolism, Fray Andrés de Olmos's *Tratado de hechicerías y sortilegios*, was inspired almost entirely by the influential demonological treatise of the Basque Franciscan Fray Martín de Castañega,[53] where idolatry and devil-worship are the central objects of concern. Written in Nahuatl, the aim of Olmos's treatise in paraphrasing Castañega's work was to convince missionaries and Indians alike that diabolism was not primarily maleficent but idolatrous. Lapsed Indians could no longer be seen as gullible simpletons who had been deluded by the devil, nor even as malicious sorcerers who used demonic power to harm their fellow beings. Much more serious than this, idolatrous Indians were active devil-worshippers, members of a counter-church set up by a devil anxious to be honoured like God. With this purpose Satan had set up his own church as a mimetic inversion of the Catholic Church. It had its 'exacraments' to counter the Church's sacraments; it had its ministers, who were mostly women, as opposed to the predominance of male ministers in the Church; and it had its human sacrifices which sought to imitate the supreme sacrifice of Christ in the Eucharist.[54]

How persuasive this nominalist rejection of Aristotelian naturalism and of the Thomist concordance between nature and grace became during this period can be seen not only in the complete disregard by contemporaries of works of a more strictly Thomist inspiration (notably Vitoria's *De magia*,[55] which deals much more with malefice than with idolatry), but also in the way in which it seemed to carry the day even among those thinkers who considered themselves to be in the mainstream of Thomist orthodoxy. This is especially clear in the thought of perhaps the most intelligent and systematic thinker to write about the cultures of the American Indians in the sixteenth century, the Spanish Jesuit José de Acosta (1540–1600).

In the work of Acosta, the rejection of the Thomist concordance

53 Martín de Castañega, *Tratado muy sotil y bien fundado de las supersticiones y hechicerías y varios conjuros y abusiones y otras cosas tocantes al caso y de la posibilidad e remedio dellas* (Logroño, 1529).
54 Georges Baudot, *Utopía e Historia en México: Los primeros cronistas de la civilización mexicana 1520–1569* (Madrid, 1983), p. 243.
55 In *Obras: Relecciones teológicas* (Madrid, 1960).

between nature and grace, albeit not made explicit, seems to be all-important. Indeed, the contrast between his treatment of what he regarded as natural and his analysis of what he thought to belong to the 'supernatural' sphere in the cultures of America is so striking that, at first sight, it is hard to believe that they are the constructs of the same mind.

As far as the 'natural' sphere was concerned, Acosta's account of the native cultures of the New World was one of the most objective and original to have hitherto appeared. In easy, fluent style, the reader is provided with a concise and lucid exposition of the nature, origins and organization of Indian cultures which clarified complex questions with confident and critical acumen. Where previous writers had been content to revert to tradition or to ancient wisdom, Acosta insisted that empirical knowledge and experience should always take precedence over the doctrines of ancient philosophers in any examination of the causes and effects of natural phenomena. Accordingly, native cultures had to be understood on their own terms, since comparisons with other races would only lead to absurd and inappropriate analogies. 'So long as they do not contradict the law of Christ and his Holy Church,' he wrote, the Indians

> should be governed according to their own laws, the ignorance of which has led to many errors....For, when the judges and rulers are ignorant of the ways in which their subjects are to be judged and ruled, they not only inflict grief and injustice on them, but they also...encourage them to abhor us as men who in all things, be they good or bad, have always opposed them.[56]

This seemed a long cry from Zumárraga and Olmos and Sahagún. Indeed, Acosta's insistence on the urgent need to assess Indian cultures on their own terms and his pursuit of causality and generality where his predecessors had been content with the mere observation and description of phenomena resembled in some ways the purpose and method of modern science. It is no doubt this quality that gained Acosta the respect of William Robertson in the eighteenth century, when the Scotsman pronounced the *Historia* to be 'one of the most accurate and best informed writings concerning the West Indies', an opinion that found a recent echo when Anthony Pagden concluded that Acosta's work had made 'some kind of comparative ethnology, and ultimately some measure of historical relativism, inescapable'.[57]

The fact that the devil had little or no room in this scheme was reflected in Acosta's frequent impatience with the opinions of 'ignorant friars' who

56   José de Acosta, *Historia Natural y moral de las Indias*, ed. E. O'Gorman (Mexico City, 1962) p. 281. See also Acosta, *De Procuranda Indorum Salute* (Cologne, 1596), pp. 483, 517.
57   Pagden, *Fall of Natural Man*, p. 200. Robertson is quoted in Brading, *The First America*, p. 184.

imagined the whole of the Indian past as a diabolical hallucination.[58] Rather than blaming the devil, Acosta was at pains to stress the natural goodness of Indian cultures. 'If anyone – he wrote – is amazed at the rites and customs of the Indians…and detests them as inhuman and diabolical…let him remember that among the Greeks and the Romans one finds the same kind of crimes and often even worse ones'. So too he reminded his readers that according to Bede, the Irish and the English, 'in their heathen days', had been no more enlightened than the Indians.[59] In their refusal to abandon their ancient rites and customs the Indians were not necessarily playing into the hands of the devil. Their behaviour, in fact, was no different from that of the bulk of the Castilian peasantry who merely needed instruction to 'submit to the truth as a thief surprised in his crime'.[60]

In all this, Acosta seemed poles apart from the demonology of his time. Even when dealing with the irksome question of conversion, Acosta's insistence on the need to preserve those pagan rites and ceremonies that did not conflict with Christianity[61] seemed to echo St Gregory the Great's advice to St Augustine of Canterbury, and was in perfect tune with the current Jesuit missionary practice which produced its most remarkable representatives in China and India with Matteo Ricci and Roberto de Nobili. But Acosta was only willing to deploy such analytical acumen when dealing with natural phenomena or with cultural expressions that could be explained from a strictly natural standpoint. As soon as he entered the field of religion proper Acosta seemed to join the nominalist camp and all his insistence on empirical knowledge and analysis was brought to a complete standstill. To enter the sphere of the supernatural was to enter the sphere of theological certainty, where the divine law was the one and only standard of truth and where the divine will was alone sovereign. Thus, when faced with the curious similarities that existed between Christian and pagan religious practices, Acosta was as baffled as his predecessors. Unlike Motolinía, however, he could find no room for providentialist hopes. Despite his conviction that in the wider structure of the divine plan good would always triumph over evil, when faced with Indian religions Acosta could not bring himself to anticipate God's intentions. To his mind, the evident similarities between Christian and pagan religious ceremonies necessarily pointed to a supernatural origin in the latter, and since it would be absurd to think of God as attempting to imitate himself, the only alternative source to account for such similarities had to be a diabolical one.

58 Acosta, *Historia,* pp. 188–9.
59 Ibid., pp. 216, 228.
60 Acosta, *De Procuranda,* p. 150; the quotation, from Acosta's *Confesionario para los curas de indios* (Lima, 1588), is from Pagden, *Fall of Natural Man,* p. 161.
61 Acosta, *De Procuranda,* p. 483.

HISTORIA
NATVRALE, E MORALE
DELLE INDIE;

SCRITTA

DAL R. P. GIOSEFFO DI ACOSTA
Della Compagnia del Giesù;

Nellaquale fi trattano le cofe notabili del Cielo , & de gli
Elementi , Metalli , Piante, & Animali di quelle:
i fuoiriti, & ceremonie : Leggi,& gouerni,
& guerre degli Indiani.

Nouamente tradotta della lingua Spagnuola nella Italiana

DA GIO. PAOLO GALVCCI SALODIANO'
ACADEMICO VENETO.

CO.N PRIVILEGII.

IN VENETIA,

Preffo Bernardo Bafa , All'infegna del Sole.
M. D. XCVI.

Plate 7. Front page of the first
Italian edition (1591) of Acosta's
Historia natural y moral.

It is true that Acosta, in Thomist fashion, would have accepted that man was capable of grasping religious truth by the mere encouragement of his own innate and natural desire for truth. But this desire seemed in itself insufficient to produce religious expressions that so closely resembled Christian religious practices, especially in milieux where Christianity had been hitherto unknown. Conversely, it was a commonplace in contemporary theological thought that Satan, the *Simia Dei*, was forever seeking to imitate his creator, so that, as Pedro Ciruelo had put it, 'the more saintly and devout the things he made men do, the greater was the sin against God'.[62] From this it followed that the more highly structured was the social order of pagan peoples, and the more refined and complex was their

62   Pedro Ciruelo, *Tratado en el qual se reprueuan todas las supersticiones y hechicerías* (Barcelona, 1628), p. 183.

civility and religious organization, the more idolatrous and perverted were the results.[63]

It was in his analysis of Indian religions, therefore, that the nominalist separation of nature and grace was taken by Acosta, with impeccable logic, to its most extreme and dramatic conclusions. Defined in the book of Wisdom as the 'beginning cause and end of every evil', idolatry had always been regarded as the worst of all sins: the means through which the Prince of Lies, moved by pride and envy, had blinded men to the true shape of God's design for nature.[64] Now, by denying paganism any natural means towards a supernatural end – unless, of course, both the means and the end could be classed as diabolic – Acosta effectively equated paganism with idolatry. Anything faintly religious in pagan cultures was necessarily the result of Satan's incorrigible 'mimetic desire'.[65] It was precisely this mimetic desire that was at the root of the existence of counter-religious practices among the Indians of America. For the devil was constantly taking advantage of any opportunity that would allow him to imitate the divine cult. In America he had his own priests who offered sacrifices and administered sacraments in his honour. He had many followers who led lives of 'recollection and sham sanctity'. He had 'a thousand types of false prophets' through whom he sought to 'usurp the glory of God and feign light with darkness'. Indeed, there was 'hardly anything that had been instituted by Jesus Christ...which, in some way or other, the devil had not sophisticated and incorporated into their [the Indians'] heathendom'. In his attempt to imitate Catholic ritual Satan had distinguished between 'minor, major and supreme priests, and a type of acolyte', and had founded 'monasteries' where chastity was rigorously observed, 'not because of any love of cleanliness...but because of his desire to deprive God, in any way that he can, of the glory of being served with integrity and cleanliness'. It was in the same spirit that Satan had encouraged 'penances and ascetic disciplines' in his honour, and sacrifices where he not only competed with the divine law, but actually tried to overstep it: for God had stopped Abraham's sacrifice of Isaac, whereas Satan encouraged human sacrifices on a massive scale. His frantic mimetic desire had even culminated in a desperate attempt to imitate the mystery of the Trinity.[66]

Such Satanic 'envy and urge to compete' became even more explicit in the devil's attempts to imitate the Christian sacraments. For he had instituted sham imitations of baptism, marriage, confession and sacerdotal unc-

63   Acosta, *De Procuranda*, p. 474.
64   Wisdom, 14: 27; St Thomas Aquinas, *Summa Theologiae*, IIa–IIae, q. 94a. 4 resp.; Acosta, *De Procuranda*, p. 486; Acosta, *Historia*, pp. 217–18.
65   I have borrowed this term from René Girard; see especially *Le Bouc Emissaire* (Paris, 1982).
66   Acosta, *Historia*, pp. 235, 238, 240, 242, 246, 248, 249, 268.

tion. More histrionically, the Eucharist had been copied and mocked by the Mexicans in their rituals involving communal banquets which, in the May celebrations of the god Huitzilopochtli, reached the level of an elaborate parody of the feast of Corpus Christi: after a long procession, the feast culminated in the communal ingestion of a small idol made of maize pastry and honey. 'Who could fail to be astonished', Acosta exclaimed, 'that the devil should take so much care to have himself adored and received in the same way that Jesus Christ...commanded and taught [to be received]!'[67]

Since, however, such similarities were a clear proof of the demonic nature of Indian religions, Acosta chose to overlook the chastity of the 'monasteries' and the asceticism of the 'penitential' practices and to stress that pagan religious ceremonies were invariably mixed with all types of 'abominations' that inverted and perverted the natural order. The unction of priests, for instance, was carried out with a substance amassed with every sort of 'poisonous vermin', such as spiders, scorpions, snakes and centipedes, which, when burnt and mixed with the hallucinogen *ololhiuqui*, had the power of turning the newly ordained priests into witches who saw the devil, spoke to him and visited him by night in 'dark and sinister mountains and caves'. Similarly, the parody of the Eucharistic host was made from a mixture of human blood and amaranth seeds; the walls of the 'oratories' were always stained with blood and the long hair of the priests had been hardened by the clotted blood of sacrificial victims. Satanic pollution and ritual filth invaded every corner of Indian religion. A manifest inversion of the Christian ideals of sacramental purity and ritual cleanliness, their ritualism culminated in the incomparably offensive practice of human sacrifice which, in an unthinkably perverted fashion, was often accompanied by cannibalism. This was not merely an 'unnatural crime' like sodomy and onanism; it was the ultimate expression of idolatry: its self-consuming nature associated it with Satanic desire itself.[68]

In his account of Indian religions, Acosta made the Indians guilty of all the idolatrous aberrations listed in the book of Wisdom:

> With their child-murdering initiations, their secret mysteries, their orgies with outlandish ceremonies, they no longer retain any purity in their lives....Everywhere a welter of blood and murder, theft and fraud, corruption, treachery, riots, perjury, disturbance...pollution of souls, sins against nature....[69]

The contrast with his assessment of Indian cultures could not be more marked, and it becomes even more striking when we compare Acosta's method with the way in which his Dominican predecessor, Fray Bartolomé

67 Ibid, pp. 266, 259–65, 255–9.
68 Ibid., pp. 262–5, 248; Pagden, *Fall of Natural Man*, p. 176.
69 Wisdom 14: 22–30.

de las Casas (1484–1566), had dealt with the same problem a few decades earlier. For Las Casas's background and intellectual concerns were very similar to Acosta's. His thought, like Acosta's, had been moulded by the theological tradition of the School of Salamanca and, consequently, like Acosta, he had grounded his anthropology upon the premise that all human minds were the same in essence, that all men were innately susceptible to moral training, and that any analysis of cultural differences needed to be based on a historical explanation. Like Acosta, too, he had insisted on the primacy of empirical knowledge as the basis of any fruitful analysis of the American reality.[70] Apart from their clear differences in style, structure and length (Las Casas's writings being as voluminous as they are convoluted), their arguments and their appreciation of Indian cultures were surprisingly similar. The one essential difference between them was that, unlike Acosta, Las Casas did not appear to have been influenced by the nominalist separation of nature and grace. This left him with the freedom to approach the supernatural manifestations of Indian cultures from an essentially naturalistic standpoint.

It is for this reason that we find no sharp contrast between the natural and the supernatural in the writings of Las Casas. Although he distinguished clearly between the two spheres, he thought it a mistake to separate them. Following Aquinas he concluded that the supernatural, albeit beyond human reason and understanding, was nonetheless as rational as the natural and that, consequently, any human desire for the supernatural was rooted in nature.[71] Although he would have agreed with St Augustine, as Aquinas himself had done, that the original initiative always came from God, he was adamant that this did not do away with the essential goodness rooted in human nature itself. The desire for God was a universal and perfectly natural phenomenon which responded to an essential human need and which sought expression in *latria*, the true worship of God. By analogy, *idolatria* was not a demonic invention, but an equally natural – albeit disordered – phenomenon, responding to a natural desire for good and emerging from an error of reason caused by the ignorance and weakness of a fallen nature. Although a degeneration of the original *latria*, idolatry tended to be the rule, the 'natural' state, among the higher civilizations whenever grace was absent. It could not, therefore, have a diabolical origin. No matter how disordered it might appear, or how much it might be used by the devil to perpetuate his perversities, the basic desire behind idolatry was essentially good: a proof, indeed, that the Indians were eager for evangelization.[72]

This, of course, did not mean that the devil was not as important for Las

70 Pagden, *Fall of Natural Man*, p. 146.
71 Bartolomé de las Casas, *Apologética Historia Sumaria*, ed. E. O'Gorman, 2 vols (Mexico City, 1967), i, p. 539.
72 For a different view see Carmen Bernand and Serge Gruzinski, *De l'Idolâtrie: Une archéologie des sciences religieuses* (Paris, 1988), pp. 45–74.

Plate 8. Fray Bartolomé de las Casas.

Casas as he was for Acosta. Indeed, the actuality of Satanic intervention in human affairs was even more pervasive in the writings of the Dominican than in those of the Jesuit, and demonic instigations were portrayed by Las Casas in more vivid and inescapable terms. As Sabine MacCormack has explained, the question of why God had given the devil power to control Indian souls for so long had been posed by Las Casas in terms that needed the devil as an active agent in the human imagination, whereas Acosta, following Suárez, opted for a historical argument that could evaluate the imagination without reference to demons.[73] It is no great surprise that the writings of Las Casas should be filled with devils deemed constantly to be transporting men and women through the air, tempting witches to obtain unbaptized infants for their cannibalistic rites, turning men into beasts,

73 Sabine MacCormack, *Religion in the Andes: Vision and Imagination in Early Colonial Peru* (Princeton, N. J., 1991), pp. 277–8. The philosophical point highlighted by MacCormack revolves around the immortality of the soul. If, as Aquinas had claimed, the soul depends on the body in order to know, was it immortal? It was in response to this question that Suárez set out to show that either the imagination was not part of the body, or there was some part of the intellect not dependent on the imagination. In my view, Suárez's preoccupation with finding a way of protecting the imagination, and therefore the soul, from material and demonic influences can only be understood in the context of the nominalist tradition that we have analysed.

faking miracles and appearing in human and animal forms.[74] Yet all these demonic actions were set by Las Casas unquestionably in the context of malefice,[75] and his demonology was more in tune with the Thomist tradition that had inspired the authors of the *Malleus Maleficarum* than with the nominalist tradition at the root of the demonology that became prevalent after the Reformation.

As we have seen, Las Casas's agreement with Aquinas on the question of the relation between nature and grace allowed him to give a naturalistic explanation to the problem of idolatry; but it also allowed him to use diabolism as a justification rather than a condemnation of Indian religions. Indeed, his insistence upon the role of demons in the imagination amounted to an acknowledgement of the possibility of religious error, including his own.[76] Where Acosta had begun his discussion with a furious denunciation of Satan as the author and fount of idolatry, Las Casas began by invoking Aristotle's criteria for a true city, only moving to a discussion of religion once he had demonstrated the essential goodness of its natural foundations. If the devil was indeed the culprit of all native vices and crimes, he could easily be brought to heel once 'doctrine and grace' were made to work on the essentially good religious expressions of the Indians.[77] In all this, Las Casas emerges as one of the last upholders of Thomist naturalism. His views on Indian religions were destined to become the last, desperate cry of this short-lived tradition. They had, ironically, much more in common with the optimism about human nature that we detected in the writings of his rivals, Cortés and Motolinía, than with the sombre pessimism that in his own lifetime he would witness permeating Christian thought.

Acosta's ambivalent analysis of the American scene, on the other hand, results from the nominalist streak in his philosophy. Without taking this factor into account, his work will inevitably seem imbued by 'a latent contradiction which he fails to resolve in any satisfactory manner' and which David Brading has explained as the result of 'his subordination of humanitarian and religious interests to political expediency'.[78] Yet, despite the clear political slant that can be detected in Acosta's triumphalist celebrations of the conquest as the fulfilment of a providential design, his work is undeniably the most able and persuasive exposition of an attitude to the Indian past that would become dominant until the first half of the eighteenth century.[79]

*

74   Las Casas, *Apologética Historia*, ed. Juan Pérez de Tudela Bueso, 2 vols, Biblioteca de Autores Españoles (Madrid, 1958), CV, pp. 299–345.
75   Ibid., esp. pp. 308–9.
76   MacCormack, *Religion in the Andes*, p. 277.
77   Las Casas, *Apologética Historia*, ed. E. O'Gorman, i, p. 183; ii, pp. 177, 178, 215.
78   Brading, *The First America*, pp. 193–4.
79   It is fascinating to observe that 'Vitzliputzli', a corruption of Huitzilopochtli, entered German folklore as one of the devils in the puppet play of Dr Faustus upon which Goethe

In stressing the importance of Acosta's work, it has been far from my intention to suggest that the Jesuit should be held responsible for the growing tendency to demonize Indian cultures. My choice of his work to illustrate this development is due to the clarity with which it highlights the nominalist streak in post-Reformation theology and the implications that this had on any assessment of Indian religions. It should be stressed, moreover, that Acosta himself would undoubtedly have been as impatient with the seventeenth-century extirpators of idolatry as he had been with those 'ignorant friars' who saw the devil at work in any indigenous practice that did not conform with European custom.[80] It is ironic, therefore, that Acosta's ambivalent insistence upon the natural goodness and the supernatural evil of Amerindian civilization should have helped to confirm the growing distrust of indigenous traditions. Jerónimo de Mendieta and Juan de Torquemada, the two influential Franciscans writing at the turn of the century, for example, chose to follow the interpretation of the facts suggested by Acosta, despite knowing and using the writings of Las Casas. Torquemada's *Monarquía Indiana*, in particular, parallels Acosta's ambivalent analysis to a staggering degree. On the one hand he presents his readers with a resolute defence of Indian cultures, overwhelming them with comparisons drawn from classical antiquity, equating Moctezuma with Alexander the Great and seeking to demonstrate the progression of Indian history from a state of savagery to one of civilization; on the other he confidently asserts that Indian religions belong, in the last resort, to the Kingdom of Darkness, that their seemingly noble expressions are in fact the product of direct demonic intervention and that even their wisest leaders and thinkers could not escape the flames of hell.[81]

All too often, observers of Indian cultures proved ill-equipped to distinguish between the natural and the supernatural spheres and, increasingly, manifestations that Acosta would have classed as harmless came to be seen as part of a wider demonic initiative to use the Indians against Christianity. It is true that the provincial councils of 1555 and 1565 reiterated the views of the ecclesiastical meetings of 1524, 1532, 1539 and 1544 by stating that Indian cultures were fundamentally good and naturally predisposed to receive the Christian faith, but at the same time they expressed doubts about the intelligence of the Indians and their capacity for piety. By the time of the third provincial council of 1585 a paternalistic attitude towards the Indians as simple-minded and pitiful belied a more fundamental preoccupation with the demonic nature of their persistent idolatrous

based his great work; thus the Mexican deity joined the group of evil spirits from which Mephistopheles was chosen. See Elizabeth H. Boone, *Incarnations of the Aztec Supernatural: The Image of Huitzilopochtli in Mexico and Europe* (Philadelphia, 1989), p. 68.
80   Acosta, *Historia*, pp. 188–9.
81   Juan de Torquemada, *Monarquía Indiana*, 3 vols (Mexico City, 1969), i, pp. 169, 217; ii, pp. 36, 81–2.

practices. A recurring recommendation of the council was the need to prohibit popular festivities and other practices that might encourage the resur-
gence of idolatry, superstition and sorcery, even ordering that 'no figures of
animals or devils be painted on the images of saints' to prevent the Indians
from thinking 'that they have to adore them like they used to'.[82] The
effects of these recommendations were soon reflected in the way in which
many clerics sought to put them into practice. In the same year as the
council, for instance, the activities of a confraternity of Indians in the
region of Chiapas were described with alarm by the Dominican Fray Pedro
de Feria:

> they call themselves the Twelve Apostles...and they go out at night and
> travel from mountain to mountain and from cave to cave, and they hold
> meetings and consultations where, under the guise and appearance of
> religion, they perform their own rites, giving cult to the Devil and plot-
> ting against our Christian religion.[83]

The same assumptions dominate the writings of the seventeenth-century
'extirpators' of idolatry. In 1629 Hernando Ruiz de Alarcón furiously
denounced the 'explicit or tacit' pacts with the devil that he readily
deduced from any Indian practice that did not conform with his expecta-
tions. The association of babies with specific animals was sufficient proof
of the pact that their parents had with Satan; the 'conjuring' of the bed at
night was a demonic imitation of the office of compline; the 'exquisite'
language that they used in their 'conjurations' had been clearly

> introduced by the devil with the aim of instilling more respect for
> incomprehensible words in the minds of the ignorant...and because, as
> a rule, those who have made a pact with the devil prefer to use the kind
> of language that cannot be understood in order to hide the pact that is
> implicit in those unintelligible words.[84]

The same attitude can be observed two decades later in the work of Jacinto
de la Serna, who borrowed the bulk of Ruiz de Alarcón's material to produce a more elaborate manual for priests working with Indians. The obsession with proving that tacit or explicit pacts were at the root of native reli-

82   Pilar Gonzalbo, 'Del tercero al cuarto concilio provincial mexicano, 1585–1771',
Historia Mexicana, 35 (1), 1986, pp. 6–7; J. A. Llaguno, *La condición jurídica del indio y el tercer
concilio mexicano* (Mexico City, 1963), p. 60.
83   Pedro de Feria, *Revelación sobre la reincidencia en sus idolatrías de los indios de Chiapa después
de treinta años de cristianos*, in Francisco del Passo y Troncoso, ed., *Tratado de las idolatrías*, 2
vols (Mexico City, 1953), i, p. 383.
84   Hernando Ruiz de Alarcón, *Tratado de las supersticiones y costumbres gentilicias que hoy viven
entre los indios naturales de esta Nueva España*, in Passo y Troncoso, *Tratado*, i, pp. 27–8, 36, 64,
115, 119, 128, 155.

gious practices permeates the work in a way that leads Serna to deduce
that the word *titzil*, meaning medicine man or healer, also means, among
the Indians, 'diviner or sorcerer...who has a pact with the devil'. He therefore denounced them as 'wolves...ministers of Satan, enemies of the precepts of the Church, total destroyers of the holy sacraments and dogmatiz-
ers of the...sparks of their heathendom'. Equally, he expanded upon Ruiz
de Alarcón's denunciation of the practice of identifying babies with animals, asserting that it pointed to the devil's efforts to blind the Indians to

> the image of God, in whose likeness they were created, so that, man
> being the most beautiful creature to have emerged from the hands of the
> Creator, they are more willing to be dogs, lions, tigers, caymans and
> other foul animals such as skunks and bats....I have brought to light all
> this doctrine...as further evidence of the well-known way in which the
> devil, by means of his pacts, deceives these miserable people...and how
> he does it out of hate for God and his creatures.[85]

It would, of course, be a mistake to generalize from this evidence and to
suggest that the tendency to demonize Indian cultures was so pervasive
that it left no room for cultural interaction and assimilation. In the course
of this book I hope to show that the modern tendency to distinguish
between a popular level of culture imbued with magic and superstition and
a more sophisticated level characteristic of the élites is, more often than
not, an artificial anachronism when applied to New Spain in the early
modern period. Moreover, the campaigns to 'extirpate' idolatry were spo-
radic and unsuccessful, and in no way comparable to the more ruthless and
officially backed campaigns in Peru. The urgent need to fight idolatry, so
characteristic of the sixteenth century, subsided notably in the seventeenth.
Not only had the Indian population itself suffered a dramatic reduction by
the combined impact of conquest and plague, but the allegedly idolatrous
practices, centring largely upon animal sacrifice and curative and preventive
rites, were a mere caricature of pre-Hispanic human sacrifice and ritualistic
cannibalism. The very fact that the extirpators were discouraged by the
Inquisition itself, suggests a much greater degree of tolerance towards
native religiosity at the official level than emerges from the more widely
available evidence.

Tolerance, however, did not imply acceptance. The deep distrust of
Indian cultures and their nagging association with diabolism persisted even
among the more favourably disposed ecclesiastics. When, in 1656, Diego
de Hevia y Valdés, bishop of Oaxaca, reminded the parish priests of his

85 Jacinto de la Serna, *Manual de ministros de indios para el conocimiento de sus idolatrías y extirpación de ellas*, in *Colección de documentos inéditos para la historia de España*, vol. 104, pp. 3, 7, 62,
83, 93–4, 139, 140–1, 162.

diocese that God had instilled in the human heart 'the desire to live according to right reason' so that 'the fire of divine love could revive from underneath the venom of false cults', he was also careful to complain about 'the Catholic ruins found amidst so much hidden idolatry, venomously lurking in the hearts of the natives and sprouting new buds from that infamous root under which our oppressed sacred religion sadly wails'.[86]

Any evidence to suggest that the Indians had converted to Christianity could be contradicted by the possibility that the devil might have taught them to continue their old rites under the guise of the new religion. It is no great surprise that, despite (or, in some cases, because of) their exemption from inquisitorial jurisdiction, Indians were often the first suspects in cases involving diabolism. When, for instance, in 1691 a group of women were thought to be possessed by the devil, the first initiative taken by the Franciscan José Olvera after his exorcisms had failed was to question an Indian healer renowned for his 'infused science'. The Indian's staunch denials of any demonic pact only served to confirm the Franciscan's, and later the inquisitors', suspicions that the apparent sanctity of the Indian was a clever trick to dissemble the pact he had with the devil. The problem was not resolved, but hopes for a solution increased after one of the sufferers remembered that an Indian woman had tried to cure her with a hallucinogen some months before. Called for questioning, the Indian explained that she had acquired her healing powers after a vision, during a long illness, when God and his saints and angels had urged her to offer a *novena* in honour of 'St Michael the Great'. The Franciscan, however, stressed that the use of hallucinogens necessarily implied a pact with the devil and thus her alleged sanctity was a sham.[87]

The tendency to link Indians with diabolism was by no means a monopoly of ecclesiastics. The devil's preference for appearing in Indian guise was reported by a Spanish herdsman in 1568, by a mestizo boy in 1617 and by a black slave in 1695.[88] In 1598, a mestizo herdsman with a figure of the devil tattooed on his arm blamed an Indian and a mulatto did the same in 1695.[89] Indians also appeared repeatedly as the principal agents of demonic compacts. They gave away 'little books' written in native dialects with instructions on how to become the devil's slaves by 'forsaking the Christian faith, God, the Virgin, the saints, the rosary and the relics', and they advised people to climb hills or to search for caves where they would find demonic assistance.[90] In 1677, the mestizo Pedro

---

86 Pastoral letter in Gonzalo de Balsalobre, *Relación auténtica de las idolatrías, supersticiones y vanas observaciones de los indios del obispado de Oaxaca*, in Passo y Troncoso, *Tratado*, ii, pp. 349, 342.
87 A.G.N., Inq., 527.9, fol. 569r–v.
88 A.G.N., Inq., 41.4, fols 295v–296r; 486(I).12, fols 53r–56r; 530.20, fol. 389r–v.
89 A.G.N., Inq., 147.6, fol. 11v; 636.4 (unfoliated).
90 A.G.N., Inq., 209.9, fols 5r–55v; 335.37, fols 181r–184v.

del Castillo, believed by the inquisitors to have a pact with the devil, confessed that he had been told by an Indian woman to climb a hill where he found a cave in which Moctezuma himself, sitting on a golden chair, had ordered him to take off his rosary and his relics and to offer his soul to the devil in return for the extraordinary powers that were granted him.[91]

The Indians also seemed to have a monopoly of magical herbs. In 1613, Francisco del Castillo, municipal councillor of Atlixco, informed the inquisitors about the widespread belief in the area that 'in the time of their heathendom' some Indians had complained to the devil about the suffering and death of many, despite the numerous sacrifices where they 'offered him their blood and cut their flesh open'. To compensate, the devil had taken them to the mountain range of Tepoztlán where he had revealed the power of many hallucinogens that, when cut at certain hours of the day, forced the devil to do the Indians' will.[92] And indeed, there is ample inquisitorial evidence pointing to the use of herbs, invariably provided by an Indian after the obligatory renunciation of the Christian faith, that gave people power to seduce lovers, escape from oppression, make money, acquire admirable skills, and cure various ailments.[93]

The close links between demonism and the Indians was occasionally even hinted at by the devil himself. During the demonic possession of Juana de los Reyes[94] in the early 1690s the devil spoke some Latin and Greek during the exorcisms, but he also spoke the regional Indian tongue Pame.[95] And in a similar case of possession recorded as late as 1748 the devil, during the exorcism, confessed through the mouth of the demoniac that he had been sent into her body by an Indian of Xochimilco.[96]

Perhaps the most illustrative example of the demonization of Indians was recorded as late as 1739 in Oaxaca, when María Felipa de Alcaraz, a Spanish woman, was found by her Carmelite confessor to be 'infested and entangled in all the crimes and offences that are opposed to our holy Catholic faith', including all manner of idolatry, blasphemy, heresy, 'Judaic sacrilege', 'sodomy with demons' and 'horrendous insults against the divine persons and the Virgin Mary'. Her accomplices included many people, but especially Indians of both sexes 'who adored the devil as God, even affirming that he was more powerful than God'. It was these Indians who played a central role in the ceremonies, usually summoned by a rocket fired by 'two Indians, male and female, who were taken up into the air by a

91   A.G.N., Inq., 633.4, fols 413r–417r.
92   A.G.N., Inq., 478.13, fols 116r–v.
93   A.G.N., Inq., 729.21, fols 494r–501v; 899.29, fols 282r–286r; 478.13, fol. 116r; 366.41; 454.14, fol. 266v; 749.19, fols 141r–148v; 525.48, fols 502r–v; 681.5, fols 269v–286v; 827.2, fols 140r–141v.
94   See below, pp. 117–18.
95   A.G.N., Inq., 538.4, fol. 514v.
96   A.G.N., Inq., 827.24, fols 356r–v.

devil while copulating carnally'. Their leader had in her possession a picture where she figured among several Indians 'coupled with each other' and involved in all kinds of different and intricate forms of sexual intercourse with her. More alarming still was the eagerness with which the many 'Jews and heretics' that frequented these ceremonies indoctrinated the Indians, transporting them through the air to their European 'synagogues' and initiating them in their 'abominable sects', with the result that the Indians then practised these errors and taught them to their children so efficiently that the practice had spread to 'all the corners of New Spain' through the diabolic apostolate of many 'masters of idolatry'.[97]

In this instance, the Indians of New Spain seem to have been incorporated into the renewed anti-Semitism that had begun to sweep through European thought from the late seventeenth century. But this was not the 'enlightened' anti-Semitism of the Spinozists and other pantheists and deists who saw in Judaism a tenacious ancient superstition that had blocked and imprisoned the mind.[98] It had much more in common with the more defensive and turgid fabrications of Johann Andreas Eisenmenger, professor of Hebrew at Heidelberg, whose *Endecktes Judenthum* (1699) had aimed at defaming the Jews through a restatement of the medieval blood-libel that Jews had killed Christian children, used their blood in their rituals, and poisoned the wells during the black death.[99] The ease with which the Indians of New Spain could be incorporated into Eisenmenger's 'infamous diatribe', as Jonathan Israel has called it, is a good indication of how deep-rooted their association with heresy and diabolism remained as late as the middle of the eighteenth century.

97   A.G.N., Inq., 867.41, fols 226r–v, 239r–240r, 241r, 257r, 266v–267r.
98   Baruch de Spinoza, *Tractatus Theologico-Politicus*, in *Works of Spinoza*, ed. R. H. M. Elwes (New York, 1951), p. 56.
99   Jonathan Israel, *European Jewry in the Age of Mercantilism, 1550–1750* (Oxford, 1985), p. 234. On medieval anti-Semitism see Miri Rubin, 'Desecration of the Host: The Birth of an Accusation', in *Christianity and Judaism*, ed. Diana Wood (Oxford and Cambridge, Mass., 1992).

2

The Indian Response

> If religion is lost among the peoples, they have nothing left to enable
> them to live in society: no shield of defence, nor means of counsel,
> nor basis of support, nor even a form by which they may exist in the
> world at all.
>
> Giambattista Vico, *The New Science*, 1109

THE PROCESS OF demonization described in the last chapter is apt to create
an impression of the Mesoamerican Indians as largely passive and unre-
sponsive. However simplistic it may seem, such an impression is not an easy
one for the historian to challenge. To the common problems that beset
modern anthropologists attempting to interpret alien cultures, the Mesoamerican world poses the further problem that most, if not all, of what we
know about it has been put through a conspicuously European filter. The
bulk of the written sources most commonly used are largely the product of
the mendicant enterprise of evangelization, in which, as Bernardino de
Sahagún put it, native cultures were to be studied as a doctor studies an ail-
ment in order better to diagnose it and prescribe a remedy.[1] Other, at first
sight more reliable accounts, such as the vast amounts of extant materials in
Nahuatl that have only recently begun to be studied,[2] are themselves the
product of an advanced process of acculturation which necessarily hinders
the efforts of students interested in pre-Hispanic cultural expressions.[3]

When we turn to the specific concepts of evil and the devil, we are faced
with the further difficulty that such concepts were alien to the Mesoamerican mind. In contrast with the typically western conception of evil as mere
absence of being or privation of good (which implied that in strict ontological terms evil did not exist), the Mesoamerican notions of evil and the
demonic were inextricably intertwined with their notions of good and the
divine. Evil and the demonic were in fact intrinsic to the divinity itself. In
the same way as in Hinduism Brahma represented both creation and
destruction, or in the works of Homer there was no clear distinction
between the concepts *theos* and *daimon*, so, too, Mesoamerican deities repre-

---

1   See above, p. 15–16.
2   The best study is James Lockhart, *The Nahuas after the Conquest: A Social and Cultural History
of the Indians of Central Mexico, Sixteenth through Eighteenth Centuries* (Stanford, Calif., 1992).
3   Inga Clendinnen, *Aztecs: An Interpretation* (Cambridge, 1991), pp. 277–93.

sented both benevolence and malevolence, creativity and destructiveness. The Nahua word *teotl*, for instance, is ambivalent, and its common translation as 'god' is misleading. Its glyph is the figure of a sun, which conveys a sense of vastness and awesomeness, but also one of difficulty and danger.[4] There is thus an equal dose of the divine and of the demonic in the word, and Sahagún can hardly be accused of inconsistency when he compares Tezcatlipoca, the great Mesoamerican deity, with *both* Jupiter and Lucifer; for on the one hand Tezcatlipoca appears as a protean majestic warlord, who is all-knowing and forgiving, while on the other he shows the face of an evil and destructive sorcerer and a withholder of rain, a seducer and a malicious trickster. Similarly, Quetzalcoatl, the benign deity associated with the sun and believed to have a special sympathy for the fate of humanity, had at the same time an evil reputation through his association with the morning star, and his twin brother, Xolotl, was depicted as a monstrous demon who operated in the underworld.[5]

These dualistic properties should not obscure the strictly monistic nature of Mesoamerican religion. Negative and destructive forces were not the enemies of positive and constructive ones. Both were essential components of the cosmos. Life came from death; creation from destruction. Disharmony was as necessary as harmony.[6] The goddess Tlaleuctli (earth lady), for instance, was the palpable rock, soil and slime on which men lived, but she was also the earth into which they were lowered at death. Revered on the one hand as a benign source of food and life, in art she was depicted as a gargantuan toad slavering blood and displaying clashing jaws at every joint in a dramatic representation of chaos. So too, Ilamateuctli (leading old woman) wore a Janus mask as a symbol of her dual role as the giver of life and the cause of death, and Tlazolteotl, the goddess of sex and fertility, was also the goddess of filth and corruption.[7] It is true that entropy eroded order, but at the same time it was fertile and it provided the energy and the substance for the reestablishment of order. Thus, opposite forces did not engage in a cosmic battle of good against evil or even of order against chaos. Although order had to be wrested from chaos through sacrifice, this did not entail any severance from chaos. Indeed, chaos was itself the source of life.

4   See Burr Cartwright Brundage, *The Fifth Sun: Aztec Gods, Aztec World* (Austin, 1979), p. 50. According to Arild Hvidfeldt, the actual meaning of *teotl* is closer to the Polynesian *mana*; the physical representation of *teotl* was called *teixiptla*. See *Teotl and Ixiptlatli: Some Central Concepts in Ancient Mexican Religion* (Copenhagen, 1958), pp. 76–100.

5   Bernardino de Sahagún, *Historia general de las cosas de Nueva España*, ed. Angel Ma. Garibay, 6th edn. (Mexico City, 1985), pp. 31–2, 58–64.

6   See Louise M. Burkhart, *The Slippery Earth: Nahua-Christian Moral Dialogue in Sixteenth-Century Mexico* (Tucson, Ariz., 1989), p. 37.

7   Sahagún, *Historia general*, p. 36; Alfonso Caso, *Los calendarios prehispánicos* (Mexico City, 1967), pp. 129–33; Juan de Torquemada, *Monarquía Indiana*, 3 vols (Mexico City, 1969), ii, p. 134.

Plate 9. Quetzalcoatl
and Tezcatlipoca.

Consequently, the European notions of good and evil, personified in the
concepts of god and devil, implied a degree of benevolence and malevolence that was totally alien to the Mesoamerican deities. The notion of a
totally good god was an absurdity in Mesoamerican thought. Such a being
would have lacked the essential power to disrupt in order to create.
Likewise, an evil devil would have lacked the power to create that would
enable it to disrupt.[8] Moreover, a god who threatened to take his place not
just as a further god in the native pantheon but as the *only* god, to the exclu-
sion of all others, was an explosive liability which put the whole cosmic
order in extreme peril.

If such was the case, however, it seems difficult to make sense of the
apparent success of the early missionaries, and especially of the euphoric
millenarianism so vividly described by Motolinía during the first years of
evangelization. But, as we have seen, it is likely that the initial enthusiasm
of the Indians to accept Christianity had more to do with the Mesoamerican tradition of incorporating alien elements into their religion than with
any conviction about the exclusivist claims of the Christian faith. To the
Mesoamericans, victory was sufficient evidence of the strength of the vic-
tor's god. A people whose glyph for conquest was a burning temple was
likely to accept the god of their conquerors not only as a matter of
prudence, but also as a welcome recruit into a supernatural pantheon

8   Burkhart, *Slippery Earth*, pp. 37–8, 124.

accustomed to the extemporaneous incorporation of foreign deities. What soon emerged, however, was that the Christian god, unlike all previous alien deities, posed a fundamental challenge to the existing system by his claim to total goodness and absolute sovereignty. More immediately alarming were the bans imposed by the Europeans on native sacrifices, for, if obeyed, they would threaten to destroy the Mesoamerican corporate relationship with the supernatural and to bring about an end to the present cosmos and a return to the original chaos.[9]

The situation finds a striking parallel in fifth-century Byzantium, where the art of theurgy, widely encouraged by the neo-Platonists after the Christian emperors legislated against sacrifices, was inspired by the mystical notion that Graeco-Roman civilization would collapse if the old gods, cults and mysteries were abandoned.[10] In the same way as in Byzantium pagans did not substitute other ways of expressing their piety, opting instead to encourage the notion that a pious individual might sacrifice on behalf of the community (a sort of 'sacrifice by pious proxy' as it has been called[11]), so too, in sixteenth-century Mexico, many Indians, to the great horror and confusion of the friars, opted to perform clandestine sacrifices on behalf of the community.

This recurring insistence on the need for sacrifice is very difficult to grasp and even more difficult to reconstruct. As Inga Clendinnen has put it, it is like trying to understand the passion of Christ solely from the observation of the Mass.[12] The notion of 'propitiation' which sees in sacrifice an offering made to the gods that provides 'nourishment' for them is too crude and functional and it fails to convey the full sense of the action. In Mesoamerican thought rhetoric and ritual were unified in an effort to sustain a social order sufficiently in harmony with the natural order to survive within it. Thus a more adequate understanding of sacrifice and, in the Mesoamerican case, of the deliberate sequence of apparently murderous and bloodthirsty acts can be gained by considering the native belief that human flesh and maize were the same matter in different transformations. Since the transformations were cyclic and the cycles constantly in jeopardy, men's actions, and human sacrifice in particular, played a crucial part in maintaining the balance.[13]

But the significance of the need for sacrifice could be seen to reside at an even deeper level. As René Girard has suggested, when considering

9   On this point see Nancy M. Farriss, *Maya Society under Colonial Rule: The Collective Enterprise of Survival* (Princeton, N. J., 1984), p. 287.

10   See J. Bregman, *Synesius of Cyrene: Philosopher-Bishop* (Berkeley, Calif., 1982), p. 47.

11   K. W. Harl, 'Sacrifice and Pagan Belief in Fifth- and Sixth-Century Byzantium', *Past and Present*, no. 128 (Aug. 1990), pp. 11–12.

12   Inga Clendinnen, *Ambivalent Conquests: Maya and Spaniard in Yucatán* (Cambridge, 1987), p. 179.

13   Inga Clendinnen, 'The Cost of Courage in Aztec Society', *Past and Present*, no. 107 (May 1985), p. 89. See also her *Aztecs*, pp. 2–4, 73–5, 91–2, 108–10, 183–4, 260–3.

sacrificial violence, modern observers suffer from an almost inescapable blind spot caused by their familiarity with the workings of the judicial system. Where such a system (defined by Girard as mere 'institutionalized vengeance') is absent, the risk of violence becomes so great and the cure so problematic that the emphasis tends to fall on prevention. Sacrifice in such cases operates by appropriating certain aspects of violence and hiding them from sight by the machinery of ritual. Without sacrifice social coexistence would be rendered impossible, since it is only through sacrifice that the destructive vicious circle of reciprocal violence can be replaced by the protective and creative circle of ritual violence.

It is possible, therefore, that sacrifice in Mesoamerica played a central role in the protection of the entire community from violence among its members. Each successive sacrifice evoked the calm produced by the original unanimous sacrificial act which transformed violence into stability and fecundity by restoring harmony to the community and reinforcing the social fabric. The gods in this context came to represent the violence that was expelled from the community in such a way that ritual sacrifices could indeed be said to offer them portions of their own substance.[14]

If this was the case, the ban on sacrifices did not merely threaten the community's corporate relationship with the supernatural; more fundamentally, it challenged those very principles upon which its social harmony and equilibrium depended.[15] In the case of Mesoamerica this danger became more immediate and compelling when the spread of Christianity and the consequent ban on sacrifices was seen to coincide with a dramatic increase in Indian suffering and mortality. Many Indians did not fail to see a connection between the two. As a native source explains, since it was the gods who kept the Indians healthy, it was only 'after their conversion to Christianity and the loss of their gods that they began to die'.[16] It is no great surprise that many Indian testimonies should flatly contradict more optimistic views of the process of conversion. In some indigenous testimonies the friars are described condescendingly by Indians as 'poor and ill' creatures to be pitied for preferring 'sadness and solitude' to 'pleasure and contentment';[17] or as 'dead men' whose habits were 'like shrouds' and who 'fell apart' at night,

14   René Girard, *Violence and the Sacred* (Baltimore, Md, 1977), pp. 8, 13–22, 144, 266.
15   Ibid., p. 49. India is perhaps the most remarkable example of the central importance of sacrifice in human culture. As Christopher Dawson put it, 'poetry and mythology, ritual and magic, education and law, philosophy and mysticism, are all interwoven in an elaborate pattern which centres in the sacrifice and is controlled and ordered by the priesthood. It is the sacrifice that makes the sun rise and controls the course of the seasons. It is by the sacrifice that the gods live, and it is for the sacrifice that men exist and through the sacrifice that they acquire wealth and success and reach beyond life until they penetrate to the innermost mystery of being.' *Religion and Culture* (London, 1948), p. 92.
16   *Papeles de la Nueva España*, ed. Francisco del Passo y Troncoso, 7 vols (Madrid, 1905-6), iv, p. 236.
17   Diego Muñoz Camargo, *Historia de Tlaxcala* (Mexico City, 1947), p. 176.

Plate 10. Tzitzimime.

turning into bones and descending to the underworld 'where they kept their women'.[18] Occasionally they are even identified with *tzitzimime*, the demonic stars of Mesoamerican mythology, the sun's enemies and monsters of death and destruction who at the end of time would descend to kill and eat the last of mankind.[19]

It was no doubt this climate of defensive uneasiness in the wake of the advance of Christianity that nurtured the theological self-assurance of Indian leaders like the Cacique de Texcoco. Before being burnt at the stake in 1539, the Cacique declared openly that since his father and his grand-

18 *Relación de las ceremonias y ritos y población y gobierno de los indios de la provincia de Michoacán*, ed. José Tudela and José Corona Núñez (Morelia, 1977), pp. 265–7.
19 *Procesos de indios idólatras y hechiceros*, ed. Luis González Obregón (Mexico City, 1912), p. 23. On *tzitzimime* see Sahagún, *Historia general*, pp. 439, 317, where they are described as 'figuras feísimas y terribles que comerían a los hombres y mujeres...los cuales han de venir a destruir la tierra...para que siempre sean tinieblas y oscuridad en todo el mundo'.

father had been great prophets and had never mentioned anything concerning Christianity, it followed that Christian doctrine was false and there was nothing true in what the friars were teaching.[20] To a lesser extent similar views can be detected in many Indian testimonies, sometimes as late as the seventeenth-century 'primordial titles' where the fury with which the missionaries destroyed Indian temples and idols and condemned Indian rites was vividly remembered.[21]

*

The existence of anti-Christian tendencies among the Indians should not be interpreted as evidence of a conscious native opposition to the new religion. In practice the process was much more flexible. The absence of an authoritative written tradition allowed a remarkable degree of adaptation, interpretation and absorption among the Indians. If it is true that the pictorial part of the system of communication could convey concepts that were beyond spoken words, investing them with a sense of timelessness, it was the oral part that carried the burden of narration, formulation and conceptualization.[22] The flexibility attainable at this level of communication can be seen at work as early as 1537, in the case of the Indian Andrés Mixcoatl, who was found wandering through the villages of the Sierra de Puebla casting spells, distributing hallucinogenic mushrooms, demanding to be worshipped as a god and preaching against Christianity. Interestingly, during his interrogation Mixcoatl explained that he had been deceived by the devil, a reply which echoed the testimony of the Indian Tacaetl who a year earlier had acknowledged that the sacrifices performed to get rain were addressed to the devil. Similarly, in 1539, the Indian Culoa Tlaspicue confessed that he was a 'prophet' and as such responsible for 'the care of the devils and of all the things they need us to do for them'.[23]

At first sight, of course, there is nothing mysterious about these testimonies, and it is tempting to interpret them merely as the result of mistranslations or even of a conscious effort by the friars to impose upon the Indians an idea that was alien to them. But too much stress on the assumption that the concept of the devil was a mere 'imposition from above' can also lead to an anachronistic reading of the process which hides the possibility that the concept might, in many ways, have made some sense to the Indians, and which exaggerates the extent to which they were trying

20   *Proceso inquisitorial del Cacique de Texcoco*, ed. Luis González Obregón (Mexico City, 1910), p. 2; Muñoz Camargo, *Historia*, p. 219.
21   Serge Gruzinski, 'Le filet déchiré: Sociétés indigènes, occidentalisation et domination dans le Mexique central, XVIe-XVIIIe siècles', Thèse de doctorat ès lettres (Paris, 1986), pp. 254, 289.
22   Lockhart, *The Nahuas*, p. 327.
23   *Procesos de indios*, pp. 9, 75, 123. On Andrés Mixcoatl see Serge Gruzinski's interesting reconstruction in *Man-Gods in the Mexican Highlands* (Stanford, Calif., 1989), pp. 36–62.

to oppose Christianity. To avoid this danger, the above examples should be set in the context of three crucial considerations. Firstly, the importance of sacrifice and the need the Indians felt to preserve it, despite the bans; secondly, the insistence of the missionaries that sacrifices were the work of the devil; and finally, the Mesoamerican understanding of deity as a compound of both good and evil, with the consequent difficulty for the Indians to conceive of a devil that was totally malevolent or even undesirable.

When these three factors are considered together, the suggestion that the Indians did not see any inconsistency in agreeing with the friars that their sacrifices were addressed to the devil should not appear farfetched. For, in spite of the friars' efforts to make the Indians see in the devil an enemy to be feared and avoided, often what the Indians saw was simply a further deity that they could incorporate into their existing pantheon. Indeed, if, as the friars insisted, it was the devil to whom the sacrifices were invariably addressed, then it is likely that the Indians would have come to see the devil as crucially important in the effort to protect and continue their sacrificial rituals. In other words, by insisting that the devil was the central object of the sacrifices, the friars were making it difficult for their neophytes to conceive of him as an enemy. They were in fact encouraging a tendency where the Indians could willingly have contributed to their own demonization.

The process can be seen at work in some of the early codices, where the devil was associated with some of the more malevolent of Mesoamerican deities, such as Mictlanteuctli (Lord of the Dead), who was often depicted as a clawed monster inducing Indians to eat human flesh or hallucinogenic mushrooms (see plates 11,12 and 13). The aim of the missionaries was to encourage an identification of the devil with evil through the mushrooms; but since the Indians traditionally attributed divinity to the mushrooms (in the *Codex Magliabecchi* the mushrooms actually appear in the colour jade, which in Nahua thought was symbolic of the supernatural and the divine),[24] many would have been persuaded of the importance and even of the divine attributes of the devil precisely because of his association with the mushrooms. It was no doubt such dangers that led some of the early friars to trivialize the devil by identifying him with non-divine Nahua concepts, such as *tlacatecolotl* ('human owl', a malevolent sorcerer associated with ghostly apparitions) in order to discourage idolatry.[25] But such efforts were short-lived. Sahagún, among others, feared that they would play down the importance of the devil. As a result, the growing obsession with diabolism and the consequent distrust of Indian cultures that we detected from the middle of the sixteenth century onwards, led to an increasing identification of Indian practices with demonic activity.

24 *Magliabecchi: Libro de la vida que los indios antiguamente hazían*, facsimile edn (Berkeley, Calif., 1903), fol. 78r; Bernardino de Sahagún, *Códice Florentino*, facsimile edn, 3 vols (Mexico City, 1979), bk. 9, fol. 142v; and see Gruzinski, 'Le filet déchiré', p. 531.
25 On this see Burkhart, *Slippery Earth*, p. 41.

Plates 11, 12 and 13 (above right). Mictlanteuctli in demonic guise inducing Indians into cannibalism and idolatry.

What needs emphasis is that the Indians often collaborated willingly in this process. Just as the association of the devil with the mushrooms had encouraged them to attribute divinity to him, so his association with sacrifices and other Indian practices that the Spaniards were eager to extirpate led to the paradoxical development of a demonic ethos among the Indians which to some extent persisted, as inquisitorial records show, throughout the colonial period and beyond. Already in the last years of the sixteenth century Indians are known to have encouraged demonic devotions. In 1597, after the Spaniard Francisco Ruiz Castrejón was found in possession of a 'little book', written in the native Tarascan tongue, where the reader was encouraged to 'offer and commend' himself to 'the Lord Lucifer', he confessed to have taken advice from a group of Indians who had urged him to stop venerating the Blessed Sacrament, saying the rosary or wearing Christian relics.[26] A year later, when a herdsman was found to have tattooed a devil on his arm next to an image of Jesus, he explained that the purpose of the figures was to remind him of the need to forsake Jesus when he worshipped the devil, for according to the Indian who had instructed him, just as the worship of God implied the abhorrence of the devil, so the worship of the devil implied the abhorrence of God.[27] Similar examples were multiplied in the course of the next two centuries, when it became a virtual rule that whoever was tempted to invoke the devil or, more specifically, to

26 Archivo General de la Nación, Mexico City, Ramo Inquisición (hereafter A.G.N., Inq.), tomo 209, exp. 9 (hereafter 209.9), fol. 5r.
27 A.G.N., Inq., 147.6, fols 18v–19v, 40r, 45r.

attempt a demonic pact would need to undergo a long search for Indians in remote mountains or caves. In such places they would invariably be asked to forsake God and the saints, take off the rosary and any Christian relic and promise to stop going to Mass, praying to God, looking at the consecrated host or observing any of the teachings of the Church.[28]

It would be a mistake, however, to generalize from the above examples and to suggest that such an anti-Christian ethos was the rule among the Indians. The evidence for such developments is characteristic of the regions on the fringe where, as James Lockhart has written, 'Spanish immigrants were few and indigenous people less than fully sedentary'.[29] It seems, therefore, that in proportion as the Christian ritual took over in the towns, and as the churches and the clergy took over from the native temples and priests, those individuals who sought to continue the native rites and practices were gradually relegated to the periphery. Given that the native conception of space was inseparable from ritual, since it was precisely the sacredness of space that gave the ethnic territory its raison d'être, it was logical that mountains, caves and other remote places should have been revitalized as a result of religious repression.[30] As late as the second half of the seventeenth century, some Indian testimonies recall how, after the arrival of the Spaniards, many Indians refused to accept the faith and went to hide in woods, ravines and caves.[31] Thus banished to the periphery, traditional rites and practices ceased to be regular community activities. But in the process they also ceased to be mere continuations of pre-Hispanic rites. The recurrence of the concept of the devil indicates that an effective affirmation of their Indian identity required the use and manipulation of Christian concepts. Just as modern Oriental and African nationalisms use an unmistakably western ideology in order to oppose the West, so the Indians appear to have used a conspicuously Christian concept in those cases when they needed to oppose Christianity. Even the mechanism of the demonic pact, complete with its pseudo-feudal oaths of fealty and vassalage, seems to have been successfully integrated into the Indian scheme by the early seventeenth century.

However marginal and peripheral, these examples shed a good deal of light upon the more confusing and haphazard processes that can be seen at work in less remote areas. In towns and cities, for instance, the way in

28 Some illustrative examples can be found in A.G.N., Inq., 454.14, fols 266v–267r; 563.3, fol. 20r; 578.5, fol. 291r.; 681.5, fols 269v–270r, 285r–285v; 788.25, fols 535r–560r; 827.1, fol. 25r. Demonic pacts and invocations will be dealt with more fully in chapter 3.
29 *The Nahuas*, p. 4.
30 On this point see Marcello Carmagnani, *El regreso de los dioses: El proceso de reconstitución de la identidad étnica en Oaxaca, siglos XVII y XVIII* (Mexico City, 1988), pp. 27–9, 49–50.
31 See, for example, the 'primordial title' of San Antonio Zoyatzingo in A.G.N., Tierras, 1665.5, fos 166r–182v; also Lockhart, *Nahuas and Spaniards: Postconquest Central Mexican History and Philology* (Stanford, Calif., 1991), p. 53.

which the Indians assimilated the concept of the devil seems to have gone hand in hand with their acceptance of the Christian message and their participation in Christian ritual. Yet it is ironical that their use of the devil had much more in common with Indian clandestine practices than with the fear and rejection of him that the friars were trying to encourage. As Nancy Farriss observed in her study of the Maya, it was, as a rule, those very Indians most eagerly involved in the Christian liturgy and ritual who were most often found to participate actively in proscribed pre-Hispanic practices. The Maya *maestros cantores*, for example, led a 'dual existence' which resulted from an 'unresolved metaphysical conflict that the friars could not understand'.[32] While in the eyes of the missionaries they were guilty of duplicity, their actions were in fact the result of a collective will determined to preserve a given set of values in the new Christian configuration.[33]

The Maya were not an exception. Diego de Landa's surprised horror at finding that the Indians had started to crucify their sacrificial victims in Yucatán finds an illustrative parallel in Tzompahuacán, in central Mexico, where, at the beginning of the seventeenth century, governor Pedro Ponce observed that the crucifix and parodies of the Mass had been incorporated into certain midnight sacrifices that the Indians performed 'according to their ancient customs'. It is interesting that only one half of the sacrifice was offered to 'the god of fire', whom the Indians had no qualms about calling the devil; the other half was reverently taken as an offering to the church.[34] Similarly, in 1656, Gonzalo de Balsalobre sent a detailed report to the bishop of Oaxaca on the 'idolatries, superstitions and vain observances' of the region, where he pointed out that the Indians had incorporated several Christian elements into their sacrificial rituals. Although the sacrifices of hens, chickens and puppy-dogs were made to 'the god of hell' – sometimes called 'the devil' without any apparent inconsistency – it was also noticed that the 'master of idolatries', an Indian called Diego Luis, insisted that the sacrifices should be performed in the church of the town on specific feast days. The feast of 'the god of thunder', for instance, was the best day to reap the harvest. The first three ears of maize should be taken to the church and flanked by three candles while penances and animal sacrifices were offered in honour of the god of thunder. Similarly, deer-hunting should be undertaken on the feast of 'the god of hell', when 'one should go to the

---

32 Farriss, *Maya Society*, p. 341. A similar phenomenon can be observed further south in Ixpimienta which seems to have become a hotbed of apostates who, nevertheless, sought collective expression in Christian ritual. See Grant D. Jones, *Maya Resistance to Spanish Rule: Time and History on a Colonial Frontier* (Albuquerque, N. Mex., 1989), pp. 107–8.

33 Carmagnani, *El regreso*, pp. 13–14.

34 Pedro Ponce, *Breve relación de los dioses y ritos de la gentilidad*, in *Tratado de las idolatrías*, ed. F. del Passo y Troncoso, 2 vols (Mexico City, 1953), i, pp. 369–80. For Landa's account of the crucifixion of sacrificial victims see Clendinnen, *Ambivalent Conquests*, pp. 88–91.

church early in the morning and light a candle on the altar of the Christ in honour of the god of hell'.[35]

The fact that the 'god of hell' was apparently attributed a Trinitarian nature by the Indians – one being with three persons who, together with the goddess of hell, was joint receiver of the sacrificial offerings – persuaded Balsalobre that this was further proof of the well-known efforts of the devil to try to mimic Christianity. Perhaps Balsalobre read too much into the ap-parent similarities, for the case has more to do with that process of reappropriation of the nomadic past, centring on fishing and hunting activities, that Marcello Carmagnani has seen at work from the middle of the seventeenth century as part of an effort to reconstitute an ethnic identity in Oaxaca.[36] But the case is also illustrative of the way in which Spanish and Christian elements had become central to the Indian sense of identity and local pride. For although it is becoming increasingly clear that indigenous structures and patterns survived the conquest on a much more massive scale than was commonly assumed, nowhere did this go hand in hand with open disbelief or continued resistance to Christianity. Just as the ostensibly Spanish-style *cabildos* of each Indian municipality became the primary vehicle of corporate representation, so too the church became the primary symbol of corporate identity. As James Lockhart has observed, the church was often felt to have been erected entirely by the community, whose strong identification with it became an important symbol of the town's existence and status.[37]

In this context, Diego Luis's insistence that the sacrifices should be performed in the church is perfectly coherent. What remains problematic is the ease with which the Indians appeared to have identified the 'god of hell' or the 'god of thunder' with the devil. The development is clearly comparable to the earlier association of the devil with the mushrooms in the codices. While the clergy expected the Indians to abandon their sacrifices by telling them that they were the work of the devil, in practice the Indians tended to see the devil as a friend rather than as an enemy precisely because of his association with the sacrifices. The problem was not so much one of agreeing with the European assumption that the sacrifices were the work of the devil, as one of failing to understand the reasons why they should be stopped.

Perhaps the best example of this process received the attention of the Mexican Inquisition in the last quarter of the seventeenth century. It involved the Indian Mateo Pérez, governor of the town of Santiago de Atitlán in the Indian parish of Juquila, in Oaxaca, who was found guilty of worshipping the devil, 'making sacrifices to him and rendering him the cult

35 Gonzalo de Balsalobre, *Relación auténtica de las idolatrías, supersticiones y vanas observaciones de los indios del obispado de Oaxaca*, in *Tratado de las idolatrías*, ed. F. del Passo y Troncoso, ii, pp. 353–4, 373–4.
36 Carmagnani, *El regreso*, pp. 50–1.
37 Lockhart, *Nahuas and Spaniards*, p. 62.

and adoration due only to God'.[38] His 'devil-worship' did not differ essentially from the activities of Diego Luis described by Balsalobre. The practice involved the sacrifice of hens and puppy-dogs and the mixing of their blood with pulque and maize before it was offered to 'the devil' amidst an elaborate ceremonial. According to an Indian witness, moreover, Pérez always insisted that the sacrifices should be performed in the church of Atitlán and especially on the feast of Santiago (St James).[39] The fact that in art St James was often associated with thunder and lightning might shed some light on Diego Luis's 'god of thunder'. The irony here is that the use of St James by the Indians with the purpose of continuing their ancient sacrifices, and the insistence by the priests and the extirpators that the sacrifices were the work of the devil, might have led indirectly to an identification of St James, as 'the god of thunder', with the devil. Indeed, some witnesses declared that on the feast of St James Pérez invoked the name of God together with the god of thunder and the devil;[40] and when Pérez himself was questioned about this he explained that he had been persuaded of the need for such sacrifices in a dream by the devil himself who, otherwise, would 'cause thunder to strike the church'.[41]

The cases of Diego Luis and Mateo Pérez point to a clear indigenous effort to incorporate elements of their own past into the Christian rituals, an effort where the use of the church and of the patron saints in the performance of their sacrifices seemed perfectly logical. It was the insistence of the Spaniards that such sacrifices were the work of Satan that led to that peculiar identification of the devil with the saints, especially those saints who, like St James, had taken over the role of some previous tutelary deity. But the identification was in no way part of an effort to oppose Christianity. Mateo Pérez was known as an exemplary Christian who 'encouraged the divine cult, the rosary and taught the Christian doctrine' and who, as *cantor* of the church of Atitlán, was actively and willingly engaged in the practice of Christian liturgy and ritual.[42] Far from opposing Christianity, Diego Luis and Mateo Pérez were engaged in an effort to reconstitute their pagan past through the appropriation and reinterpretation of Christian elements. Despite the inevitable distortions that this process entailed, it is clear that the devil, together with the saints, soon came to form an integral part of indigenous cosmology.

*

38   A.G.N., Inq., 615.1, fols 1r–212v. This is one of the few cases in the Inquisition that deal with an Indian. It was made possible by Pérez's claim to be a mestizo until the Inquisitors decided otherwise and brought the trial to an end.
39   A.G.N., Inq., 615.1, fols 1r, 4r–v., 116v, 25r.
40   A.G.N., Inq., 615.1, fol. 65v.
41   A.G.N., Inq., 615.1, fols 116v–118v.
42   A.G.N., Inq., 615.1, fols 79v, 100v.

The above developments shed some light upon the insistent association of Indians with demonic activity that we have detected in inquisitorial records throughout the colonial period. But it would be dangerous to ignore that they are peculiar to the southern region of Oaxaca, while similar examples for the rest of Mexico are very rare. The case of Yucatán, where Nancy Farriss and Grant D. Jones have pointed to a similar collective effort to reconstruct an ethnic identity by the appropriation and reinterpretation of Christian elements,[43] suggests that such developments are peculiar to remote and relatively unacculturated regions where, moreover, the comparative violence and intolerance that accompanied the missionary enterprise led to the development of a more markedly defensive ethos among the Indians. The situation contrasts sharply with developments in central Mexico, especially those areas where the early Franciscans left their mark. Indeed, in contrast to the negative Indian memories of the conquest and to the identification of friars with *tzitzimime* and death, Indian testimonies from central Mexico are full of romantic evocations of the sanctity, humility and chastity of the friars, with the memory of the first years of conversion as a golden age when the message of the gospel finally liberated them from the yoke of idolatry.[44]

Such evidence points to a process of conversion where, underneath the growing distrust of native beliefs among clerics and intellectuals, the identification of Christian saints with native deities was often tolerated and even encouraged. The early development of cults such as those of the Virgins of Guadalupe and Ocotlán on the sites of the native goddesses Tonantzin and Xochiquetzalli would be inexplicable otherwise. The case of Our Lady of Ocotlán has been given added interest by a document recounting the apparition where the Franciscan author Fray Martín Sarmiento de Hojacastro openly states that even when it was not clear whether the Indian saw the Virgin Mary or the goddess Xochiquetzalli or, indeed, some other pagan deity, the confusion was of no consequence so long as it might encourage the Indians to come eventually to venerate the mother of God. Similar developments, he concluded, should be encouraged as powerful tools in the process of evangelization.[45] And indeed, in the neighbouring area of San Juan Tianguismanalco St John the Apostle was readily identified with the youthful manifestation of Tezcatlipoca; and in Santa Ana Chiautempan, St Anne, grandmother of Jesus, adequately took the place of the grandmother goddess Toci.[46]

43   Farriss, *Maya Society*; Jones *Maya Resistance*.
44   *Papeles de la Nueva España*, iv, p. 220, vi, pp. 15-16, 29; A.G.N., Tierras, 1665.5, fol. 183r; 2674.1, fol. 13r.
45   I draw on Hugo G. Nutini, 'Syncretism and Acculturation: The Historical Development of the Cult of the Patron Saint in Tlaxcala, Mexico (1519–1670), *Ethnology*, 15, no. 3 (July 1976), pp. 310–16; see also his *Ritual Kinship*, 2 vols (Princeton, N.J., 1980–4), i, ch. x.
46   Nutini, 'Syncretism and Acculturation', pp. 306–7.

It must be pointed out that the claim of the Hojacastro document, as it has come to be known, to date from 1547, when the Virgin was believed to have appeared to the Indian Juan Diego Bernardino, is highly questionable. Hugo Nutini's argument that it provides adequate proof of a process of 'guided syncretism' encouraged by the Franciscans has been rightly criticized by James Lockhart as incompatible with what is known of the attitudes of the friars in the middle of the sixteenth century. Moreover the style and the subject matter of the document are much more characteristic of seventeenth-century accounts of apparitions, and in any case it would be difficult to date it before 1647, when the first account of the Guadalupe apparition, upon which the Hojacastro story seems to be based, began to circulate.[47] However that may be, and even if it dates from the late seventeenth century, the Hojacastro document points to the existence of a strong unofficial tradition that tolerated the persistence of pre-Hispanic elements and their incorporation into the ceremonies and rituals of Christianity. The trend is especially evident in the recurrence of themes such as the story of the Magi in Nahuatl songs and plays throughout the colonial period, as well as of stories that stress the essential goodness of pagan traditions.[48] Perhaps the best example is the Nahuatl play about St Helena and the Holy Cross, preserved for posterity by Manuel de los Santos y Salazar, the Tlaxcalan collector and editor of the late Nahuatl annals, who copied or revised the text in 1714. In a revealing passage Constantine's conversion to Christianity is strategically placed after a eulogy of the emperor for honouring the ancient Roman gods, who are acknowledged as great and powerful, 'for they have put at his feet his various enemies, who greatly feared him'.[49]

Turning to the devil, the absence in central Mexico of evidence to compare with the examples of Diego Luis and Mateo Pérez in Oaxaca suggests that the process of identification might have followed a similar pattern to

47 Lockhart, *The Nahuas*, pp. 549–50, n. 170. The name Juan Diego Bernardino is not a common Indian name in the sixteenth century and it is more likely to be a compound of Juan Diego, the hero of the Guadalupe story, and Juan Bernardino, Juan Diego's sick uncle. The best recent study of the Guadalupe cult is Edmundo O'Gorman, *Destierro de sombras* (Mexico City, 1986).

48 Lockhart, *The Nahuas*, pp. 407–8. Lockhart notes the apparent paradox that the vast majority of the extant copies of the plays are very late, while the basic themes correspond to the early years of Franciscan evangelization. This suggests the existence of a dynamic unofficial tradition seeking to affirm the Indian past in a Christian context.

49 Ibid., p. 400. Lockhart points out the 'strangely contradictory message about religion'. Yet in the context of the unofficial tradition preserved by the Indians and apparently tolerated, or perhaps even encouraged, by the friars, the message is perfectly coherent. In Lockhart's literal translation from the Nahuatl the passage reads: 'Constantine arriving, honours his gods. For that reason he was able to overcome his enemies. May everywhere be praised valiant Constantine, deserving to be feared everywhere. Powerful are his gods, for they have put at his feet his various enemies, who greatly feared him. Now he has recognized the precious child of God; now he has received baptism.'

that of the Virgins of Ocotlán and Guadalupe. Indeed, it could well be that the absence of cases comparable to the ones observed in Oaxaca and Yucatán is explicable in terms of a lack of concern among clerics in the face of similar developments. Instead, the scattered pieces of information that are at present available from central Mexico seem to fit into a pattern of gradual assimilation and incorporation of the Christian notion of the devil into the Indian mental world. Just as it was hoped that the identification of the Virgin with a native goddess would lead eventually to the veneration of the Virgin, so too it was hoped that the identification of the devil with the more malevolent representations of the native deities would gradually lead the Indians to repudiate the devil and his works. Already Sahagún's *tzitzimime* seem to combine the worst elements of both indigenous deities and Christian devils, in such a way that, as Louise Burkhart has put it, 'they seem to have stepped right out of a converted Nahua's nightmare'.[50]

Although in the early stages such methods seem to have reinforced rather than contradicted Nahua understandings, a clearer differentiation between morally positive and morally negative supernatural beings had begun to sink in by the end of the sixteenth century. In 1598, for example, a mestizo called Juan Luis defended himself against an inquisitorial accusation by blaming Gabriel Sánchez Mateo, an Indian from Xochimilco, for having advised him to pray to the devil. When called for questioning, the Indian willingly confirmed Juan Luis's testimony and stated that nobody had taught him to pray to the devil and to ask for his help, but that the desire to do so had been 'born in his heart' after remembering how

> the Indians, in their antiquity, used to invoke the devil seeking his help and how the devil used to help them; and that, in order that the devil would come to help him, he had forsaken God and his saints, because the devil flees from them, and thus he had turned away from them so that the devil would come.[51]

There is a clear interplay in this testimony between an emerging Christian concept and a receding pre-Hispanic memory. Gabriel Sánchez Mateo had assimilated the concept of the devil as the enemy of God and his saints. Yet this did not prevent him from seeing the devil as a friend whose help could be invoked just as the Indians used to do 'in their antiquity'. It was precisely this identification of the devil with the pre-Hispanic rites that the friars hoped would eventually persuade the Indians to reject the devil and their ancient practices. But at this stage the development was still very much in that 'middle ground' that the Dominican Diego Durán had described so aptly only a few decades earlier when he had come across an

50   *Slippery Earth*, pp. 55–6.
51   A.G.N., Inq., 147.6, fol. 45r.

Indian who persevered in his 'idolatry'. 'Being reproached for the evil that
he had done', writes Durán,

> he replied: 'Father, you should not be alarmed that we are still *nepantla*'.
> And wanting a better understanding of what he meant by that word and
> metaphor which means 'to be in the middle', I again asked him to
> explain in which 'middle' they were. To this he said that, since they were
> not yet firmly rooted in the faith, I should not be alarmed, for they were
> still neutral and held on to neither to one law nor to the other; or, in other
> words, that they believed in God but at the same time they reverted to
> their old customs and rites of the devil.[52]

The same opinion is found in more coherent form in the remarkable set
of *Coloquios* composed in Nahuatl in the 1560s under the direction of
Bernardino de Sahagún. After the Franciscans have proclaimed the existence of the Christian god and the consequent falseness and perversity of
the native deities, whom they equate with demons, the indigenous priests
openly acknowledge the Christian god, but at the same time argue for the
preservation of their own divinities, who from time immemorial have provided the Indians with spiritual and material sustenance.[53]

*

It would be tempting to see the tendency to 'nepantlism' among the Indians
as evidence of the incompatibility of the two sets of beliefs, or of the
absence of a 'mutual middle ground between a sacrifice-oriented monism
and a soteriologically oriented matter/spirit dualism'.[54] But such an interpretation seems to read too much into the contemporary intellectual
assumption that Christianity and paganism were mutually exclusive alterna-
tives from which the Indians had to choose and between which they might
switch back and forth as the forces of good and evil struggled for their
souls.[55] At the practical level, the kind of Christianity that the Indians had
to contend with was not so much the Christianity of the intellectuals and
the extirpators as that 'local' religion which William Christian has
unearthed so meticulously in sixteenth-century Spain and whose points of
contact with the Mesoamerican world were innumerable.

As Christian has shown, the saints in Castile were widely regarded as the

52 Diego Durán, *Historia de las Indias de Nueva España e islas de Tierra Firme*, 2 vols (Mexico
City, 1967), ii, p. 3.
53 Bernardino de Sahagún, *Coloquios y Doctrina Cristiana*, ed. Miguel León Portilla (Mexico
City, 1986), pp. 146–55.
54 Burkhart, *Slippery Earth*, p. 188. A commonly held opinion; see, for example, Gruzinski,
Man-Gods, pp. 18, 42, 44, 50.
55 Farriss, *Maya Society*, p. 293.

resident patrons of their communities, very much in the same way as the
tutelary deities were perceived by Mesoamericans. Most vows were made in
response to some natural disaster, and, although men and women
approached the saints as advocates of the community, some reports point to
a belief that the saints were capable of inflicting harm on communities if the
latter did not observe their sacred contracts. Each Castilian village had its
own calendar of sacred times, marked on the village memory by natural dis-
asters or other supernatural signs which had become solemn contracts with
the saints. Everyone thus knew that it was a collective responsibility, going
back in time and ahead into the future, to observe these sacred contracts
and that dire consequences could follow lapses. As much as in Mesoamerica,
therefore, religion in sixteenth-century Castile was a corporate affair involving the propitiation of a host of supernatural beings who displayed
benevolent and malevolent attributes.[56]

   Thus the view of the extirpators and of too many subsequent thinkers
that Christianity sat, in its purity, like a layer of oil over Mesoamerican
magic is a highly misleading one. For the Christian religion was itself inter-
mingled with a great deal of magic. Necromancers, enpsalmers and
conjurers of clouds often competed directly with parish priests in early
modern Castile. Inquisition records show that many of them were themselves clergy or religious, sometimes involved in such practices as dealing
with locusts by holding them up for trial and excommunicating them, or
holding matches with wizards to see who was best at chasing clouds.[57] It is
true that they were widely regarded with suspicion and often accused of
having sided with the cause of Satan; but even so, it could not be denied
that the Church itself had its own arsenal of orthodox and legal prayers and
exorcisms to be used on similar occasions.

   It is a mistake, therefore, to regard all magical practices as standing outside official teaching and worship. In the context of a world-view where
humanity was permanently assailed by hostile armies of demons, against
which the appropriate official remedy was the incantatory (a manual invocation of the cross or names of Christ), magical practices can hardly be
regarded as mere constructs of the folk imagination. As Eamon Duffy has
explained, the bulk of them were 'built into the very structure of the liturgy,
and formed the focus for some of its most solemn and popularly accessible
moments' such as 'the Rogation processions, the administration of baptism
and the blessings of salt and water every Sunday and of wax candles at
Candlemas'.[58] There thus existed a symbiotic relationship between the
official orthodox remedies and the apparently superstitious practices that

56   William A. Christian, Jr, *Local Religion in Sixteenth-Century Spain* (Princeton, N. J., 1981),
pp. 33, 97, 124, 142, 174–7.
57   Ibid., pp. 29–30.
58   *The Stripping of the Altars: Traditional Religion in England c.1400–c.1580* (New Haven and
London, 1992), p. 279.

became the most common objects of concern and criticism among the educated. The *Malleus Maleficarum*, for instance, specifically recognized that many popular practices, though fallen into the hands of 'indiscreet and superstitious persons', were entirely sacred in origin and legitimate when applied by pious people, whether lay or religious. And even when such remedies as holy water, the sign of the cross, holy candles, church bells, or consecrated herbs had failed, the *Malleus* recommended the use of popular magic provided it did not involve demonic invocation or transfer of diseases. Sacred words worn round the neck, or placed by the sick or given them to kiss, constituted an entirely lawful practice, even if the user could not understand the words, for 'it is enough if such a man fixes his thoughts upon the divine virtue and leaves it to the divine will to do what seems good to his mercy'.[59]

If by the middle of the sixteenth century such practices had come under deep suspicion, the line between 'magical' and 'orthodox' remedies remained thin. In seventeenth-century Mexico it is interesting to observe that those very people who were especially suspicious of Indian magical practices often found themselves working almost on identical assumptions to those they were so keen to condemn. Jacinto de la Serna, for instance, had no qualms about attributing the healing powers of an Indian to a demonic compact; yet, in the very same passage, he describes how he himself performed a similar healing practice on his Indian servant Agustina:

> Seeing that there was no remedy...nor any adequate knowledge of the ailment that would point to the suitability of a homely cure, it so happened that I had in my possession a piece of bone from the saintly and venerable body of Gregorio López....With the utmost devotion known to me...I gave her a tiny piece of the bone to drink in a spoonful of water.

Agustina's subsequent recovery was, to Serna's mind, evident proof that 'the saintly Gregory had performed two miracles: the one, to return that convalescent woman to health...and the other, to help spread the rumour that she had been bewitched'.[60]

Not only is there no essential difference between Serna's healing rite and those practised by Indians, there is even open competition between them in

---

59 *Malleus Maleficarum*, pp. 381–7; Duffy, *Stripping of the Altars*, p. 285. Keith Thomas, *Religion and the Decline of Magic* (Harmondsworth, 1978 edn) p. 588. The application of sacramentals to this-worldly concerns, often seen by historians as a mark of the superficiality of late medieval religion, was also legitimated by the liturgy. An excellent brief discussion of the significance of sacramentals at this time is R. W. Scribner, *Popular Culture and Popular Movements in Germany* (London, 1987), pp. 1–49.

60 Jacinto de la Serna, *Manual de ministros de indios para el conocimiento de sus idolatrías y extirpación de ellas*, in *Colección de documentos inéditos para la historia de España*, vol. 104, p. 58.

a way very similar to that described by William Christian between conjurers and parish priests in Castile.[61] What was under attack, therefore, was not the belief in the magical utility of certain objects. Such belief was scientifically accepted: it stemmed from current systems of classification that assumed the existence of correspondences and analogies between different parts of creation which, as late as 1702, still allowed a group of physicians in Puebla to ask permission from the Inquisition to attempt a cure for epilepsy with the use of the skulls of hanged men.[62] In such a context, attacks on magic, and especially Indian magic, did not stem from the fear that it was superstitious or irrational or even 'wrong' but, on the contrary, that it was powerful and efficacious and, therefore, dangerous. Recourse to magic was a practice accepted by both cultures and understood and put into effect in very much the same way.

If this was true of the likes of Jacinto de la Serna, it was even more so of the average Europeans and Africans who had steadily begun to populate the new continent. The clear differences that the immigrants necessarily encountered between the New World and the world they had left behind led them increasingly to rely on the Indians not only for the physical knowledge of the environment but, more often, for the local spiritual forces that they understood so much better.[63] The recurrent involvement of Indians in inquisitorial cases dealing with diabolism suggests that a large number of people opted to defer to the Indians' superior knowledge of their world and its spiritual forces. But, likewise, the meticulous care that the inquisitors took to deal with such cases is a clear indication that even those who chose not to defer to Indian magic were far from denying its reality and efficacy.

And the process did not flow only in one direction. From the beginning Christian 'magic' was believed by the Indians to be efficient, and its association with the dominant sectors of society gave it a charisma that native magic, for all its local efficacy, lacked. Indian healing rites soon came to be accompanied by Christian prayers and invocations, and hallucinogens like peyote and ololiuhqui are known to have been associated with Christ, the angels, Mary, the Child Jesus, the Trinity, St Nicholas and St Peter.[64] In an

61 Identical developments have been found recently in Counter-Reformation Catalonia, for which see Henry Kamen, *The Phoenix and the Flame: Catalonia and the Counter-Reformation* (New Haven and London, 1993), p. 236, and in Counter-Reformation southern Italy, for which see David Gentilcore, *From Bishop to Witch: The System of the Sacred in Early Modern Terra d'Otranto* (Manchester and New York, 1992), pp. 94–113.

62 A.G.N., Inq., 724.1.

63 On this point see Julio Caro Baroja, *Vidas mágicas e Inquisición*, 2 vols (Madrid, 1967), i, p. 49.

64 On the 'christianization' of Indian healing rites see, for example, A.G.N., Inq., 513.31, fol. 110r; 687.2, fols 14r–277v; 781.54, fols 609r–644v; 1121.8, fols 229r–233v. On the association of hallucinogens with saints etc. see A.G.N., Inq., 303.19, fols 78r–80r; 510.23; 510.133; 317.21; 339.34; 356(II).126; 727.9; 746.12; 781.54; 912.72.

illustrative example recorded by Serna, an Indian healer called Catalina claimed that she had not been taught the art of healing by any human person but directly by God. An angel, she claimed, had appeared to her saying:

> 'Do not be sad, Cata, God has sent you this gift to relieve you from your poverty and great misery, that you may get chilli and salt with it; with it also you will have the power to heal wounds by the mere touch of your tongue....' And after saying this...he crucified her, nailing her hands to a cross; and it was while she was nailed to the cross that she was taught the art of healing.[65]

Despite widespread fears that such examples were further proofs of the perfidious ways of Satan to keep the Indians under his grip, there are no signs here of any clandestine persistence of idolatry or of any sort of opposition to the Christian faith. Such examples point more in the direction of a process where the Indians were piecing their cosmos together in the new Christian configuration, a process that entailed a gradual shift from the 'nepantla' position, noticed by Durán, towards a less obviously syncretic devotion to the Christian saints.

It was inevitable that in this nascent form of Christianity, many of the Christian friars, hermits and ascetics should have adopted features formerly associated with the native shamans and demigods, like the *naguales* who, before the conquest, had led a life of sacrifice, fasting and sexual abstinence. With the introduction of Christianity many *naguales* came into conflict with each other and were gradually forced into defensive and destructive attitudes that only served to further their association with demonic powers.[66]

The vacuum left by the native shamans was adequately filled by the many hermits, ascetics and 'venerables' that began to populate New Spain's hagiographic literature from the late sixteenth century onwards.[67] That the prestige of such men should have depended upon their power as wonderworkers, or that men and women should have sought them in the same way as they had formerly resorted to pagan shrines or healers, is often seen as

---

65   *Manual de ministros*, p. 165.
66   On this see Gonzalo Aguirre Beltrán, *Medicina y Magia: El proceso de aculturación en la estructura colonial* (Mexico City, 1963), pp. 98–103.
67   Among the most representative works are the Dominican Francisco de Burgoa, *Palestra historial de virtudes y ejemplares apostólicos* (Mexico City, 1670), the Augustinian Matías de Escobar, *América Thebaida, Vitas Patrum de los religiosos ermitaños de N.P San Agustín*, 2nd edn (Mexico City, 1924), and the Jesuit Andrés Pérez de Ribas, *Historia de los triunfos de nuestra Santa Fe entre gentes de las más bárbaras y fieras del nuevo orbe* (Madrid, 1645). On Franciscans there is an interesting manuscript compiled by order of Bishop Juan de Palafox, giving details of the lives of fifteen saintly friars in the first three decades of the seventeenth century; 'Informaciones de quince religiosos venerables de esta provincia de San Diego de México...' Archivio Generale dei Frati Minori, Rome, MS. T. 10.

evidence of the limitations of the missionary enterprise or even of the non-Christian character of Spanish American Catholicism.[68] Yet the climate of these years is no less genuinely Christian than that of the early centuries of the middle ages, which saw the rise of the cult of the saints, to which Gregory of Tours contributed so much.[69] Behind its syncretic mixtures, it was in this twilight world that the Indians came face to face with a transcendent power in which the harsh realities of existence no longer dominated their lives and where human suffering and misfortune could find a remedy. Indeed, it was precisely in this world of mythology – of the cult of the saints and their relics and their miracles – that the vital transfusion of Christianity with Mesoamerican tradition was most successfully achieved. For it would have been very difficult for a people without a tradition of written literature or philosophy to assimilate the metaphysical distinctions of Christian doctrine or the subtleties of medieval scholasticism. When, however, the new religion was manifested to the Indians visibly in the lives and example of men seemingly endowed with supernatural powers, it became incomparably more accessible to them. The process of conversion in New Spain was carried out not so much by the teaching of the new doctrines as by the manifestation of a new power. Just as in the European 'dark ages' the hermits and the monks had been the apostles of the new faith among the pagans of Europe, so now the ascetic friars and 'venerables' became the principal channels of Christian culture among the Indians of Mesoamerica.[70]

The process was not so much one of assimilation or even of acculturation, but rather one of contradiction and contrast. The friars impressed the

---

68   The same view has been vigorously argued in the case of pre-Tridentine European Catholicism by Jean Delumeau, *Catholicism between Luther and Voltaire: A New View of the Counter-Reformation* (London, 1977), passim. For Mexico and Italy, Delumeau's argument is taken up by Serge Gruzinski and Jean-Michel Sallmann, 'Une Source d'ethnohistoire: Les vies de "venerables" dans l'Italie méridionale et le Mexique baroques', *Mélanges de l'école française de Rome*, 88.2 (1976), pp. 789–822.

69   Peter Brown, *The Cult of the Saints: Its Rise and Function in Latin Christianity* (London, 1981), pp. 106–27. On competition between saints and sorcerers in Late Antiquity see his 'Sorcery, Demons and the Rise of Christianity: from Late Antiquity into the Middle Ages', in his book *Religion and Society in the Age of St Augustine* (London, 1972), pp. 129–30. See also Valerie Flint, *The Rise of Magic* (Oxford, 1991), pp. 64, 248, and Alexander Murray, 'Missionaries and Magic in Dark-Age Europe', *Past and Present*, no. 136 (Aug. 1992), pp. 188–90. It is fascinating to observe that the principal hagiographical writings of Gregory of Tours (the four books on the miracles of St Martin, the Life of the Fathers, the book of the miracles of St Julian of Brioude and the books of the Glory of the Blessed Martyrs and the Glory of the Confessors) are remarkably similar in spirit to Spanish American hagiographical writings such as Matías de Escobar's *America Thebaida* or Francisco de Burgoa's *Palestra Historial*.

70   For the same process during the European dark ages see Christopher Dawson's remarkably perceptive account in his Gifford Lectures of 1948–9, published as *Religion and the Rise of Western Culture* (London, 1950), pp. 32–43. I am heavily indebted to these pages for what follows.

Indians because they represented a way of life and a scale of values that opposed virtually everything they had hitherto known. But the contrast was not one of 'civilization' against 'barbarism', for at the practical level of preaching and catechesis the Christian religion did not try to impose a civilizing mission or to instil any conscious hope of material well-being or social advancement. Its message was primarily one of divine judgement and salvation and it sought expression in the eschatological distinction of the present world and the world to come. Through original sin the human race was enslaved to the powers of evil and was sinking deeper under the weight of its own guilt. The only way for humanity to extricate itself from this wreckage was by the way of the cross and the grace of the crucified redeemer.

This stern doctrine was presented with deep conviction by the early Franciscan missionaries, imbued as they were with the spirit of Colette of Corbie and of Bernardino of Siena who, looking back to Joachim de Fiore, had identified St Francis with the angel of the Apocalypse who would unlock the seal of the sixth age and inaugurate the age of the Holy Spirit.[71] But the doctrine came with peculiar force to the declining world of Mesoamerican civilization, a world in which poverty and exploitation, illness and death had become the unavoidable facts of daily experience. If the world was visibly falling to pieces, it was also believed that the millennium was imminent. It was natural that the newly converted Indians should have turned their eyes in hope to the other world.

Consequently, the intense asceticism of Indian Christianity in Mesoamerica is not to be explained as a mere imposition of the Franciscan way of life, for at a much deeper level it responded to an urgent and essential psychological need. Its marked otherworldliness, moreover, differed emphatically from much that we have come to associate with the word in its modern pietist form, with its individualist, subjective and idealist connotations. Nothing could be further from the otherworldliness of Mesoamerican Christianity, which was collective, objective and realist. Although the world to which it aspired was outside history and beyond time, it was nonetheless the ultimate end towards which time and history were moving. Furthermore, the Church could claim to possess a corporate experience and communion with the eternal world in the sacred mysteries. Just as the Mesoamerican world had found its centre in the ritual order of sacrifice around which the whole life of the community revolved, so now the Christian liturgy came to hold a similar position. And just as in the European dark ages the impoverishment of material culture did not prevent an enormous creativity in the field of liturgy, so, too, indigenous art forms in

71 Georges Baudot, *Utopía e Historia en México: Los primeros cronistas de la civilización mexicana 1520–1569* (Madrid, 1983), pp. 82–92. On Joachimism see Marjorie Reeves, *The Influence of Prophecy in the Late Middle Ages: A Study of Joachimism* (Oxford, 1969).

sixteenth- and seventeenth-century New Spain came to the service of the Christian liturgy in a way that was as spontaneous as it was genuinely Christian in spirit.

Whatever else might be lost and however dark might be the prospects of Mesoamerican society, the Christian liturgy came to provide a new principle of unity as well as a means by which the mind of the Indians could be attuned to a new view of life and a new concept of history. For although the new liturgy came to hold the same key significance as the sacrificial rituals of the Mesoamerican world, its spiritual content was very different. On the one hand, the Mesoamerican ritual order was conceived as the pattern of the cosmic order and its central mysteries were the mysteries of nature itself, manifested and represented in the dramatic action of myth and sacrifice. On the other, the Christian mysteries were essentially related to the mystery of eternal life, and although they were tuned into the cyclical life of nature in the liturgy, their central object of concern was the redemption of humanity brought about by the incarnation, death and resurrection of Christ. Additionally, since all these articles of the Christian faith were historically situated, the Christian mystery was also a historical mystery. Instead of the nature myths that were at the centre of the Mesoamerican ritual order, the Christian mystery was based on a sacred history, and the Christian liturgy itself developed into a historical cycle where the progress of humanity, from creation to redemption, was seen to unfold.

It is in this climate of ascetic otherworldliness and corporate liturgical expression that the best sense can be made of what has misleadingly come to be known as the 'spiritual conquest'. What we see at work is not so much an imposition of a new way of life but a manifestation of a new spiritual power that the Indians came to find virtually inescapable. No matter how many similarities there might have been between the cult of the saints and the sacrificial propitiation of the old tutelary deities, in practice the cult of the saints became inseparable from the Christian liturgy and the commemoration of the feasts of the saints provided an element of corporate identity and social continuity by which every community and every town found its liturgical representative and patron. Moreover, the Indians came to view this liturgical participation in the mysteries of salvation with an overwhelming sense of realism. It is hardly an exaggeration to suggest that the Christian liturgy had become for them the only context in which the passing of the old ritual order could be explained and raised on to a plane where eternity had invaded the world of time and where creation had been brought back to the spiritual source that kept it in being.

In the midst of this process of transfusion, the growing distrust of indigenous cultures and the tendency to demonize the Indian past that we detected from the middle of the sixteenth century onwards were doubly tragic. It was, to a great extent, the feeling of frustration derived from this tendency (and especially from the ensuing prohibitions to ordain a native

Plate 14. Baptismal font incorporating many indigenous art-forms.

Plate 15. Depiction of the Resurrection imbued with indigenous symbolism; particularly striking is the use of human bones and maize as symbols of life.

clergy) that led to the many Indian efforts to appropriate the Christian ritual and to incorporate it into their autochthonous liturgical practices. Such initiatives were especially in evidence in those areas where Christian priests were scarce or indolent. It is known that often, when a priest failed to turn up on a feast day, an Indian would readily step in and celebrate a 'dry mass', as the variant of the Mass which omitted consecration was known.[72] The increasing discouragement of such practices as 'abusive' and 'dangerous' from the time of the first Mexican provincial council in 1555, led to their association with idolatry and diabolism. Yet, despite the initial misunderstandings that we have looked at, which led to the somewhat ironical collaboration by many Indians in the process of their demonization, the devil that came to dominate Indian mythology by the middle of the seventeenth century had very little in common with the devil that theologians and inquisitors had increasingly come to see at the centre of idolatry. The numerous testimonies in the Inquisition linking the practice of demonic pacts with clandestine Indian rituals do not find parallels in the bulk of Indian testimonies known to us. Indeed, the apparent inconsistency of Indians who accused themselves of idolatry and then denied ever having made a pact with the devil, or possessing a written compact, was so recurrent that it had to be specifically considered as a serious theological problem at the end of the seventeenth century.[73] In those rare cases when Indians were summoned for questioning at inquisitorial courts, they invariably expressed a bewildered consternation at the common assumption that their seemingly extraordinary powers were derived from a demonic pact.

Such was the case of the Indian Antonio de la Cruz who, when questioned in 1691 about the alleged demonic possession of a group of women, declared that he knew the cause of the possessions and assured the inquisitors that he could 'cure' the victims. Yet he furiously denied that his knowledge was derived from a pact with the devil. On the contrary, it had come to him directly from God, through 'infused science'. It was the witch responsible for the *maleficium* who had made a pact with Satan, whom she worshipped in the shape of a goat. All remedies would thus be inefficacious until the pact was dissolved, and this would come about if the demoniacs made three acts of contrition and then said the *Salve Regina* three times with devotion to the Blessed Virgin.[74]

There is no trace of any syncretic mixture or of any pre-Hispanic remnant in Antonio de la Cruz's diagnosis. Not only did he see the devil as an enemy, he also knew him to be inferior and subordinate to God, since divinely infused science would be sufficient to bring about his defeat. So, too, his suggested 'cure' for dissolving the pact was in tune with the tradi-

---

72 Constantino Bayle, *El culto del Santísimo en Indias* (Madrid, 1951), pp. 34–6.
73 See Diego Jaymes Ricardo Villavicencio, *Luz y método de confesar idólatras*, 2 vols (Puebla, 1692), ii, pp. 3–7.
74 A.G.N., Inq., 527.9, fols 569r–569v.

tional Christian view that an essential weapon against the devil was repentance, a conscious turning away from sin, which necessarily involved the
acts of contrition that Antonio had recommended. Moreover, since the
Virgin Mary had increasingly come to be seen as the Christian's most powerful ally against Satan,[75] Antonio's recommendation to say the *Salve Regina*,
much more than a mere disguise to gain the favour of the inquisitors, was a
pious practice in tune with traditional Catholic orthodoxy.

This example could have been transposed virtually intact to contemporary Catholic Europe. Its orthodoxy is likely to be far more representative of
Indian religion as it had evolved by the middle of the seventeenth century
than the more syncretic examples from peripheral and remote areas which,
precisely because of their heterodoxy, have come down to us in greater
detail. If anything of the old pre-Hispanic order was remembered by the
Indians at this stage, it was largely in the form of disjointed residues which
lacked a unified pattern and which no longer formed part of the mainstream
of the religious system. In contrast to the views of the scattered priests and
extirpators who saw in these remnants proof of a ubiquitous Satanic
mimetism, the Indians, and indeed the bulk of the population, seem to have
regarded them as cultural expressions that were perfectly at home in a
Christian culture.

This does not mean, of course, that the devil was not an essential element
in Indian Christianity. As Serge Gruzinski has observed, more than half the
visions that afflicted Indians during the colonial period seem to have been
of a diabolical nature, with Satan being the most recurrent, followed closely
by demonic monsters, hell and the damned, in that order.[76] But it would be
a mistake to interpret such developments as mere expressions of the process
of demonization, for there was little difference between such visions and
those that afflicted contemporary Europeans or, indeed, the bulk of
Christians in the early modern period.

However terrifying, there was nothing in this image of the devil that
could be used against Indian cultures. Their corporate and deeply liturgical
character provided age-old and well-tested defences against demonic
attacks, where Indians were more commonly associated with celestial rather
than demonic beings, as we know, for example, from the life of the charismatic lay friar Juan Pobre, who in the 1620s was allegedly assisted by
angels, appearing to him in the figure of Indians, to collect alms and food
for his convent.[77] The Indian devil was not, in other words, the devil of José
de Acosta and the early modern demonologists, but the more malleable

---

75   On this see Maximilian Rudwin, *The Devil in Legend and Literature* (La Salle, Ill., 1959), pp.
178–9. On the growth of Marianism in the middle ages, Rosalind and Christopher Brooke,
Popular Religion in the Middle Ages (London, 1984), pp. 31–4.
76   'Le filet déchiré', pp. 465–8.
77   Gruzinski and Sallmann, 'Une source d'ethnohistoire', p. 796.

devil of the monastic hagiographies and *exempla,* whose most confident exponent in the New World had been Bartolomé de las Casas.

*

It is hardly surprising, given the above evidence, to find very few movements of Indian resistance, however nativistic or even anti-Spanish in purpose, that at the same time adopted an anti-Christian attitude. As a rule, rebellions or movements that opposed the status quo were at pains to stress rather than to deny their Christian identity. The group of native *fiscales*[78] who set themselves up independently as a Catholic priesthood in order to render cult to their own miraculous image of the Virgin during the Tzeltal revolt in Chiapas in 1712, provided a distant echo of a similar attitude already observable a century earlier in Yucatán, when in 1610 two Maya Indians had proclaimed themselves pope and bishop, offered Mass, administered the sacraments and ordained their own native clergy to assist them.[79] As the eighteenth century wore on, such nativistic movements became more numerous and virulent, often adopting attitudes that on a first reading seem imbued with anti-Christian feeling. For example, in the 1760s a group of Indians who were in possession of an arsenal of machetes, knives and pistols in the Sierra de Puebla were apparently convinced that the God of the Spaniards was the devil, that the Catholic priests were demons, and even that the Virgin of Guadalupe had lost her powers.[80] And only a few decades later a group of Indians were found in the mountains around Mexico City resisting the Church and fighting the priests, interrupting their sermons and preventing them from administering the sacraments.[81] There were hints of a millenarian expectation in these movements, since they looked forward to a time when the Spaniards would pay tribute to the Indians and serve them. More alarming still, in their attacks against the Church and the priests, and even such popular images as the Virgin of Guadalupe, they seemed, on the surface, to have abandoned the efforts of former Indian movements of resistance to stress a Christian identity.

The most detailed and illustrative example of this trend is the case of Antonio Pérez Pastor, 'the Shepherd', which came to the attention of the Inquisition in 1761, when Domingo de la Mota, an Indian parish priest, found more than one hundred Indians engaged in 'idolatrous practices' out of whom he arrested sixty-four in Chimalhuacán alone, where Antonio Pérez had declared himself high priest. Among those accused was the mestiza Luisa de Carrillo. She confessed that she had gone to see Pérez, who

---

78 *Fiscal* was a church steward, the highest indigenous ecclesiastical official in the district.
79 Farriss, *Maya Society,* p. 318.
80 A.G.N., Ramo Criminal, 308, fols 1r-92v.
81 A.G.N., Ramo Bienes Nacionales, 976.39.

was well known as a healer, because she was about to give birth. Apparently Pérez had advised her not to have the baby baptized in church, but to give it to the Indians instead. Having agreed to this, Luisa was paid with some maize and given 'communion' by Pérez, three times, with three kernels of maize each time. Later, Luisa's husband explained that the baby had then been duly baptized by the Indians in a ceremony where the blood of a pigeon that had been 'offered to the Most Holy Trinity' was used instead of the chrism and holy oil.[82]

It was during this ceremony that Mota had surprised them, and had been shocked to discover that the principal object of their devotion was a figurine

> made of wood in the shape of a woman...seated on a chair, her shoulders covered with a shawl...and, instead of a skirt, she wore a yellow altar pallium where the Most Holy Name of Jesus had been embroidered. She wore a silver palm hat and carried a wooden walking stick, and she was known by them as Our Lady the Virgin of the lily, the palm and the olive. They thought the image had appeared miraculously, but also claimed to have brought it out of purgatory themselves.

The 'idol', which, as Mota explained, had been placed on an altar with flowers and candles, and to whom the Indians prayed on their knees, was not a true image of Our Lady because 'her breasts were naked and monstrous and her face resembled more that of a man than of a woman'. When the figurine was examined by Antonio de Medina, the archbishop's special envoy, it had been found to contain 'in a broken segment of the head, a pigeon's heart, and in the stomach, an altar-wine bottle filled with the menstrual blood of a virgin, a small maize cob, some palms and other herbs'.[83]

One can imagine Mota's consternation and that of his assistants when confronted with such evidence, especially when further testimonies revealed that Antonio Pérez was involved in a campaign to denigrate the Church and its ministers. When he heard confessions he persuaded his penitents that they were poor because they 'went to church, which was hell', and because they 'listened to the priests, who were devils', and because they believed in 'the God of the priests, who was false'. He ridiculed the images and paintings of the churches, insisting that they were the mere work of human hands and that the Indians 'should do better to commend themselves to the drunkards than to the saints', and he seemed especially anxious to vilify the sacrament of the Eucharist, urging his followers not to believe in it and flogging those Indians who refused to believe in his God, 'who was none other than the Virgin that they adored'.[84]

82 A.G.N., Inq., 1000.21, fol. 294v.
83 A.G.N., Inq., 1000.21, fols 295v–296r.
84 A.G.N., Inq., 1000.21, fols 292r–293v.

Pérez's openly 'anti-establishment' belligerency is quite unprecedented and it contrasts sharply with earlier cases of heterodoxy. For example, the sacrifices of Mateo Pérez in Oaxaca, recorded almost a century before and analysed above, show none of the signs of Antonio Pérez's militant opposition to the established Church. Indeed, Mateo Pérez could not regard himself as anything but a good Christian who devotedly carried out his duties in the Church and gave good example to his neighbours. It is doubly ironical, therefore, that the far more aggressive case of Antonio Pérez in Chimalhuacán should have been the product of a much higher degree of acculturation and of a much better understanding of the tenets of Christianity. For, whereas Mateo Pérez in Oaxaca was still very much in the *nepantla* position where saints and devils adopted the attributes and functions of the old tutelary deities in what was an essentially polytheistic pantheon, Antonio Pérez Pastor in Chimalhuacán was deeply monotheistic. His aggressive anticlericalism was, therefore, much more the product of Christian acculturation than Mateo Pérez's pious devotion to the local church and cult. Nowhere is this contrast more in evidence than in the two men's respective attitudes to the devil. On the one hand, Mateo Pérez in Oaxaca seems to have no clear notion of the devil as understood by Christianity; as we have seen, his devil had more in common with the old tutelary deities which were neither wholly good nor wholly bad but which nonetheless needed to be propitiated in order to stave off any ensuing calamity. On the other hand, Antonio Pérez Pastor in Chimalhuacán seems to have had as clear a concept of the Christian devil as he had of monotheism. Indeed, his deployment of the concept of the devil against the established Church is identical to the use of the same concept by the extirpators of idolatry against the Indians. Very much in the same way as the Indians had been demonized by the extirpators, so now Antonio Pérez Pastor and his followers were demonizing the established Church and its ministers.

It is therefore a mistake to see in this and similar movements expressions of a widespread anti-Christian ethos among the Indians. It is not the Christian religion that is under attack here, but the established Church. If the Church was evil and 'hell', it was not because it was Christian but because it seemed to sanction a system which appeared to the Indians to contradict the essential tenets of the gospel. Similarly, if the priests were 'devils' it was not because they were Christian but because they were bad Christians. In fact, it was precisely in the Christian message that the Indians found the most efficient means to voice their grievances and to redress the balance. Antonio Pérez said Mass, heard confessions, administered baptism and the Eucharist, witnessed marriages, and insisted that worship should be given to the true God and not to the God of the priests who had come to represent a gargantuan appetite for money and food.

What the Indians were against was not Christianity, nor even the Catho-

lic Church as they had come to know it through the corporate and liturgical evangelization of the mendicant friars, but the increasingly detached and
oppressive conduct of the secular clergy and the official hierarchy. During
the second half of the eighteenth century the clash between official and
unofficial forms of piety would become much more acute as a result of the
policies of the new Bourbon ministers, who were engaged in a systematic
attack on corporate forms of religious expression. Both utilitarian and
'dirigiste' in their political philosophy, these ministers found asceticism dis-
tasteful and corporate piety wasteful in its encouragement of a sumptuous
and elaborate liturgy. Instead they favoured clerics of a Jansenist persuasion
who preferred the study of the Church Fathers and scripture to scholasticism, and who stressed the conciliarism of national hierarchies against
canon law theories of papal sovereignty.[85] At the same time they sought to
reaffirm the Council of Trent's insistence on the importance of episcopal
authority and the central role of the parochial clergy, thus inevitably coming into conflict with the corporate popular devotions which had been as
central to the mendicant missionary enterprise as they now were to Indian
religiosity and communal identity.[86]

Consequently, the late eighteenth-century movements of Indian resistance do not represent a clash between Christianity and a reemerging form
of syncretic Indian paganism, but between two conflicting forms of
Christian culture. On the one hand there was the official culture that looked
back to the Tridentine exaltation of the secular clergy at the expense of the
regular orders and forward to a simple form of piety which favoured good
works at the expense of Baroque rhetoric and mysticism. On the other,
there was the traditional culture of the Indians and the mendicants which
looked back to the medieval ideals of corporate and liturgical piety and forward to a millenarian kingdom where the Indians would rule their own
destiny. It was no accident that as Antonio Pérez condemned and vilified
the secular priests he also honoured the memory of the two mendicant friars, a Dominican and a Franciscan, who had respectively taught him the art
of healing and helped him to locate the images of the Virgin and of Christ
which had become the centre of his devotion.[87] Pérez's own account of his

85   Owen Chadwick, *The Popes and European Revolutions* (Oxford, 1981), pp. 392–439.
Spanish Jansenism is the subject of Joël Saugnieux, *Le Jansénisme espagnol du XVIIIe siècle*
(Oviedo, 1975) and *Les Jansénistes et le renouveau de la prédication dans l'Espagne de la seconde moitié
du XVIIIe siècle* (Lyons, 1976).
86   The best brief study of this movement in Mexico is D.A. Brading, 'Tridentine
Catholicism and Enlightened Despotism in Bourbon Mexico', *Journal of Latin American Studies*,
15 (1983), pp. 1–21, which includes a long extract from a remarkably illustrative document
where Indian *mayordomos* complain to their bishop about the official attack on feasts and processions.
87   This information is found in the Archivo General de Indias, Seville, Audiencia de México
1696. Here I rely on Serge Gruzinski's transcription in *Man-Gods*, pp. 105–7. I have profited
from Gruzinski's meticulous, albeit somewhat speculative, reconstruction of the case.

early years as a healer at once throws us back into that world of hermits and ascetics that populate seventeenth-century hagiographies. He recalls how the Dominican taught him to cure,

> advising me to use...eggs, soap, milk, cooking oil, mint or tomato skins.... He taught me cures for everything.... For all my treatments I recite the *Credo* as the holy Church teaches it... and I add these words: 'in the name of the most holy Trinity, of the Father, the Son and the Holy Spirit. Amen.' I put my trust first in God and only then in the herbs. When he is on his way to recovery, the sick man recites the act of contrition. I do all that because the Dominican friar told me to.[88]

If such instances can be read as proofs of the patent failure of the extirpators, they point no less clearly to the success of the mendicant method of evangelization. For despite his deep sense of Indian and local identity, there is nothing in Antonio Pérez's attitude that cannot be understood in terms of Christian culture. Indeed, similar movements were not unknown in Spain itself where, as William Christian has shown, many legends of the return of images to country sites reflected a sense of liberation from parish control and can be seen as expressions of the resistance of local religion to the growing claims of the Church, or simply as statements of peasant or rural 'otherness'.[89]

More significantly, the case of Antonio Pérez points to a method of evangelization that allowed for a gradual absorption of a corporate and liturgical religiosity which would succeed in creating a culture that was genuinely Christian without doing violence to local customs and traditions. The piecemeal and gradual way in which the Indians accepted and appropriated the new religion left them in freedom, if the need arose, successfully to oppose official manifestations of Christianity from an essentially Christian standpoint. To put it crudely, Antonio Pérez, when confronted with the attacks of an official brand of Christianity, was capable of genuine heresy.

On a more theological level this meant that the tendency to separate nature and grace and to demonize alien cultural traditions does not seem to have sunk to the levels of practical catechesis and corporate religiosity. The devil that we see at work here is still very much the medieval devil of hagiographies and *exempla*, a devil who, despite being God's grand cosmic antagonist, was nonetheless completely subservient to him and even susceptible to manipulation through natural means.

---

88   Ibid.
89   *Local religion in sixteenth-century Spain*, p. 91.

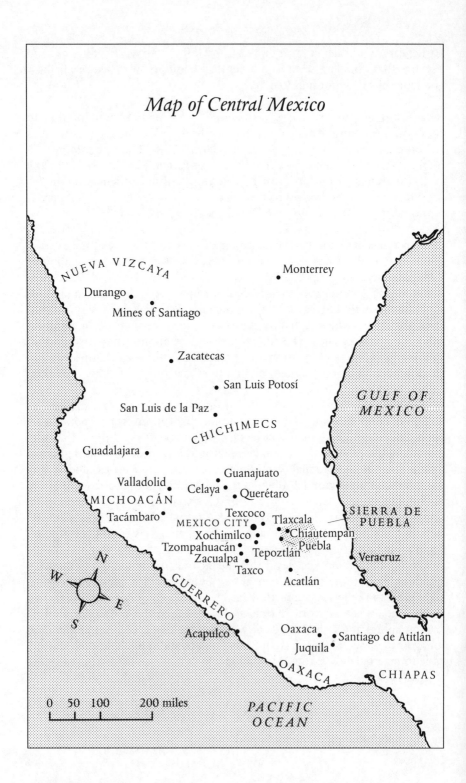

Map of Central Mexico

NUEVA VIZCAYA

Durango •

• Mines of Santiago

Monterrey •

• Zacatecas

• San Luis Potosí

San Luis de la Paz •

CHICHIMECS

Guadalajara •

Guanajuato
Valladolid • Celaya • • Querétaro

MICHOACÁN

Tacámbaro •

Texcoco
MEXICO CITY • Tlaxcala
Xochimilco • • Chiautempan
Tzompahuacán • • Tepoztlán Puebla
Zacualpa • Taxco •

GUERRERO

SIERRA DE
PUEBLA

• Veracruz

GULF OF
MEXICO

Acatlán •

Acapulco •

Oaxaca •
• Santiago de Atitlán
Juquila •

OAXACA

CHIAPAS

0 50 100   200 miles

PACIFIC
OCEAN

N
W · E
S

3

The Demimonde

The best seed ground for superstition is a society in which the fortunes of men seem to bear practically no relation to their merits and efforts.

Gilbert Murray, *Five Stages of Greek Religion*, p. 164

THE EVIDENCE PRESENTED in the last two chapters points to an apparent incongruity in the image of the devil in New Spain during the early modern period. On the one hand, there is the philosophical and theological trend to separate nature and grace and consequently to increase the importance of the devil's powers over men and women while, on the other, there is the pastoral and catechetical trend to preserve a more medieval notion where the devil was held at bay by the liturgy and by a moral system still very much based on the seven deadly sins. The way in which magical practices were approached by those who were closest to the religious needs of the Indians does not suggest any fear of demonic intervention or any obsession with idolatry such as we detected in the bulk of theologians and intellectuals after Acosta. As we have seen, this also seems to have been the case among the Indians well into the eighteenth century and beyond.

When we turn to the other sectors of the population, and especially to that growing and ill-defined group of mestizos, mulattos and *castas*,[1] a good starting-point is provided by the existence of a classic mestizo account of the Mesoamerican past and the Spanish conquest. For if something distinguishes the work of Fernando de Alva Ixtlilxóchitl from the bulk of Creole and Peninsular interpretations of the Amerindian past, it is his deliberate omission of any reference to the devil and his alleged influence upon native idolatry. Like his great Peruvian counterpart, the Inca Garcilaso de la Vega, Ixtlilxóchitl interpreted the Mesoamerican past as an enlightened period inspired and guided by the basic tenets of the natural law. It is true that his vision came nowhere near Garcilaso's mythical reconstruction of the Inca world as a utopia of enlightened pagans, a myth so powerful that it still

---

1 *Casta* was the generic term used for the various groups that resulted from racial mixture. On the complexities of this process see Magnus Mörner, *Race Mixture in the History of Latin America* (Boston, 1967). For New Spain the best study is Jonathan Israel, *Race Class and Politics in Colonial Mexico 1610–1670* (Oxford, 1975).

managed to capture the rationalist wit of Voltaire in the eighteenth century.[2] Yet he was in fundamental agreement with Garcilaso's view that the Indians had discovered the one true God long before the arrival of the Spaniards. If he was not as blatant as Garcilaso in claiming that this discovery had been achieved through the natural light of reason, he nonetheless asserted that the Mesoamericans had been taught the tenets of civilized morality by Quetzalcoatl-Huemac, taking care to place his alleged 'mission' firmly in the first century as a clear hint that Quetzalcoatl might have been St Thomas the Apostle.[3] Implicit in this hint was the need that Ixtlilxóchitl felt to legitimate the indigenous past in an intellectual context where the natural world was deemed irredeemable without Christianity, but the subtlety of the hint also points to the mestizo's wish to reassert the value of the Mesoamerican world on its own terms. Thus, Ixtlilxóchitl's interpretation of Mesoamerican history down to the eve of the conquest evokes Las Casas and culminates in a mythical portrayal of Nezahualcoyotl, the king of Texcoco, whom our author celebrates as 'one of the wisest men in the world...who rallied together all the philosophers and sages of his time' and who, through his own study and meditation of the 'divine mysteries', came to the knowledge of the one true God and to the realization of the existence of heaven and hell. Although Ixtlilxóchitl could not deny the widespread practice of human sacrifice and was thus prevented from echoing Garcilaso's claim that the Incas had suppressed such practices together with superstition, idolatry and cannibalism, he was nonetheless careful to insist that the kings of Texcoco had come to deplore such atrocities, allowing them to continue only as a matter of political prudence.[4]

The vision of Ixtlilxóchitl, like that of Garcilaso, could not contrast more sharply with the widely accepted contemporary trend to demonize the Amerindian past. Indeed, in many respects the devil became more active after than before the conquest in the writings of the two mestizos, entering the scene as 'the Father of Discord', in Garcilaso's words.[5] Such contrasting views cannot be separated from the personal experiences of those who voiced them. Although both Ixtlilxóchitl and Garcilaso were proud of their Spanish ancestry and refused to follow Las Casas in his condemnation of the conquest as the work of Satan, they were equally proud of their Indian

2   Voltaire's description of El Dorado in *Candide* is based on his reading of Garcilaso; see John Butt's Introduction to Voltaire, *Candide* (London, 1946).

3   Fernando de Alva Ixtlilxóchitl, *Obras históricas*, ed. E. O'Gorman, 2 vols (Mexico City, 1975), i, p. 204.

4   Ibid., i, pp. 385–447; ii, pp. 61–137. Ixtlilxóchitl's main source is clearly the Codex Xolotl; see C. E. Dibble ed., *Códice Xolotl*, 2 vols (Mexico City, 1980). Garcilaso's views on the Inca past, and especially on natural law, can be read in his *Comentarios Reales de los Incas*, 2 vols (Buenos Aires, 1943), i, pp. 66–82; ii, pp. 27–30.

5   Inca Garcilaso de la Vega, *Historia General del Perú*, 3 vols (Buenos Aires, 1944), iii, p. 301.

Plate 16. Nezahualpilli,
Lord of Texcoco
(1472–1515).

ancestry and conscious of the suffering that Spanish colonization had
brought about. Garcilaso remembered bitterly how his Indian mother had
been given by his Spanish father to a common foot-soldier as his wife in
order to marry a Spanish woman twenty years his junior; and Ixtlilxóchitl
would witness how the Spanish viceroys refused Texcoco the right to figure
as a capital city, with the result that by the end of the sixteenth century the
descendants of Nezahualcoyotl were forced to plough the fields to eke a
meagre subsistence which was further reduced by demands for tribute from
royal officials who refused to recognize their noble status.[6]

These experiences were not exceptional. It was precisely those frequent liaisons between Spanish men and Indian women that led Miguel
de Cervantes to refer to the New World as 'that great lure of licentious

6 D. A. Brading, *The First America: The Spanish Monarchy, Creole Patriots and the Liberal State
1492–1867* (Cambridge, 1991), pp. 255, 275.

women',[7] but it was the equally frequent abandonment of such liaisons as
soon as Spanish women became available that led to a rapid growth of an
unrecognized group of mestizos, whose marginalization and the ensuing
urban vagrancy and idleness were to become one of the great concerns of
viceroy Luis de Velasco.[8] The situation was not made any easier by the
influx of black slaves, especially the 'creole negroes',[9] who proved to be
much less submissive than the *bozales*[10] and who contributed to the rapid
growth of dangerous bands of runaway slaves culminating in the famous
Yanga revolt (1607–11).[11] Meanwhile, Peninsular Spaniards found themselves free to pursue ambitions that in Europe would have been the
monopoly of the aristocracy and became increasingly prone to denigrate
mestizos and castas by identifying them with the vile plebeians of traditional European society.[12]

The situation was ripe for a defensive reaction among the underprivileged where the concept of the devil could be turned against the oppressors.
Just as Garcilaso and Ixtlilxóchitl had omitted any association of the devil
with the Amerindian past and only brought him in to explain discord and
greed among the Spaniards, so too the oppressed and underprivileged
could interpret the conduct of their oppressors as the result of demonic
influence. We have seen some examples of this tendency among the Indians
in the eighteenth century. In more extreme cases the reactions could even
lead to an appropriation of demonic powers. As Michael Taussig has shown
in the case of the slaves in the Bolivian tin mines, enslavement and exploitation often appear to have inadvertently delivered a special mystical power
to the underdog in colonial society. Through their very attempts at suppres-
sion, and especially through their persistent identification of heterodox
practices with diabolism, the oppressors ironically validated devil-worship
itself: they invested the devil with a power that the oppressed could appropriate by standing to their oppressors as the devil stood to God.[13]

At first sight it might seem puzzling that the evidence for New Spain
does not point to a development along these lines among the mestizos and
castas. To some extent this suggests that the levels of oppression and
exploitation were considerably lower in New Spain than in Upper Peru. But
the situation in New Spain might also, and more significantly, result from

7   Quoted by Mörner, *Race Mixture*, p. 26.
8   There are several extant letters expressing Velasco's concern. See especially Biblioteca
Nacional de Madrid, 3636, II, fols 80v–81r, 116v–117r, 124v–126r, 154v, 167r.
9   The first group of evangelized slaves and those who had been born and raised in New
Spain.
10   Black slaves transported directly from Africa.
11   Gustavo Aguirre Beltrán, *La población negra de México* (Mexico City, 1984 edn), pp.
157–8; Israel, *Race, Class and Politics*, pp. 68–71.
12   Mörner, *Race Mixture*, p. 55.
13   Michael T. Taussig, *The Devil and Commodity Fetishism in South America* (North Carolina,
1980), pp. 42–3.

the fact that the image of the devil that prevailed among mestizos and castas was not that which had come to dominate philosophical and theological
speculations, but the more medieval image of him that the friars had so successfully preached to the Indians. There was little in this image of Satan,
often appearing as a figure of mirth, that the oppressed could effectively
deploy against the oppressor. Rather than siding with the cause of Satan,
black slaves were more often scandalized by any hint of demonic activity.
Such was the case of Ana and Baltazar Marabán, slaves in the mines of
Zacapula, near Taxco, who in 1605 made the sign of the cross and kissed
the crucifixes on their rosaries, imploring a friend 'for the love of God' to
abandon his evil and dangerous practices after he had shown them some
'little papers' that an Indian had given him 'to give him courage and win in
fights'.[14] Nor were slaves prone to team with each other against a common
oppressor. More often they readily gave evidence against fellow slaves suspected of demonic activities, seeing them as more serious threats than any
oppression they might suffer in common. When Gabriel Escudero Rosas
noticed some 'disturbances and noises' in his house shortly after purchasing
a slave called Cristóbal in 1655, three slaves in the same household willingly testified against Cristóbal in the courts of the Inquisition. Fortunately
for him the inquisitors were not convinced by the evidence that the slave
had made a pact with the devil.[15] But the case of Cristóbal was not exceptional. Slaves were in fact rarely found guilty of demonic complicity. In the
many inquisitorial cases where they are accused of diabolical compacts or
invocations it is common to find that they had fabricated the story with the
purpose of getting a hearing at the courts of the Inquisition where they
could voice their grievances. An extant letter of the mulatto slave Juan de
Morga, written to the Inquisition in 1650, is revealing in this respect. After
accusing himself of bigamy, blasphemy and a demonic pact, he states that
he has many other things to declare,

> for I serve a very cruel man in Zacatecas and as long as they keep me
> here I shall continue to live by this law and to deny God and his
> saints…and I shall go to hell if I do not declare and confess [these
> things].[16]

And Jacinto de Zavala, also a mulatto slave, likewise explained to the
inquisitors in 1674 that the main reason why he had told many people that
he was a witch and had a pact with the devil was that his master treated
him very badly and had threatened to send him to a textile workshop, and

14 Archivo General de la Nación, Mexico City, Ramo Inquisición (hereafter A.G.N., Inq.),
tomo 276, exp. 2 (hereafter 276.2), fol. 11r.
15 A.G.N., Inq., 444.4, fols 436r–443r.
16 A.G.N., Inq., 454.14, fols 255r–255v.

that he would rather be a prisoner of the Inquisition, where he would be treated well both in body and soul.[17]

Similar strategies to escape maltreatment by seeking a hearing at the courts of the Inquisition were so common[18] that sometimes inquisitors did not even need to be persuaded by the suspects. In 1695 the black slave José de Messa, feeling afflicted and oppressed in a textile workshop, told his confessor that he had called the devil, saying 'Is there not a devil somewhere who might help me out of these labours in exchange for my soul?' Since then he claimed that the devil had appeared to him constantly, causing him 'great fear'. Urged by his confessor, he agreed to denounce himself at the Inquisition, but, even before he was called for questioning, the inquisitors had deduced (wrongly, it would seem), from evidence attesting to his devotion to the rosary and to the Virgin Mary, that Messa's story was a shrewd fabrication and dismissed the case without further ado.[19]

More than a vengeful spirit that could be rallied by the oppressed, the devil appears here more as a powerful trickster that could be used in cases of affliction and then forgotten. It is true that in many cases he appeared as a more compelling force. Messa had actually called the devil and feared him, while Zavala and Morga, even while using the devil as an excuse to get a hearing at the Inquisition, nonetheless accepted that they had carried out a formal pact with him where they had renounced the Christian faith. But this does not point to a situation even remotely comparable to that found by Taussig in the Bolivian tin mines. Even in the silver mines, the system in New Spain was supported by a well-paid and geographically mobile labour force made up primarily of voluntary workers. Far from encouraging oppression, the mines operated as much for the benefit of the workers as for the owners, with the former often acting as virtual partners, if not active rivals, of the latter.[20]

This does not mean, of course, that a sense of frustration and anger emanating from oppression and maltreatment and finding an outlet in demonic beliefs did not exist. Prisoners in particular often saw the devil as a powerful means to assist them in their escapes. In 1598 the mestizo Juan Luis claimed that one of the main motives behind his decision to make a pact with the devil was that he would help him escape from any prisons that his 'enjoyment of all manner of turpitude and dishonesty' might lead him to;[21] and the prisoner Diego de Lugana claimed in 1622 that his black friend

17   A.G.N., Inq., 629.1, fol. 71r.
18   On this point see Solange Alberro, *Inquisición y sociedad en México 1571–1700* (Mexico City, 1988), pp. 462–72.
19   A.G.N., Inq., 530.28, fols 389r–416r.
20   On this see P. J. Bakewell, *Silver Mining and Society in Colonial Zacatecas 1546–1700* (Cambridge, 1971), pp. 124, 128; and D. A. Brading, *Miners and Merchants in Bourbon Mexico 1763–1810* (Cambridge, 1971), pp. 146, 148–9.
21   A.G.N., Inq., 147.6, fol. 3r.

Bartolo had escaped by virtue of a figure of the devil he had painted on some part of his body and that, since he had a similar figure, his escape was imminent.[22] Despite recurring failures,[23] the practice persisted throughout the colonial period.[24] In 1704 the warder of the court prison of Guadalajara reported that Tomás de Santiago, a mulatto accused of murder, was known to brag that he had a pact with the devil who had assisted him in his escapes from many prisons in the past. Further investigations revealed that Santiago had been instructing many prisoners to fast in honour of the devil on certain days and to 'light candles to him after taking off their rosaries and throwing them away'. Some days later Nicolás de Luna, one of the prisoners who had refused to follow Santiago's instructions, saw an enormous cat go in through the cat-hole in the dungeon 'causing him great fear and consternation, for the cat was too large to have gone through such a small hole'. After Luna had invoked the favours of Our Lady of Guadalupe, the cat disappeared into the larger dungeon next door where he was seen talking to Tomás de Santiago for a while before disappearing again. Presently the door opened and one of the prisoners, full of excitement, exclaimed 'Blessed be the Most Holy Sacrament!' – a reaction that put their rescuer to flight and infuriated Santiago, who told the euphoric prisoner that his stupidity had ruined everything.[25]

No matter how malleable or even mockable the devil was perceived to be, the above example suggests that those who actually made a diabolical pact were often conscious that they had made a positive choice to enter the opponent's camp. Once there, any acknowledgement of God, any reference to the mysteries of the faith or any manifestation of Christian devotion was not only invalid but positively detrimental. As countless examples attest,[26] before signing the pact and offering their soul to the devil, postulant devil-worshippers were asked to forsake Christianity and to remove their rosaries and any other Christian relics they might have. Thereafter they became sworn enemies of the Christian faith, often even adopting a kind of anti-religion where any association with Christianity was seen as an act of infidelity. The bold mestizo Juan Luis asserted in 1598 that he believed the devil to be more powerful than God and to be capable of 'knowing the things that men have hidden in their hearts, just as God knows them'. He had thus worshipped the devil

22 A.G.N., Inq., 335.44, fols 206r–207v.

23 See, for example, the frustrated attempts of Jusepe Pérez (1639) and Juan Bautista 'el noble' (1670) in A.G.N., Inq., 387.13 and 515.17 respectively.

24 Among other illustrative examples see the cases of Agustín Navarro (1692–97), A.G.N., Inq., 539.16, fols 172v–176r, and José Ventura (1740), A.G.N., Inq., 863 (unnumbered), fol. 179r.

25 A.G.N., Inq., 728.6, fols 214r–215v.

26 See above, p. 50, n. 28.

Plates 17 (right) and 18 (below). The Devil in the popular imagination, *c.*1790.

in the same way as he once used to worship God whom, by the command of the devil, he had forsaken together with the Most Holy Virgin,
his Blessed Mother, and St Michael the Archangel and all the saints, and
he had offered himself to the devil in body and soul, and had never since
been to confession or to communion, nor had he prayed, attended Mass
or shown any devotion to the crosses...for he ran away from churches
and sacred places.[27]

And in 1608 the mulatto Juan Francisco, 'a man who carries the devil with
him and worships him...[and] has never been seen at Mass or uttering the
name of God...or of Jesus...or of Our Lady', was accused of throwing four
images from the altar of a devout Indian, trampling over them and spitting
furiously.[28]

Such whole-hearted demonic devotion was rare, however, and in the
majority of inquisitorial cases of invocation or pact, the devil appears more
as a second-best than as an object of exclusive worship. As a rule people
turned to the devil as the last option left after God and the saints had
ignored repeated requests. In 1572, the Spaniard Juan Bautista de Luque,
who claimed to be a good, God-fearing Christian, asked the inquisitors to
give him a 'salutary penance' to atone for saying in a moment of doubt, 'Let
the devil be my help, for I have seen that God does not want to help me'.[29]
And the Spaniard Alonso Cordero de Mendoza, after some Indian women
had run away from him in 1621, was heard to exclaim, 'O devils! Come and
grant me your favour, for God has left me so abandoned that I no longer
think that he exists'.[30]

But it was states of anger and desperation that more aptly gave rise to
such reactions. In 1602 the Spaniard José de la Rosa was accused by his
sister-in-law of invoking the devil, 'burning with anger' because of a problem with a horse, and saying:

> Devils! Please come to get me now! Do not tie my hands, for this soul
> belongs to you. Help me! Do not leave me now, for I do no service what-
> ever to God. Devils! Please help me and I shall forsake God, dead or
> alive![31]

And in 1680 another Spaniard, Juan de Ledesma, was accused by Catalina
de Villaela of throwing his rosary on the floor and calling the devil in a
state of angry desperation.[32]

27 A.G.N., Inq., 147.6, fol. 3r.
28 A.G.N., Inq., 283.16, fol. 100v.
29 A.G.N., Inq., 46.10, fols 47r, 57r.
30 A.G.N., Inq., 486(I).19, fols 83r–83v.
31 A.G.N., Inq., 452.59, fol. 263r.
32 A.G.N., Inq., 640.1, fols 1r–1v.

As we might expect, it is cases involving slaves and servants that provide the best examples of this trend. In 1614 the mulatto Diego de Cervantes confessed that he had called the devil after the steward of a textile workshop had burnt his feet with boiling water as a punishment for sloth. Angry and afflicted, he had said to himself in front of a crucifix, 'I do not believe that there is a God in heaven, nor do I wish to die in the faith of God, but in that of the devil'.[33] And it was after his master had whipped him that, in 1647, the mulatto Monserrate had decided to go to a cave to make a pact with the devil.[34] Similarly, it was only after she had been whipped and told that she was a bad Christian by the nuns of the convent of San Bernardo that, in 1686, María Juana de San Ignacio had said that 'if all that was true, then she did not want God but the devil, who was charming, and that she would make a pact with him'.[35] And it was also after his master had beaten him and forbidden him to go out that, in 1762, Mariano Manuel de Rojas, 'blinded by his anger', had thrown his rosary on the floor and had torn to pieces a print of St Gertrude, calling the devil to assist him with some money to buy his freedom.[36]

If something characterizes the above examples it is their unpremeditated impulsiveness. They are all circumstantial cases responding to an immediate urge where the purposeful plan that the mechanism of the pact involved was absent. Any opposition to Christianity that might be detected in them was dominated by a subjective introspection that led almost inevitably to repentance and confession. It is true that trust in the temporal power of the devil might have seemed natural to some, especially at a time when Christian teaching linked the world, the flesh and Satan together as the chief enemies of the soul.[37] If, as was commonly accepted in contemporary teaching, the devil was 'the lord of this world', his help would be seen by many as more efficacious than God's when it came to the pursuit of worldly things. It was this logic that led the Spaniard Juan de Villavicencio to scandalize a friend in 1602 by saying that he longed to see the devil; after the friend had made the sign of the cross and invoked God and his saints believing that Villavicencio had gone mad, the latter replied that, on the contrary, he was the saner of the two, for the friendship of the devil was much better for the acquisition of material things.[38] The attitude had in no way diminished towards the end of the colonial period; in 1749, the

33   A.G.N., Inq., 301.35, fol. 237v.
34   A.G.N., Inq., 429.9, fol. 368r.
35   A.G.N., Inq., 520.116, fols 176v–177r.
36   A.G.N., Inq., 1037.11, fols 321r–323v.
37   See, for example, the influential catechism of Jerónimo de Ripalda, *Doctrina Christiana, con una exposición breve...*(Burgos, 1591). The opinion was widely shared and by no means a monopoly of Catholics. Thomas Cooper in England portrayed the devil as 'exquisitely skilful in the knowledge of natural things'; see Keith Thomas, *Religion and the Decline of Magic* (Harmondsworth, 1978 edn), p. 565.
38   A.G.N., Inq., 452.72, fol. 303r.

Spaniard Antonio de Castrejón confessed to having invoked the devil six times asking for gold and silver, and in 1758 the priest Francisco Ignacio de Castillo sought advice from the Inquisition concerning a woman who had lit a candle to the devil to bring a man 'back to her friendship'.[39] Indeed, so skilful was the devil deemed to be in worldly affairs that his help was even sought for seemingly virtuous motives. In 1717, the Spanish blacksmith Juan Antonio de Gamboa confessed that he had tried to make a pact with the devil so as to 'remedy his temporal needs' and thus 'help his mother and sister'.[40] The Spanish tailor Diego Enríquez wrote a letter to the Most Holy Sacrament in 1728 promising never to gamble again while, to quote the inquisitors, 'in a sacrilegious mixture' he 'mortgaged his soul to the devil', allowing him to do whatever he wanted with him if he ever gambled again.[41] And in 1744 the mulatto woman Jacinta Ramírez, 'having every formal intention of lighting some candles to Our Lady of Sorrows, wishing her son to be relieved of all hardship and labour [while in prison] …nevertheless lit a candle to the devil' because she had heard that he specialized in helping prisoners.[42]

Yet behind and above this apparently widespread trust in the temporal power of the devil, it is not difficult to detect an ever present and overriding fear of God. To call on the devil's immediate help in unfavourable circumstances might prove more efficacious than to submit patiently to the divine will in a heroic display of the cardinal virtue of hope; but to linger too long in the devil's service would inevitably lead to much more lasting and fearful consequences. True, in some rare cases the very fear of hell and eternal damnation could lead people to seek the devil's friendship in the hope that he would spare them such torments after death. The illustrious mestizo Juan Luis actually thought that Satan and his demons 'were not tormented with eternal grief and sorrow', but spent their days

> flying through the air in idle pleasure and communicating with many people like himself; and that among the souls that God had created, beside those that, through their good works, would be destined to the beatific vision of their Creator, and those that, through their evil deeds, would be eternally tormented,…there must be a third group of souls that would fly through the air with the said devils in infinite and idle pleasure.[43]

But Juan Luis is by no means a characteristic example, and most people were only too aware of the precarious nature of demonic negotiations. If, as

39 A.G.N., Inq., 901.16, fols 277r–277v; 929.24, fols 355r–355v.
40 A.G.N., Inq., 777.24, fol. 210r.
41 A.G.N., Inq., 811.11, fols 414r–414v.
42 A.G.N., Inq., 884.4, fol. 215r.
43 A.G.N., Inq., 147.6, fol. 3v.

we have seen, demonic invocations made in a state of desperation or anger
were often irresolute, those made in less pressing circumstances were altogether riddled with doubt. In 1624 the Spaniard Bartolomé de la Coba y
Castillo accused himself of invoking the devil 'ten or twelve times', offering
him his soul and a written pact of slavery in exchange for help, but repented
and asked for God's mercy when he realized that the devil would not listen
to him.[44] The mulatto Jusepe Pérez's more fortunate attempt to get the
devil's attention only led to repentance and contrition after the devil
appeared to him in 1639 and asked him to take off his scapular.[45] And in
1711 the Spaniard Antonia de Osorio accused herself of writing 'Devil: I
shall give you my soul if you give me what I must have', only then to tear
the letter to pieces and to insult the devil telling him that God was more
powerful than him.[46]

Some acts of repentance displayed an emotion worthy of the religious
fervour associated with enclosed conventual piety. On realizing his guilt in
1717, Juan Antonio Gamboa 'shed copious tears' with 'great contrition and
a sorrowful heart' and, with 'deep devotion to the divine blood of Our
Saviour Jesus Christ', he resolved to recite the rosary daily.[47] Less devout
souls contented themselves with the thought that they would repent and go
to confession as soon as the devil came to their aid and granted their
request. It was precisely in that mood that in 1749 the mestizo Luis de Silva
had worshipped the devil as God, only while asking his favours, even in the
knowledge 'that it was a monstrosity'.[48] Countless similar cases proved
inefficacious, but they ended up in the confessional anyway. Indeed, it was
only because of the decision of those involved in demonic practices to confess their guilt and request a 'salutary penance' from the Inquisition that so
many cases of demonic invocation carried out in private have come down to
us. If the number of cases involving diabolism is an indication of the ubiquitous power then attributed to the devil, the large proportion of
self-accusations points to the scrupulous sense of guilt that afflicted the
majority of those who succumbed to his seductions.

*

In the context we have described, Satan's cause seemed so hopeless that the
reader might well wonder why the inquisitors spent so much time and
energy taking him seriously. Most temptations were limited to particular
urges and desires and, insofar as they moved the sinner to repent, they were
not merely inefficacious but actually counterproductive. In many instances
they can be seen as the foolish instigations of a pitiable spirit whom God

44   A.G.N., Inq., 518.106, fols 477r–479v.
45   A.G.N., Inq., 387.13 (unfoliated).
46   A.G.N., Inq., 752.18, fol. 215r.
47   A.G.N., Inq., 777.24, fol. 210v.
48   A.G.N., Inq., 918.18, fol. 245v.

had allowed some power over men only in order to lead them to repentance. And if this was true of individual temptations, it was no less true of the theological understanding of the role of the devil. Even in the exaggerated Augustinianism of the time, original sin could still be seen as the *felix culpa* that had made possible the redemption of humanity. In the incarnation, God had turned Satan's original victory into his most humiliating defeat, and all the plots and instigations of the devil would only serve to deepen this humiliation while the repentance of sinners would constantly lay bare the loving mercy of God.

There was, as we have seen, plenty of evidence to convince the inquisitors that the above view was essentially correct. But perhaps nowhere was Satan's impotence more clearly exemplified than in the way he seemed to set about sexual temptation. His most nagging instigations in this field seemed to centre upon timid and irresolute characters whom he would tempt repeatedly to seek his help in their efforts to satisfy their sexual lust only then to disappoint them by failing to comply with their wishes. In 1621 Fray Antonio de Bilbao reported the case of a timid young Spaniard from Acatlán in southern Puebla, who had given him permission, after his last confession, to inform the inquisitors that he had called the devil many times, offering him his soul in exchange for his help in enamouring a woman, carrying an image of the devil next to his heart and visiting a nearby cave that had become a well-known focus of demonic power. It had been the devil's indifference to his requests that had persuaded the penitent to return to the Christian fold.[49] A similar feeling of disappointment was experienced by the young *pardo*[50] Guillermo José, who in 1702 accused himself of invoking the devil's help, offering him his soul and his body and indulging in what the inquisitors called a 'ritual with pollution' when, after an 'emission *propis manibus*', he had implored the devil to take his semen to the girl he wanted to enamour.[51] Then again, in 1748 the Spanish muleteer Francisco Solano de San Miguel, prompted by his 'notable weakness' in sexual matters, resolved 'as a last resort' to use 'certain herbs' that might 'lull women to his carnal desires', but on realizing the inefficacy of the herbs he concluded that it was all a trick of the devil.[52] And in 1768 the Spaniard Antonio José del Castillo remembered how at the precocious age of six he had invoked the devil and taken off his rosary, 'wishing to sin with his aunt', an action that he repeated at the more realistic age of sixteen when, 'inflamed with desire for a woman', he had exclaimed 'Prince of darkness come!' and '*Triquis triquis* devils come out!' Again, it was the futility of such attempts that moved Castillo to repentance.[53]

There were, of course, many instances where the devil did seem to com-

49 A.G.N., Inq., 486(I).57, fol. 278r.
50 *Pardo* was the term commonly used for Indian mulattos.
51 A.G.N., Inq., 721.25, fol. 327r.
52 A.G.N., Inq., 913.14, fol. 399v.
53 A.G.N., Inq., 1000.20, fol. 288v.

ply with the sexual needs of those who sought his help. As we might expect, our illustrious mestizo Juan Luis had no doubt that the devil had helped him to seduce 'more than one hundred Indian virgins and two married women',[54] while only a year earlier, in 1597, the mulatto Francisco Ruiz de Castrejón was reported to have asked the devil to help him to enamour women by relying on a 'sacrilegious mixture' of the words from the Angelus, *verbum caro factum est*, and the forsaking of God, the Virgin Mary and the saints. When called for questioning, the mulatto confessed that he had seduced 'all types of women' with the help of a little book where he had offered his soul to 'the devil Satan'.[55] Almost a century later, in 1689, the mulatto Cristóbal Franco was reported to have seduced many women with the help of the devil, some herbs and the tongue of a snake,[56] while in 1692 the mulatto Esteban de los Angeles bragged that a friend had managed to undress a woman in the street with the help of the devil and some powders he had given him.[57] But all these instances involve characters whom one would expect to have succeeded regardless of any demonic assistance. The sexual drive of the likes of Juan Luis and Francisco Ruiz de Castrejón was not a negative passion to remind them of their weakness but a dynamic urge that nurtured their voracious ego. The help of the devil in this field was not essential or even necessary, but a mere added extra. Juan Luis's main motive for making a demonic pact was to seek help while herding, carding wool or breaking in horses, all of which he did with 'unbelievable speed and efficiency';[58] while Francisco Ruiz de Castrejón confessed that his principal motive for seeking the devil's help was to consolidate his power over other people whom he liked to keep firmly under control.[59]

Thus it seems that the devil's apparent preference for confident and self-assertive types had little to do with sex. Indeed, I know of no instances where success in sexual adventures through demonic aid did not go hand in hand with an increase in social ascendancy, normally reflected in a hubristic display of bumptious skills; and always it was the acquisition of such skills that took precedence as a motive for invoking the devil's help. In 1655 the mulatto Juan Andrés, well-known for his 'amazing skill' in the carding of wool, stated that the two tattoos of the devil he had on his arm also helped him to win fights.[60] Two other mulattos were reported in 1705 to have signed with their own blood a demonic compact with the purpose of be-

54   A.G.N., Inq., 147.6, fol. 16r.
55   A.G.N., Inq., 209.9, fols 5r–5v, 58r.
56   A.G.N., Inq., 674.19, fol. 142r.
57   A.G.N., Inq., 681.5, fol. 269r.
58   A.G.N., Inq., 147.6, fol. 15v.
59   A.G.N., Inq., 209.9, fol. 38v. 'Avía hecho el d[ic]ho pacto para que nadie se le aventajasse ni le echasse el pie adelante'. The devil was also believed responsible for the 'outstanding' and 'dazzling' bull-fighting skills of Cristóbal Franco and Esteban de los Angeles's friend. (A.G.N., Inq., 674.19, fol. 142r; 681.5, fol. 269r.)
60   A.G.N., Inq., 636.4 (unfoliated).

coming stronger at loading and carrying water.[61] In 1727 the mulatto José Padilla told his confessor that his father had taught him to make a pact with the devil to help him excel in bullfights as well as in fights.[62] And in 1744 the Spaniard Luis de Jiménez accused two mulattos of invoking the devil whenever they had something to load, or whenever they saw themselves 'embroiled in a conflict', adding that they had offered him a drink that would supposedly make him more agile.[63] So widespread was the devil's reputation as a dispenser of markedly masculine skills that when the mulatto slave Antonia de Noriega escaped from her master disguised as a man, she thought it wise to 'call and invoke the devil' and, with the help of some herbs, became proficient in bullfights, gambling, and the breaking in of horses; she also became so confident in fights that she even killed many of her opponents.[64]

To many, the close association of diabolism with self-assertive worldly achievement was almost axiomatic. In some isolated instances the concurrence is even known to have taken place among seemingly practising Christians. Such was the case of the mulatto Baltazar de Monroy who, in 1704, was reported to brag about his acquaintance with the devil and to insist to his friends that it was very easy to see him and to make a pact with him in order to obtain herbs and powders to attract women, while swearing that it was all true, 'in the name of God, the Blessed Virgin and the holy cross'.[65] But as a rule self-assertive diabolism was markedly irreligious. The boastful and inflated self-centredness that devil-worship was prone to encourage was at war with the community-oriented nature of religious practice and ritual. Having forsaken God and the Church and thrown away any Christian relics in their possession, devil-worshippers were apt to see in religion a rather effeminate affair. Best suited to timid and insecure types, Christianity became worthy only of the kind of scorn and ridicule poured upon it by the mulatto Pedro Hernández in 1605, when he mocked Ana Baltazar's scruples and pious concern for his soul after he had bragged about his demonic practices;[66] or of the arrogant indifference of the mestizo José de León who, while employed as a servant in the palace of the Count of Santiago de Calimaya in 1652, was reported to make a point of eating meat on Fridays and missing Mass on Sundays and feast days while 'bragging about his courage and manliness' and never missing an opportunity to trivialize religion, saying that 'his friend the devil' would help him against 'the justice of the Church'.[67]

*

61   A.G.N., Inq., 729.11, fols 391r–392r.
62   A.G.N., Inq., 788.25, fols 536v–537r.
63   A.G.N., Inq., 883.21, fols 226v–227r.
64   A.G.N., Inq., 525.8, fols 502r–506v.
65   A.G.N., Inq., 727.18, fol. 504r.
66   A.G.N., Inq., 276.2, fols 9r–11r.
67   A.G.N., Inq., 442.7, fols 191r–201r.

It is perhaps no accident that most of the cases of self-assertive diabolism should come from a group of people engaged primarily in herding and riding activities; for such groups would come to constitute what was in many ways a world apart in New Spain. Drawing on the marginal culture developed among mestizos, mulattos and a number of social misfits who had not found their place among Spaniards or Indians, shepherds and cowherds gradually developed a lore that partook of Indian, African and Iberian magic and which spread throughout the more or less geographically defined region stretching to the southwest into Michoacán and to the north into Zacatecas and Nueva Vizcaya.[68] Until the middle of the sixteenth century, this area had been a sparsely populated frontier zone between the inhospitable northern wasteland and the central fertile valleys. With the discovery of rich silver deposits in Zacatecas (1546) and Guanajuato (1550), however, there began a great mobilization of population and a cycle of land appropriation, giving rise to that complex rural middle class that became the mark of ranchero society.[69]

The more or less generalized economic prosperity that ensued from this process should not obscure the downward pressures exerted on many through the laws of inheritance and what David Brading has called the 'remorseless fertility' of ranchero women. Although some rancheros found security in the priesthood, the majority were forced to seek their living as miners or muleteers, with the lower stratum being driven further down the scale to eke a livelihood close to the margins of subsistence. Within single families the impoverished children of former hacendados often mingled with ambitious new men of enterprise; yet the latter's rise to prosperity rarely exceeded beyond one generation. Indeed, a sudden fall from the level of a prosperous farmer to that of a smallholder was a general worry that bore little relation to race or social background.[70]

In this climate, assertiveness was part and parcel of subsistence itself, and those who excelled tended to develop presumptuous attitudes in a way that was not only natural but widely expected. When the Spanish cowherd Juan Fernández was accused in 1568 of having made a pact with the devil, he bragged openly in front of the inquisitors about the number of cows he could control with the mere sound of a horn while transporting them via Querétaro from Michoacán to Mexico City;[71] and Francisco Ruiz de Castrejón explained in 1598 that he had become more conceited and less

68   Serge Gruzinski, *Man-Gods in the Mexican Highlands: Indian Power and Colonial Society 1520–1800* (Stanford, Calif., 1989), p. 111; Gonzalo Aguirre Beltrán, *Medicina y Magia* (Mexico City, 1963), p. 113.

69   P. W. Powell, *Soldiers, Indians and Silver* (Berkeley, Calif., 1969), pp. 157–71; François Chevalier, *La formación de los grandes latifundios en México* (Mexico City, 1956), pp. 46–50; G. M. McBride, *Land Systems of Mexico* (New York, 1923), pp. 82–102.

70   D. A. Brading, *Haciendas and Ranchos in the Mexican Bajío* (Cambridge, 1978), pp. 163, 157.

71   A.G.N., Inq., 41.4, fol. 308v.

considerate of others after an Indian had given him a 'little book' with figures of the devil which had empowered him to do very impressive tricks with horses and cows.[72] Around 1660 the Spaniard Manuel de Tovar Olvera was suspected of having made a pact with the devil because of the way he bragged about being able to control single-handed a herd of mares that in normal circumstances 'would have kept ten or eleven men very busy', and because his mare could carry a pot of honey on its tail without spilling a drop.[73] And in 1706 the mulatto Nicolás Rodríguez was reported to brag about the valour and courage he derived from the protection that a figure of the devil he had painted on his back gave him in his adventures as a robber in San Luis de la Paz.[74]

If the unpredictable and competitive nature of herding and riding activities was good seedground for hubris, it is unlikely that the peculiar demonic ethos that we have seen to accompany it would have developed without the ubiquitous presence of the Chichimecs. The reputation that this fiery and half-subdued group of Indians came to acquire for their skill in the manipulation of demonic power had spread dramatically as early as the first years of the seventeenth century. Already in 1605 the mulatto Pedro Hernández in Taxco knew about

> a cave in the land of the Chichimecs...where those who want to get or ask for certain things to grow in valour go into, and at the entrance they find many snakes and toads and other bugs, and going further in they find a man sitting whom they may ask for what they want, and the man sitting gives them little papers to increase their valour...and those who thus go in and out of the said cave become good cowmen.[75]

And as far north as New Mexico the Spaniard Luis de Ribera confessed in 1630 that 'in a farm in the land of the Chichimecs' he had obtained a little book with figures of the devil that helped him to control the cattle.[76]

This recourse to Indian knowledge was in many ways a natural development. As we saw in chapter 2, newcomers were prone to rely on the local knowledge of the natives for the manipulation not only of the physical environment but also of those spiritual forces seen as peculiar to the region. This tendency was obviously much more common in the alien, unpredictable and often mysterious landscapes that cowmen and shepherds had to contend with. Their very remoteness made natural landmarks such as mountains or caves acquire sacred connotations that in urban areas would be reserved for shrines and churches. Among the Chichimecs, it is known

72 A.G.N., Inq., 209.9, fols 40v–41r, 57v.
73 A.G.N., Inq., 568.1, fols 5v, 32v.
74 A.G.N., Inq., 735.3, fol. 11r.
75 A.G.N., Inq., 276.2, fol. 9v.
76 A.G.N., Inq., 366.41, fols 403r–403v.

that mountains and caves, especially those associated with springs or water reservoirs, often had their own *chan* or tutelary deity. It was no doubt the guardians and propitiators of these sacred spots who were so often identified with the devil by many who sought their help. Having been slowly relegated to remote rural regions where they could continue their ancient practices in secret, these 'nonconformist' leaders often also assimilated and appropriated many Christian elements, sometimes even associating hallucinogens with Christian saints, Christ and the Virgin Mary. And many herdsmen were quick to adopt such practices. The indefatigable Hernando Ruiz de Alarcón noted that the cowmen of northern Guerrero attributed 'divine virtues' to many herbs, especially to peyote and ololhiuqui, 'and thus they venerate them as sacred and carry them around the neck like relics'.[77]

But a movement in the opposite direction, where the Indians appropriated many of the attributes of the devil, is not to be discounted. As we saw in chapter 2, the association of hallucinogens with the devil encouraged by the missionaries sometimes ironically led the Indians to collaborate actively in the process of their own demonization. Although as a rule this was only a stage in the process of the emergence of a more genuine Indian Christianity, the tendency was seen to persist well into the seventeenth century and beyond in remote and relatively unacculturated areas, notably Oaxaca and Yucatán. In the land of the Chichimecs this tendency became even more extreme. For the Chichimecs were not only comparatively unsubdued and unacculturated; they actually became formidable adversaries once they had adapted to Spanish methods of war, seeking to jeopardize the Spanish presence in the region and on countless occasions posing a serious threat to it.[78]

This attitude of active opposition helps to explain the anti-Christian stance of many Chichimec leaders. Before the conquest, for example, Indian holy men like the *naguales* were renowned for supernatural powers that could be either benign, such as the production of rain, or malevolent, such as the invocation of frost and hail. Significantly, shortly after the arrival of the Spanish the *naguales* lost their socially productive attributes. They came to constitute an exclusively conservative force, seeking to preserve the stability of Indian societies by opposing all innovations and reasserting their power through an ability to kill unfaithful Indians and to keep Spaniards and castas in a state of psychological insecurity through a display of malevolent supernatural power.[79] But such efforts to preserve a native identity could also be carried out in less inflexible ways. The evidence suggests that the persistent association of hallucinogens and indeed of any manifestation

77   Hernando Ruiz de Alarcón, *Tratado de las supersticiones*, in *Tratado de las idolatrías*, ed. Passo y Troncoso, ii, p. 53.
78   On this see *The Cambridge History of Latin America*, ed. Leslie Bethell, 10 vols (Cambridge, 1984–92), i, pp. 187–90.
79   On this see Aguirre Beltrán, *Medicina y Magia*, pp. 98–105.

of heterodox supernatural power with the devil came in many cases to con-stitute a useful tool in the process of resistance. As God's greatest cosmic antagonist, the devil, or at least some of his supernatural attributes, could be welcomed by less anti-innovationist Chichimec leaders. The process gave rise to a truly remarkable process of cultural interaction where pre-Hispanic sacred spots like mountains and caves became centres of a type of diabolism that on occasions could have been transported directly from Europe. Around 1612, for example, the young Spaniard Juan de Puelles, seeking 'help and favour in his job as a herdsman... so as to be freed from every kind of fall and gore', had gone to a cave near the mines of Santiago where he had been told that he would see 'an old man who was known to be the devil'. The old man agreed to help him 'on condition that he made a promise, signing it with his name written in his own blood, that he would be his'. Then, 'as a sign of slavery to him', the old man (now believed to be the devil) painted shackles on his arms, ordered him to kiss his feet, which were 'like the claws of a rooster', and finally, in unmistakably European fashion, made him 'kiss the arse of a he-goat', after which Puelles became a very competent herdsman for a period of nine years.[80] Equally illustrative was the case of the mulatto shoemaker Francisco Rodríguez, who in 1657 was reported to have advised many people to visit a 'cave in the midst of cliffs and crags' near Celaya, where 'with a mere writ of slavery' one could become 'brave, a good bullfighter, a good rider, a good lover and very rich'. Inside the cave Rodríguez claimed to have seen many extraordinary things, including a silver chair on which whoever sat would be 'exposed to very great dangers'. After making the pact, he had been given some herbs to use as relics and he had become a good rider and bullfighter and he always found money in his pocket, except when he wanted to give alms. He had been welcomed by an old man who had introduced him to a group of col-leagues, 'and they were all devils... because, although they were very elegantly dressed, they all had horns'.[81]

*

It is difficult to determine to what extent this development was the result of a Chichimec initiative to assert their cultural identity by means of an active opposition to Christianity. The existence of similar cases outside the land of the Chichimecs (one of them, complete with the adoration of the he-goat, as far south as Tacámbaro in the heart of Tarascan Michoacán[82]) suggests that the spread of this type of western diabolical folklore was more the

80   A.G.N., Inq., 486(II).98, fols 542r–542v.
81   A.G.N., Inq., 563.3, fols 20r–20v.
82   A.G.N., Inq. 568.1, especially fols 34r & 37v. Other illustrative cases were reported in Guadalajara in 1743 (A.G.N., Inq., 912.46) and in Temascaltepec in 1758 (A.G.N., Inq., 986.7).

responsibility of cowmen and shepherds than of Chichimec Indians. Yet it is significant that by the second half of the seventeenth century the devil seemed to have taken over most of those rural sacred spots that in pre-Hispanic days had been dedicated to local tutelary deities. In seeking the supernatural help of Indians, therefore, cowmen and shepherds in turn presented them with a western spiritual force that the Indians could readily appropriate. In this process of symbiotic exchange, however, the devil would soon lose all the attributes associated with the more capricious and ambivalent tutelary deities and would emerge not only as the undisputed enemy of God, but also as the chief opponent of the status quo.

To some extent, this emerging role of the devil as a political opponent helps to explain the puzzling inquisitorial persistence in persecuting an otherwise apparently impotent spirit. But however real the political motivation of the inquisitors might have been, it would be a rash anachronism to overlook the essentially theological reasons for their concern with the spread of diabolism. No matter how futile or redundant the devil's efforts might appear at first sight, even the certainty of his ultimate failure did not mean that Satan could not win some very real temporary victories and even lead a large proportion of humanity to eternal damnation. Indeed, it was an accepted theological truth that the devil could succeed in damning the majority of the human race and still be the loser, for a single soul that was saved was infinitely more valuable than millions of damned souls.

Consequently, no matter how logical or commonplace his help to confident extroverts and his disregard for timid introverts might appear to the modern observer, to the early modern inquisitor, and indeed to early modern men and women in general, the devil presented a much more threatening picture. His help to self-assertive herdsmen could have been interpreted as a deliberate tactic to bring about a more radical and self-centred conversion away from God, thereby preventing, as far as possible, the common and counterproductive reaction leading from repentance to confession to a return to the life of grace. Conversely, Satan's contempt for the sexual weakness of timid introverts could have been seen as resulting from his age-long experience; for a desperate quenching of an introverted sexual passion was apt to lead to a sense of unfulfilment that was ripe ground for repentance and contrition.

At the same time, the devil's apparent preference for assertive characters in no way implied that his tactics for controlling more timid introverts were any less effective. In fact, the devil was seen just as hard at work in the self-centredness of guilt-ridden introverts as in the self-assertiveness of confident extroverts, and the results were often more satisfactory in the former than in the latter. The sense of guilt was just as self-centred and oblivious of God as the self-assertiveness of pride, and from the point of view of the devil it had the added advantage of being inherently barren. Whereas assertive characters experienced a sense of achievement and pleasure that, in line with the orthodox Christian doctrine of the goodness of creation, was legitimate and pleasing to God, the attitude of guilt-ridden introverts was totally negative; their relegation of God to oblivion could even lead them to the hatred of self, which was the doorstep of despair.

Therefore, when faced with the nagging threat of the repentance of those who had sought his help, the devil could still be seen as capable of bringing out one of his strongest cards. The skill with which he was believed to do this occasionally misled even self-assertive characters. When Francisco Ruiz de Castrejón decided to repent or, as he put it, to 'leave the vice', the devil appeared to him in a dream 'like a dog with horns' saying: 'Why are you thinking of abandoning me? One day you will need me again!' And after he persisted in his decision, taking his 'little book with figures of the devil' to one of the Jesuit missionaries who had solemnly burnt it, the devil had chased him in the shape of 'a fire-spitting cow', threatening to kill him if he went to confession.[83]

It was a similar fear that prevented Juan de Puelles from going to confession after he had made a pact with the devil around 1612,[84] and the same problem afflicted Luis de Ribera who, in 1630, described how he constantly saw the devil in visions and dreams, threatening him and 'appearing visibly' to him because he wished to repent, turn to God and go to confession. Subsequently he reiterated that even if the devil had not tormented him so much, he would have found it impossible to go to confession because of the fear that the realization of the enormity of his sin had brought about in his soul.[85] And more than a century later, in 1743, the mulatto José Manuel de Estrada told the inquisitors in Guadalajara that he had been persuaded by his friend Manuel López to make a pact with the devil that would not only make women 'go mad about him', but also turn him into a very good rider and herdsman. Yet, because he had done everything half-heartedly and with fear, never actually throwing his rosary away but only hiding it under his saddle and never actually signing the written pact, Manuel López had started to maltreat him and denigrate him and the devil frequently appeared to him in the shapes of men and women, causing him deep tension and anxiety.[86]

It thus seems that despite the prevalence of the more medieval notion of a malleable and even mockable devil who was strictly under God's control, the more threatening and overpowering early modern conception of him was not a mere monopoly of theologians and demonologists. Especially among those who did not have access to the liturgical defences of communal forms of worship, diabolism and self-centredness inevitably became bed-fellows. Where this self-centredness was confident and assertive, it

83 A.G.N., Inq., 209.9, fol. 56v.
84 A.G.N., Inq., 486(II).98, fol. 542v.
85 A.G.N., Inq., 366.41, fols 403v, 410r.
86 A.G.N., Inq., 912.46, fols 134v–136r.

6. La Deseeperacion.

Periit finis meus, & spes mea
a Domino. Thr. c. 3. v. 18.

Plates 19 (right) and 20 (below). The fear of Hell
and eternal damnation in popular literature.

7. La Eternidad de las Penas.

Dolor meus perpetuus, & plaga
mea desperabilis renunt curari. Jer. 15.

managed to preserve and even to develop many of the more humorous and folkloric attributes of medieval diabolism; but when confidence gave way to insecurity and a sense of guilt (a development which, as we have seen, was not uncommon even among the more assertive characters) the individual was left virtually powerless in the grips of a seemingly overwhelming supernatural force. In some extreme cases the devil seemed almost to have usurped God's omnipotence. In 1731 the free black Atanasio Florentino declared that the devil had granted him the power to exorcize other demons with an efficacy unknown to saintly men, at the same time insisting that, no matter how frightful he felt his behaviour to be, it would be impossible for him to repent, because on the day of his birth the planet Saturn, then at its peak, had predestined him incorrigibly to evil.[87]

This somewhat incoherent testimony suggests that the inescapable and overpowering image of the devil that came to dominate early modern thought found some echoes in the bulk of society. But for the most part these echoes were scattered and infrequent and, as a rule, it was the more malleable figure of medieval demonology that tended to dominate. This does not mean, of course, that early modern demonology was an inaccessible and over-intellectualized construct fit only for a minority of theologically trained minds. It does suggest, however, that the nominalist streak that we detected at the heart of post-Reformation diabolism, with its tendency to separate the natural and the supernatural spheres, rendered the devil increasingly impotent in the natural world. It is no great surprise, therefore, that the social sphere should duly cease to interest him and that his attention should be turned, with an increasingly disturbing punctiliousness, to the inner realms of the individual soul.

---

87 A.G.N., Inq., 834.19, fol. 387r.

4

The Interior Castle

I have often asked myself whether, taking a larger view, philosophy
has not been merely an interpretation of the body *and a misunderstand-*
ing of the body.

Friedrich Nietzsche, *The Gay Science*

IN 1613 THE inquisitors of Mexico City concluded that the Spanish priest
Alonso Hidalgo was 'mad'. As 'an obedient child of the Roman Catholic
Church', Hidalgo had finally decided to ask the holy tribunal to 'have
mercy on him' because he had committed 'many crimes, excesses and evil
deeds' against God, the Virgin, the saints and the Church. All this he
claimed to have done

> in deed as well as in word, from the earliest day I can remember until
> the present...denying all the precepts of our holy faith...having
> renounced...the Holy Trinity, and Our Lady, and the whole of the celes-
> tial court, and having denied the authority of the pope, believing myself
> to be greater than God and rendering obedience to the devil, for I am
> certain that Beelzebub, the prince of the devils, is inside me.

Throughout these years he had grown in the conviction that salvation was
impossible for him. He had not been properly to confession, going only 'in
order to comply and not saying the truth but many lies and frauds to satisfy
the priests'. His sense of being already damned was so overpowering that
whenever he said Mass he suffered innumerable afflictions

> which were so sad and desperate that I could barely walk under the
> weight of so many fantasies and of the realization that I could hardly
> stand up during Mass and that it was no longer possible to excuse myself
> from the task of saying it, for I had said many Masses, even after I had
> despaired of the mercy of God.

Not even the fear of death had made him change his attitude. During a serious illness he had tried to remember his sins, but realizing that

> my sins were so numerous and detestable that it was impossible [to

remember them], I abandoned the effort wishing rather to die like a beast, without the sacraments. And although this time I made a resolution that if God raised me from my bed I would not say more Masses until I had gone to confession, I did not comply.... And during a further illness I did not go to confession although I thought I would die.... And seeing myself in such a poor state, not knowing what to do, I decided to hang myself amidst a thousand chimeras and desperations; and it seemed to me that the devils took me to the hospital of Our Lady, grabbing me by the neck...and one devil with two horns and throwing flames of fire carried me off to a wall where he hung me on a peg and made me drink very quickly from a flask...what seemed to me to be the blood of Our Lord Jesus Christ.... [And] I imagined that, since I had to say Mass the next day, it seemed that there had been an explosion which confounded the clockwork of the heavens, and of many actual heavens that I saw in my imagination, and of many hells; and I saw large quantities of the blood of Christ appear before me like a whirlwind.... And another loud sound of thunder made me think that the world was being torn asunder and that the consciences of men were crumbling in a way that not even God could help them.... It was after I awoke from this rapture that I realized that I was possessed by Beelzebub, with whom I spoke and who reminded me of many things I had long forgotten. So many indeed are the incongruities and heresies that I have said while speaking to the devil ...that I think I must be guilty of a hundred thousand heretical tales... and I have pretended to be mad because I was ashamed of appearing before this holy tribunal.[1]

To the modern reader, the opinion of the inquisitors that Father Hidalgo had lost his mind will undoubtedly seem adequate and even commendable. But in the context of seventeenth-century spirituality the issue was not so simple. Indeed, behind its obvious exaggerations and its confused and desperate style, which no doubt influenced the opinion of the inquisitors, Hidalgo's testimony reveals many characteristics that can be seen as paradigmatic of the spirituality of the age. *Mutatis mutandis*, the case of Hidalgo is strikingly similar to those of many mystical writers of the period, in particular that of the famous French Jesuit Jean-Joseph Surin.

It was only two decades after the case of Hidalgo, in 1634, that Surin was put in charge of a French Ursuline convent in Loudun where a large number of the nuns were showing alarming symptoms of being possessed by demons. A profound mystic, Surin decided not to rely exclusively on exorcism, but to seek to instruct the nuns in the secrets of the mystical life

---

1   Archivo General de la Nación, Mexico City, Ramo Inquisición (Hereafter A.G.N., Inq.), tomo 478, exp. 67 (hereafter 478.67), fols 409r(bis)–411v(bis).

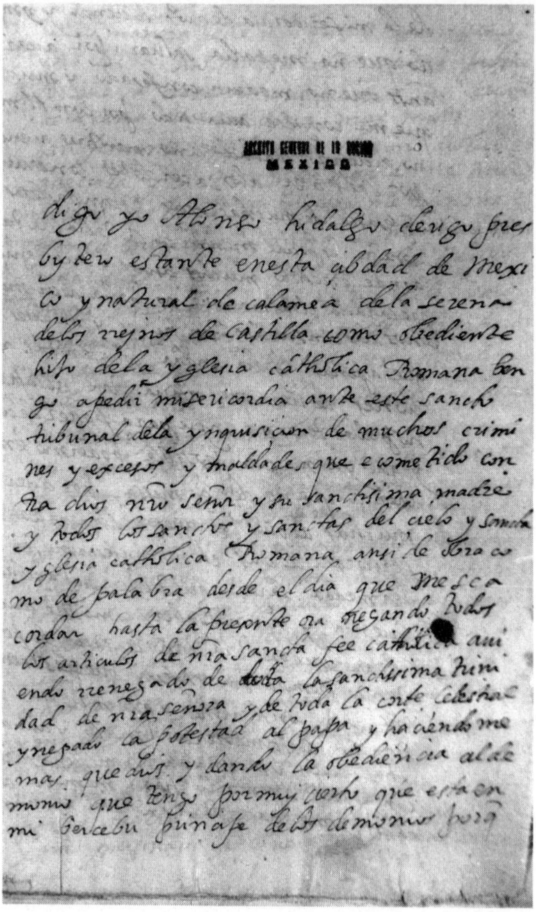

digo yo Alonso hidalgo clerigo pres
bytero estante enesta ciudad de Mexi
co y natural de calamea dela serena
delos reynos de castilla como obediente
hijo dela yglesia cathólica Romana ben
go apedir misericordia ante este sancto
tribunal dela ynquisicion de muchos crimi
nes y excesos y maldades que e cometido con
tra dios nro señor y su sanctissima madre
y todos los sanctos y sanctas del cielo y sancta
yglesia cathólica Romana ansi de obra co
mo de palabra desde el dia que me se a
cordar hasta la presente ora negando todos
los articulos de nra sancta fee cathólica avi
endo renegado de la sanctissima trini
dad de nra señora y de toda la corte celestial
y negado la potestad al papa y haciendo me
mas que dios y dando la obediencia al de
monio que tengo por muy cierto que esta en
mi Berzebu principe delos demonios porq

Plate 21. First page of Fr Hidalgo's letter to the inquisitors.

and to persuade them that the only way to defeat the devils was to give a total and unconditional obedience to God. Seemingly weakened by such methods, the devils sought vengeance by possessing the Jesuit so forcefully that he had to abandon his mission, returning to Bordeaux in the autumn of 1636. After a further, short-lived effort to help the nuns, Surin would spend the subsequent twenty years of his life in a state of virtual insanity. He came to believe that his 'true' soul had been turned into a mere passive spectator of the horrendous tortures and *maleficia* that constantly afflicted his other, diabolical soul. Yet all these things were as nothing when compared to the terrifying conviction that he was irredeemably damned. The knowledge of eternal damnation which tormented Satan and his army of demons had permeated every corner of his being and had convinced him that he had the obligation to act in accordance with that 'sentence', doing evil consciously. Yet Surin still sought to do good, thus going, according to his logic, against God's will:

for, just as there is nothing more important than to observe the impeccable order with which God governs the world, and that which governs hell consists in that it is a place of evil, there is nothing more horrible than to put something good in a place destined for evil, just as it would be a disorder to put evil in paradise.... That is why my most horrendous crime consisted in the fact that I still hoped and wanted to do good.[2]

Having thus prevented him from doing the will of God, the devil seemed to enjoy filling the Jesuit's mind with all kinds of blasphemous and heretical thoughts, even suggesting to him that he should take his own life. In a state of delirium reminiscent of Father Hidalgo's, Surin would spend whole nights contemplating suicide, holding a knife to his neck or thinking of jumping out of the window, which he actually did once, but managed to survive.[3]

Despite marked differences in style and circumstance, the accounts of Surin and Hidalgo follow a strikingly similar logic. Both men were excessively scrupulous and deeply conscious of their incorrigible malice; they both concluded that they were already damned and that any attempt to avoid their terrifying destiny would only lead them to commit even worse sins (doing good against the will of God in Surin's case, and saying sacrilegious masses in Hidalgo's); they both reached an extreme state of despair and attempted suicide; and they both came to believe that they were possessed by the devil.

In strict terms, the last of these symptoms, which from a modern perspective appears as the most serious, was in fact the only one that left some room for hope. As Surin himself insisted, diabolical possessions were frequently a sign of divine favour and mercy. There were countless ways in which God could make use of a possession in order to 'purge' a favourite soul in preparation for the mystical union. Once this possibility was accepted, all diabolical instigations to blaspheme, to renounce God, to commit 'impure acts' or even to despair of divine mercy could be seen as ideal means to combat self-love, especially when the individual soul was humbled to the degree of thinking that it might even have committed those horrors voluntarily.[4]

Consequently, the way in which both Hidalgo and Surin seem to have overcome their state of despair on the basis of their firm conviction of being

2 *Lettres spirituelles du P. Jean-Joseph Surin de la Compagnie de Jésus*, ed. L. Michel and F. Cavallera, 2 vols (Toulouse, 1926–8), ii, p. 54.

3 The events of Loudun are dealt with in detail in Jean-Joseph Surin, *Triomphe de l'amour divin sur les puissances de l'enfer en la possession de la Mère Prieure des Ursulines de Loudun* (Avignon, 1829), pp. 11–147. The details of his subsequent mental state are in *Lettres*, i, pp. 127–8; ii, pp. 1–152. There is an excellent summary in Leszek Kolakowski, *Cristianos sin iglesia: La conciencia religiosa y el vínculo confesional en el siglo XVII*, trans. F. Pérez Gutiérrez (Madrid, 1982), pp. 302–13.

4 *Lettres*, ii, passim.

possessed by the devil, far from being ironical, is actually perfectly logical. To many scrupulous souls a demonic possession, much more than a simple misfortune, often appeared as a clear explanation and justification of their own malice. In such cases, rather than an enemy, the devil would appear as a perfect and even welcome scapegoat.

What is perhaps the most illustrative inquisitorial example of this tendency in New Spain was recorded in 1717 and concerns Sor Margarita de San José, a professed nun in the convent of Jesús María in Mexico City, whose doubts about the articles of the faith had become, in the words of her confessor, 'a constant temptation while she is awake and even sometimes when she is asleep'. At all times she was afflicted by temptations to

> take off her rosary, throw away her relics, scourge a holy crucifix, go to communion without going to confession, take the sacred form out of her mouth and stab it and fry it in oil. She feels as if some kind of fury and rage [*cólera y rabia*] oppressed and inflamed her heart, moving her to fury, disturbing her judgement and alienating her reason, as if she was being violently enraptured and thus she runs out of sung Mass during the creed.

Tempting her 'continuously to offend God', the devil had led her to write a warrant of slavery to him on the feast of the Assumption, which she did in a state of rapture 'as if driven by a foreign power which had also forced her hand to sign "the slave of Satan"' instead of her own name or the alternative 'slave of Our Lady of Sorrows' that her confessor had recommended as an exercise in self-abnegation. Whenever she tried to 'think lovingly about God or Our Lord Jesus Christ' she was struck dumb; and when she was advised to frequent the company of pious and virtuous nuns she would burst into loud laughter 'as if driven by a strange impulse'.

From such evidence her confessor deduced that she was either 'mad and insane' or 'bedevilled'; but he soon dismissed the first possibility because it seemed incongruous to him that Sor Margarita behaved perfectly sanely at all times except when religious subjects were brought to her attention. It thus followed that she was 'spirited, obsessed, enraptured, bedevilled or possessed by the devil, which is what she herself has conjectured' and which was attested by the fact that, after she asked to be exorcized, 'she wrote to me explaining that Lucifer wanted the ceremony to be performed with a black stole, and not with a white or a red one'. (In a subsequent questionnaire Sor Margarita explained the logic behind Lucifer's instruction: black was symbolic of hell, while white and red symbolized purity and the blood of Christ respectively.)[5]

There is, of course, nothing in Sor Margarita's symptoms that cannot be

5   A.G.N., Inq., 1029.6, fols 182r–184r, 191r.

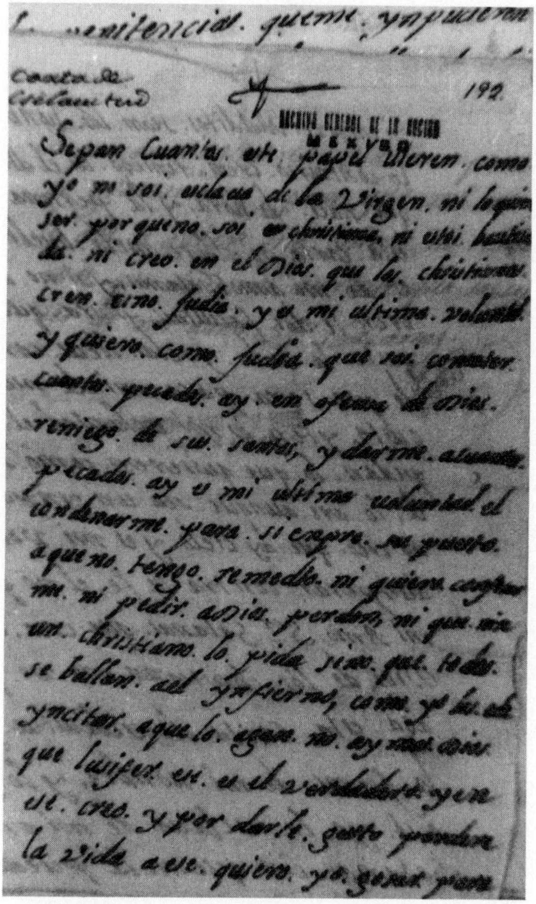

Plate 22. First page of Sor Margarita's written pact with the Devil.

adequately interpreted from a strictly modern standpoint. Indeed, from a psychological perspective they could constitute a straightforward case of neurotic delusion. Her devils, in Freud's words, could be seen as 'bad and reprehensible wishes, derivations of instinctive impulses that have been repudiated and repressed',[6] and her conduct could be the 'expression of a rebellion on the part of the *id* against the external world: of its unwillingness (or incapacity) to adapt itself to the exigencies of reality'.[7] In such a context, Sor Margarita would seem to be facing an inner conflict between her own reality (*ego*) and the ideal that she was meant to be pursuing (*superego*) which, through a failed repression, had encouraged the development of a subconscious hate of religion that she could not explain as belonging to

6   Sigmund Freud, 'A Seventeenth-Century Demonological Neurosis', in *Standard Edition of Complete Psychological Works* (London, 1961), xix, p. 72
7   'Loss of Reality in Neurosis and Psychosis', ibid., p. 185.

herself. The only outlet was to attribute these subconscious urges to an external force; and since in the context of the time such a force could only be seen as diabolical, Sor Margarita could have opted for the logic that we have already observed in the cases of Hidalgo and Surin by investing the devil with the convenient role of scapegoat.

Thereafter Sor Margarita could feel free to express her furious hate of religion as if it emanated from a force outside her control and responsibility. She could fearlessly confess that she had committed sacrilege three times by taking communion in a state of mortal sin with the specific purpose of offending God; the second time she had taken the wafer out of her mouth and had thrown it on a tomb in disdain and the third time she had trampled over it and spat on it. Likewise, she had torn a print of Our Lady to pieces and had thrown it in an 'indecent place' after spitting on it and treading on it, and she had slapped and spat on an image of the child Jesus and scourged a holy crucifix furiously. It is hardly surprising that she often lost her temper with the priests while they preached at Mass, especially if they mentioned the Holy Trinity. Although she admitted to have followed her confessor's advice and asked Our Lady's help during these temptations, she always, deep down, wished that 'the Enemy' should possess her body. That this last wish had been fulfilled could be attested from the way in which her body trembled during the recitation of the creed and especially while saying *et incarnatus est*, as well as from her complete inability to look at the holy sacrament and the 'intense inner forces' that prevented her from kneeling during the consecration. Finally, the logic of our interpretation can be adequately confirmed by Sor Margarita's own admission that her sacrilegious confessions and communions were due to her failure to confess the sins 'against the sixth commandment', which leaves little doubt about the presence of erotic urges in her.[8]

For the historian, however, the interest of such experiences is not so much to be found in the way in which they point to pathological states or psychiatric complexes, but rather in the fact that they allow some understanding of the spirituality of the time, and particularly of the way in which the doctrines which it inspired fitted into the contemporary ideological climate. In this sense, psychological interpretations of cases such as Hidalgo's and Sor Margarita's, however illuminating they might be individually, are of little help. At times they may even hinder our understanding. Notice, for example, that the cases we have analysed are only exceptional insofar as they represent extreme developments of tendencies that were not just accepted but actually recommended at the time. What to us might seem a clear case of neurosis or sexual repression could just as clearly have appeared to contemporaries as a sign of virtue or Christian perfection. This, indeed, is one of the most recurring and disconcerting characteristics of the

---

8   A.G.N., Inq., 1029.6, fols 185r–190v.

hagiographic literature of the seventeenth and eighteenth centuries in New Spain. In her biography of María de San Joseph, for example, Sebastián de Santander y Torres quotes a letter from the alleged saint where she explains:

> I can assure you that for every virtue that I must and want to exercise I have in me a devil that contradicts it. Of this I have no doubt at all, for it is clear to me that it is so and they force me to say so many and such terrible blasphemies against Our Lord that they can only be contained in the horrendous iniquity of them who force me to say them; all this they do with such great violence that I press my teeth together with all my strength and it seems to me that I can still feel my tongue uttering them...[and] because of the many battles that I have to sustain with them I am in such a state that with every effort that I make my bowels are pushed out.

Not even in her most virtuous thoughts and 'revelations' did the devils leave her alone. When she felt a divine impulse to found a convent in Oaxaca the devils at once came to cause her a 'great confusion' making her 'lose her senses' while they said:

> Look at her! See how happy and proud she is. This simple, silly and alienated blockhead thinks that, just because the bishop has approved them, all the lies and rackets that we hammered into her head are true. She consoles herself...believing that all those frauds and chimeras that we concocted and stuffed her conk with and which she used to deceive her candid and innocent confessor whom she has made to swallow such unbelievable rubbish were true revelations.... Oh, what a fine day it will be when...they declare her a deluded hypocrite and a bedevilled cheat! They really will give her then...the prize that her revelations deserve![9]

The extraordinary fact about such diabolical instigations is that they do not seem to have become a source of anxiety; on the contrary, they were seen as clear symptoms of spiritual progress. Indeed, the more powerful and vivid were the demonic attacks, the more worthy of respect and admiration were those who suffered them. Sor María de San Joseph only grew in virtue after it was revealed to her that 'God had allowed three infernal spirits to torment her for eight years'; and there were many more that came by night in troops so numerous that when she saw them 'with the inner vision of the soul' they seemed to her to be scattered in her cell 'as if they were pins'. They beat her, tormented her and mocked her, depriving her of sleep throughout the night and leaving her 'so shattered, crippled and breathless'

9 Sebastián de Santander y Torres, *Vida de la Venerable Madre María de San Joseph* (Mexico City, 1723), pp. 176, 194.

that she had to drag herself out of her cell in the mornings and lean faintly against the walls on her way to choir. Then they filled her head with scruples, suggesting that all her actions were sinful so that she would act with fear in everything. In their attempts to stop her praying, which would be an unforgivable source of scandal to her sisters, they hid the words of the breviary from her sight; but since Sor María often knew the words by heart, they then tied up her tongue and paralysed her jaw. They constantly filled her head with evil thoughts. On one occasion so many devils attacked her at once that she thought she had been transported to hell itself, and the torments she received were 'so cruel' that she felt how her body 'crumbled into tiny pieces'. After this, she wrote,

> I came back to my senses and they left me for the space of an hour, during which I could enjoy the favours and mercies granted to me by my Lord, which were very great. Then…they returned…but I had been so admirably…comforted…that it all seemed like nothing and I was only willing to suffer more and more.[10]

To the modern reader, such attitudes inevitably appear riddled with a morbid masochism. But in the hagiographic literature of the time they had become normal and recurrent symptoms of what were considered to be truly saintly lives. It was actually to be expected that diabolical torments should increase in proportion to the degree of virtue and patience displayed by the victims. In his biography of Sor Michaela Josefa de la Purificación, the Mercedarian friar Agustín de Miqueroena remarks on the 'prolix illnesses' that afflicted this saintly woman, caused by the way in which 'the furious ministers of the most enraged rabble took turns to beat her body repeatedly and with unbounded tyranny'. Her sisters would pray unceasingly for her, but this would only serve to augment the fury of the 'rabid… ministers of the infernal tyranny' who, 'like rigourous…slayers of her innocence' would inflict such terrifying torments on her that she often felt 'as if her body was being torn to tiny pieces and her bones had been dislocated from her natural joints'. These and worse things she suffered gladly. What seemed a more 'cruel' and 'rigorous martyrdom' to her were all the 'exterior signs' that the torments left on her body. For Sor Michaela 'was so naturally serious and so hostile to anything exterior, that she would undoubtedly have suffered twice as many illnesses had she been spared the need to suffer such exterior signs'.[11]

In the case of Sor Sebastiana Josefa de la Santísima Trinidad, it was similarly believed that God had allowed the devil to take advantage of every

10   Ibid., pp. 169–71, 175–6.
11   Agustín de Miqueroena, *Vida de la V. M. Sor Michaela Josepha de la Purificación* (Mexico City, 1755), pp. 25–6.

opportunity to insult her and torment her. 'Countless were the occasions', wrote her biographer,

> when the devil carried the venerable mother through the air, moving her from top to bottom and from the floor again he carried her up to great heights; then from side to side with incomprehensible violence, as if she was only a light piece of straw, so that excessive pains spread all over her body. Often she found herself in the deep dungeons of hell itself... and on each occasion she experienced new martyrdoms and sorrows that seemed to drive her to her death.... Many times the devils acted as cruel ministers who crucified her, causing her extreme and agonizing pains with the excessive impiety and cruelty with which they carried out their task.

They would constantly play tricks on her, as she wrote to her confessor, tempting her sisters to

> hate me and insult me... delaying me on my way to choir, so that I miss the most important parts of the divine office.... Whenever I try to rest he afflicts me, taking me to filthy places... holding me back, making me forget where the choir is, making me think that I have missed communion and that by the time I go to chapel they will have finished prayers.

And, of course, during the rare moments of peace she enjoyed 'she gave thanks to her sweet Husband for the benefits she had received... but always thirsty for more sufferings'.[12]

*

The nagging role of the devil in early modern conventual piety is so alien to our understanding of Christian spirituality that it is difficult to understand how it came to be regarded as an orthodox development. It is true that the idea that God could, and often did, allow the devil free reign with the specific purpose of obtaining a greater good was commonplace in traditional theology. But the above examples go well beyond a mere divine permission. It was almost as if the devil had been turned into an indispensable means to salvation. In the words of Valdés,

> Very few saints placed in the high altar of glory have been untouched by the hand of the devil. For, given that this cursed craftsman has always shown a great skill in cutting, edging and polishing, God has seen fit to grant him a general licence to refine, polish and adorn with his hand all

---

12   Joseph Eugenio Valdés, *Vida admirable y penitente de la V. M. Sor Sebastiana Josepha de la SS. Trinidad* (Mexico City, 1765), pp. 287, 291–3, 294–7.

those who, in his wise providence, he has destined to fill the eternal niches that are found in heaven's immense reredos.[13]

This notion of the devil as a mere instrument of God went hand in hand with a notion of God which was rooted in the nominalist tendency to separate nature and grace. Indeed, Valdés's view was in full agreement with the teachings of Surin, for whom, as we have seen, the difference between the natural and the supernatural was not merely a difference of degree but a fundamental rupture 'between heaven and earth, between the finite and the infinite'.[14] According to this view, the goodness of human actions could not be measured in terms of their effects, however good these might be, but only insofar as they resulted from the unconditional abandonment of the self to the divine will 'in the same way as a good servant does not do good works but only the will of his master'.[15] In strict terms, nature and goodness became virtual antonyms. Since God was the only autonomous value, human actions were incapable of deriving any value whatsoever from themselves. To suppose otherwise would amount to affirming that a given subject other than God was a possible source of goodness, which in turn amounted to denying the sovereignty of God. Indeed, the value of a good work could not even be derived from its concordance with divine law, for the latter could not claim any autonomous existence outside the divine will.

Surin's 'extreme monism', as Lezsek Kolakowski has called it,[16] was inseparable from a complete rejection of the Thomist concordance between nature and grace. The problem was not simply that men and women could not collaborate with grace, but that they should not even try to do so. The human will should be extinguished to the point of bringing about a 'holy hate of self' and an 'absolute repudiation of everything human'.[17] Christian men and women should at all times believe themselves to be the worst of sinners, who justly deserved to be hated and condemned by God to the eternal punishments of hell. Only thus could their souls be liberated and come to the realization that God had put them to the test and even allowed them to commit horrendous sins with the sole object of purifying them.[18]

The teachings of Surin are characterized by many of the elements associated with Quietism, as expounded in Miguel Molinos's *Spiritual Guide*. In them we find not only the principle of *extinctio virum proprium*, advocating a

---

13   Ibid., p. 285.
14   *Lettres*, ii, p. 388.
15   Jean-Joseph Surin, *La guide spirituelle pour la perfection, divisée en sept parties* (Paris, 1836), p. 73.
16   *Cristianos sin iglesia*, p. 317.
17   Jean-Joseph Surin, *Les fondements de la vie spirituelle, tirés du livre de l'Imitation de Jésus-Christ* (Paris, 1667), pp. 330, 256.
18   Ibid., pp. 300–3.

passive self-annihilation, but also that peculiar gnostic hate of the world and of creation, leading to the idea that temptations and even sinful acts have their seat in the lower part of the soul, while the 'apex' of the soul remains undisturbed by them. The separation of the two halves of the soul that Surin perceived so vividly was just as marked in Molinos, complete with the belief that the devil was the master of the lower half.[19] The 'spiritual martyrdom' that Christians had to undergo on their way to the mystical union in Molinos's *Spiritual Guide* is virtually indistinguishable from the bulk of current spiritual doctrine. 'Your invisible enemies', he writes, 'will persecute you with scruples, with lustful suggestions, with unclean thoughts', since it was God's will that we should be assailed by

> thoughts against the faith, horrible temptations, violent and troublesome suggestions of impatience, pride, gluttony, lust, anger, blasphemy, cursing and despair…horrible desolations, unceasing and teasing suggestions of evil, violent temptations of the enemy,

all of which had to be suffered in patient perseverance, 'quietly and resignedly', for 'God will value your peace and resignation more than if you formed good resolutions'.[20]

It is true that such views were always regarded with suspicion in official circles and that the exaggerated teachings of Molinos were categorically condemned in 1685. But the condemnation did not do away with the propitious atmosphere that had led to the emergence of Quietism. Indeed, it is impossible to understand Molinos outside the wider tradition of the French Oratory, which was the tradition of Francis de Sales and Frances de Chantal, of John Eudes, of Bérulle, of Lallemand and Surin; a tradition which was deeply Augustinian and whose distrust of nature and the body could be traced back even to the most orthodox writers of the Counter-Reformation. When, for instance, Molinos insists that we should become dead to ourselves, 'like a lifeless corpse', and allow the divine will to rule our lives, he is echoing St Ignatius;[21] and when Surin writes that the devil inhabits our nature, while God our spirit,[22] he could fall back on the undisputed authority of St Teresa, who had only welcomed 'supernatural

---

19 *Guida espiritual que desembaraza el alma…*(Rome, 1675) II, 11.

20 Quoted in R. A. Knox, *Enthusiasm: A Chapter in the History of Religion with Special Reference to the XVII and XVIII Centuries* (Oxford, 1950), p. 281.

21 'He who lives under obedience', writes St Ignatius, 'ought to allow himself to be carried and directed by divine providence…as if he were a lifeless body which allows itself to be carried to any place and to be treated in any manner desired, or as an old man's staff which serves in any place and in any manner whatsoever in which the holder wishes to use it.' *The Constitutions of the Society of Jesus*, trans. George E. Ganss, S.J. (St Louis, Missouri, 1970), pp. 248–9.

22 *Lettres*, i, p. 256

experiences' when they were as far removed from the 'natural' as possible; for 'it is where the natural is united to the supernatural that the devil can do most damage'.[23]

In the context of this separation, the early modern distrust of creation, particularly the natural inclinations of the body, is easier to understand. It is on this basis that a popular eighteenth-century Mexican preacher insisted that 'purity' was 'the highest of the virtues', since 'through no other are men made so similar to the angels'.[24] Indeed, Christians should always be on their guard and take meticulous care to avoid anything that might awaken in them any kind of sensual desire. To illustrate this point the same author recounts an apocryphal story where St Bernard had allegedly

> laid eyes upon a woman on one occasion, inadvertently, and, notwith-standing his lack of consent, yet he chastised himself so severely that he plunged his whole body into a tank of freezing water from which he was rescued on the verge of expiring. Oh what laudable modesty is effected by those who know the dangers of losing their way in the crooked path of the senses![25]

In very much the same spirit it was regarded as an act of exemplary virtue that Sor Antonia de la Madre de Dios should 'turn a blind eye or a deaf ear' to any words that might awaken a sensual desire in her, and this not only in the course of her daily activities but even during her readings of the lives of the saints or the divine office or sacred scripture![26] The distrust of the sensual and its increasing identification with the demonic became an orthodox and undisputed issue in the spirituality of the time, often even receiving authoritative confirmation from established and recommended authors. In his biography of Bishop Juan de Palafox, Antonio González de Rosende states that

> according to the doctrine of St Paul, man…is made up of a repugnance and contradiction between the spirit and the flesh; and his miserable make-up is a living and never ending battle. For the flesh tends to what is contrary to the spirit, and the spirit yearns for what is opposed to the flesh, which amounts to saying that they both aim to destroy and subject one another…[and] it is a constant [teaching] of theology and every document of faith that the devil's intentions are not that the spirit should prevail against the flesh…but the reverse.

23   *Interior Castle (Las Moradas)*, book iv, ch. 3.
24   Juan Joseph de Escalona y Calatayud, *Instrucción a la Perfecta Vida* (Mexico City, 1737), p. 21.
25   Ibid.
26   José Jerónimo Sánchez de Castro, *Vida de la V.M. Sor Antonia de la Madre de Dios* (Mexico City, 1747), pp. 239–41.

Consequently, and in sharp contrast to the medieval tradition, it was in the area of 'intellectual communication' where the devil could do least damage. His efforts were always centred on the senses, where he was capable of

> feigning lights or forming voices, and it is here where all the fabrications and chimeras of his illusory tricks are forged. Yet, always astute and resourceful...he endeavours to preserve and protect the senses, which are the district of his jurisdiction; and thus, all the effects produced by the gifts of his hand are sensitive...[and] never will his delights, visions or voices lead to those extreme and inflamed desires of the love of God...where the soul seeks to undo itself for that Supreme Good and to destroy its body, despising it and mortifying it with penances.[27]

This rejection of the body resulted from a radical interpretation of the Pauline opposition of the spirit and the flesh which is quite new in Christian spirituality. There was, of course, a long and recurring ascetic tradition in Christian history where the distrust of the body was expressed just as forcefully. But the early modern identification of the flesh *exclusively* with the body and the senses as Satan's chosen realm, and its propagation as an orthodox doctrine, was unprecedented. No matter how perishable and weak the human body might be, traditional Christian doctrine had always affirmed its intrinsic value. As Peter Brown has observed, even St Paul's 'brutally dualistic image' of the body as 'an earthen vessel...sown in dishonour', 'already glowed with a measure of the same spirit that had raised the inert body of Jesus from the grave'.[28] The war of the spirit against the flesh was not an image of the body's intrinsic depravity but a sign of the human resistance to the will of God. Consequently, sexual renunciation as a desirable option developed in early Christianity not as an expression of the rejection of the body but as a means towards a transformation that would unite the human body to the victorious body of Christ.[29]

Very little of this affirmation of human nature remained in early modern spiritual literature. The pendulum seemed to have swung quite drastically from the Tridentine concern over good works and free will towards an exaggerated Augustinianism commonly associated with Jansenism and

---

27 Antonio González de Rosende, *Vida del Ilustríssimo, y Excelentíssimo señor Don Juan de Palafox y Mendoza* (Madrid, 1762), pp. 596–7, 600.
28 Peter Brown, *The Body and Society: Men, Women and Sexual Renunciation in Early Christianity* (London, 1990 edn) p. 47
29 Ibid., pp. 48–57. Brown's remarkable treatment of sexual renunciation in the thought of St Augustine – possibly the man most frequently blamed for the allegedly Christian aversion to sex – is very suggestive. 'Augustine was exceptionally careful to point out, in frequent, patient expositions of the letters of Paul, that *the flesh* was not simply the body: it was all that led the self to prefer its own will to that of God. The *concupiscentia carnis*, indeed, was such a peculiarly tragic affliction to Augustine precisely because it had so little to do with the body. It originated in a lasting distortion of the soul itself.' Ibid., p. 418.

Quietism, but by no means peculiar to them. The emphasis again fell on a religion of the heart, where a direct personal access to God could be achieved with little intellectual background or liturgical expression. The sacraments were by no means dispensed with, but there was a tendency to see them as a barrier interfering with the truer worship of the heart. The Divine Office, in particular, was no longer seen as a joyful communal cele-bration, but as an obligatory exercise of obedience and self-abnegation where, moreover, the pious exposed themselves to the devil's most artful tricks on the imagination.

At the root of this lay a theology where grace no longer perfected nature but destroyed it and replaced it. The pious Christian should decry human nature as the basis for any kind of spiritual truth. David should not wear the panoply of Saul, lest the divine will, which was only communicated to the pious if they chose to reject the flesh, should be lost in the miasma of man's intellect, fatally obscured by the fall.

Thus it was that ascetic practices ceased to be aimed at a detachment from disorderly worldly attractions and became painful exercises of self-abnegation where the enemy was no longer, strictly speaking, sin or disorder, or even the devil, but nature itself. Since on a personal level the enemy was the body, the devil's instigations were often seen as useful, even necessary, benefits on the road to salvation. Whenever Sor Sebastiana Josefa de la Santísima Trinidad found herself free from the horrendous torments with which the devil 'crushed her body', making her feel as if her bones 'crumbled into tiny pieces', she would 'thank her sweet Husband for such benefits...always, however, thirsty for more torments'.[30] It was, in fact, only when the devil played directly on the natural inclination of the senses that he could do positive damage. Of the many 'frightening images' that the devil used against Sor Sebastiana, those that most 'afflicted her heart' were the ones he used to appear to her in human shape, for then he would 'place himself before her very eyes in unmentionable dishonesty and extreme turpitude and filth, moving her imagination with horrible suggestions and wakening in her heart furious flames of sensual fire'.[31]

The concurrence of this rejection of the body, and its consequent advo-cacy of sexual repression, with the emergence of what has come to be known as the bourgeois society, has often been remarked on. As Michel Foucault put it, sexual repression is 'emblematic' of bourgeois morality.[32] What needs more emphasis, however, is that, seen from the perspective of the place that the devil had come to occupy in this development, the phe-nomenon can be explained equally well as an expression of the widespread nominalist-inspired tendency to reject the possibility of a concordance

30 Valdés, *Vida admirable*, p. 287.
31 Ibid., p. 286.
32 *The History of Sexuality: An Introduction*, trans. R. Hurley (Harmondsworth, 1981), p. 17.

Plate 23. The Devil's role in salvation: St Rose of Lima in Satan's arms.

between nature and grace, and of the consequent voluntaristic conception of God which turned the devil into a mere instrument of the divine will.

*

By far the most illustrative example of the trend we have been analysing is the bizarre case of the demoniacs of Querétaro, which came to the notice of the Mexican Inquisition in the last months of 1691. There can be little doubt that the most important factor leading to the growth of an awareness of the diabolic at this time was the missionary activity of the newly arrived Franciscans of Propaganda Fide, who founded their first college in Querétaro in 1683. Their activities included popular preaching, the conversion of unevangelized rural areas and the spiritual ministry of the towns and cities in which they had set up colleges, but it was the popular missions that, according to Fr Lino Gómez Canedo, mostly gained for them the

admiration of the people. 'They constituted events of extraordinary reso-
nance in each city and town', he writes, with an impact that was 'chiefly
attributable to the rigour of their penance, which was as disinterested as it
was indefatigable'.[33]

In his monumental chronicle of the colleges, Fray Isidro Félix de
Espinosa has left a vivid account of the ideals of the founders and of the
extraordinary penances of his coreligionists. 'Since the venerable founder of
this apostolic college was an ecstatic man', he writes with reference to the
college of Querétaro, he organized the regular life of the missionaries

> in such a way that they would never have a moment of idleness, so that
> the common enemy would always find them alert.…Sleep was so scarce
> that they barely had a moment's rest. As soon as the hours of choir were
> finished at two-thirty, all of them, in holy emulation, busied them-
> selves…walking the Via Sacra with crosses, ropes and crowns of
> thorns.…As lovers of the cross and of the crucified…they constantly
> devised new ways of transferring His aching image…onto themselves.
> With pious obstinacy they forced their lay brethren to become their
> fierce executioners by slapping their faces, tugging them with ropes and
> scornfully trampling over them.…On the eve of important festivities
> they added more penances to their mortifying fasts: some ate sitting on
> the earth, others carried heavy crosses around the tables, others kissed
> the feet of their brethren confessing their defects and sins.…

Soon after their first college was founded in Querétaro in 1683, 'the seed of
the divine word' was seen to spread to 'all the corners of the city'. The friars 'preached with words filled with the spirit' and they soon claimed to
have brought about the 'universal reformation of customs'. Feasts and
celebrations stopped and so did public games, dances and comedies.
'Relaxation' was checked in such a way that the 'celebrated gaiety of the
city of Querétaro' could no longer be recognized. 'Querétaro', a man was
known to have commented,

> is no longer Querétaro. For some Fathers of the Cross have come to it
> and they are so impertinent that they have brought an end to all the cus-
> tomary festivities; now everything seems very sad; harps and guitars are
> no longer heard; all are prayers and sermons and the place has lost its
> former gaiety.

This man, Espinosa commented, was 'surely one of those about whom the
Holy Spirit says that they are happy in doing evil and that they glory in

---

33 See his introduction to Isidro Félix de Espinosa, *Crónica Apostólica y Seráfica de todos los
colegios de Propaganda Fide de esta Nueva España*, ed. Lino Gómez Canedo (Washington, D.C.,
1964), pp. xxviii–xxix.

their most depraved deeds'. But now the good work of the missions had stifled such people. If formerly the 'delicious terrain' of Querétaro had been 'an incentive to many a sin', now, 'its moderate way of life and the frequentation of the sacraments' had turned it into 'one of the most exemplary cities in the world'.[34]

In this fervid mood of enthusiasm, the Franciscans seemed at pains to channel people's religious aspirations into the mould of a rigorous asceticism which they had come to see as the only way to virtue. The success of their sermons and processions could be observed in the radical changes that they had brought about in the life-style and customs of the city, particularly the way in which numerous women, 'otherwise the natural enemies of silence', were seen to leave their husbands in order to follow the friars without saying a word. Some were reported to shed copious tears during the three-hour-long sermons and then to urge the friars to begin again; others were seen readily to exchange their 'scandalous dresses' for coarse Franciscan habits, as a visible pledge of their eagerness for sanctity and ascetic suffering.[35]

Such stories of radical conversion were seen by contemporaries with varying degrees of credulity. But the situation became more highly charged when it began to be widely rumoured that many of the women who frequented the missions and had taken Franciscan habits were showing marked signs of being possessed by demons. On 13 December 1691 the commissary of the Holy Office in Querétaro, Juan Caballero y Osio, wrote to the inquisitors in Mexico City informing them that every evening after the sermons a new demoniac emerged from the Franciscan mission. Having witnessed one such event, he attested to the truth of the rumours that the women threw themselves violently on the ground, covering their eyes when the friars brought them communion, resisting the host 'with all sorts of scowls and smirks', while others screamed madly, insulted the Virgin Mary and spat contemptuously on the hands of the priests and on the crucifixes and relics that they used during the ceremonies.[36] Scarcely a month later, the Spanish merchant Diego Nabrijo confirmed that Francisca Mejía, a devout young woman who attended the Franciscan missions assiduously, was evidently possessed and had been exorcized by several friars. He explained that he himself had witnessed some of the exorcisms and had heard how the devil actually spoke through the mouth of the demoniac, stating that his name was Gorra and that he and another devil had entered Francisca's body an hour earlier while she changed a vest where the friars had put a powerful relic. This acceptance by the devils of their ultimate weakness against sacred objects had given the friars some hope. Nabrijo had seen how the victim's belly 'after growing to an unnaturally large size',

---

34   Fray Isidro Félix de Espinosa, ibid., pp. 173–6.
35   Ibid., pp. 183, 189, 193.
36   A.G.N., Inq., 527.8, fol. 486r–v.

had returned 'to its normal being' by the mere touch of a relic. Yet the powers that the devils seemed to have been allowed to exercise by God were extraordinary. Nabrijo had been horrified by the numerous bite-marks left by the devils all over Francisca's body, while 'other invisible beings' furiously tore her Franciscan habit to pieces, claiming that the number of demoniacs would increase daily.[37]

Such disjointed fragments of information were to be confirmed and expanded by Fray Pablo Sarmiento, at that time preacher and guardian of the Franciscan College of Santa Cruz de Querétaro, in a long letter to the inquisitors dated 2 January 1692. Anxious to defend the Franciscan position in face of the growing scepticism of the other religious orders, in particular the Carmelites, Jesuits and Dominicans, Sarmiento decided to recount his whole, first-hand experience in the matter.

He claimed that the affair had begun on 10 August 1691, when Francisca Mejía's mother had anxiously called him, asking for help with her daughter who 'seemed to have gone mad'. Fray Pablo, however, soon grew aware that Francisca's behaviour 'could not proceed from a natural cause and even less from any inner fiction of her own', for she was totally dumb and her mouth was so stiff that it could only be opened by the application of relics. Yet, whenever this was achieved, she immediately felt insufferable pains in other parts of her body and she was frequently tormented by violent convulsions. At times her body was suspended in the air and often it turned 'so stiff that not even the strength of many robust men was sufficient to bend her frail arm but an inch'.

All this left Sarmiento with no doubt that Francisca was possessed and accordingly he began to exorcize her. After only two or three 'conjurations', 'God willed that one of the devils should ascend to the creature's tongue' to reveal that he and other spirits had been put inside Francisca's body by a group of witches – the most notable of whom was 'the mice-sucker' (*La Chuparratones*) – and that Fray Pablo could help her feel better by administering those 'holy drinks' that were recommended in authorized manuals of exorcism such as the *Flagelum Demonuum* [*sic*].[38] Sure enough, once the devil's advice had been followed, Francisca began to expel many foul objects from her body, notably 'four avocado stones, about half a pound of river pebbles resembling small nuts, a cow bone..., a small toad, then a snake...which came out of her ear' and which Fray Pablo burnt 'in holy fire', spreading a 'foul pestilence' around the neighbourhood. Noticing that Francisca had recovered 'a little' Sarmiento felt confident enough to order the devil to leave. To his great delight, Francisca looked visibly relieved

37 A.G.N., Inq., 523.3, fols 307r–308r.
38 This is almost certainly Girolamo Menghi, *Flagellum Daemonum: Exorcismos terribiles, potentissimos et efficaces...*(Venice, 1587 and many other editions). I am grateful to Stuart Clark for this reference.

after the devil had promptly obeyed his command. But his triumph was short-lived. The same devil returned only eight days later and solemnly stated that the witches had sent him back 'to service the maleficium' which was 'renewed every moon'. Thereafter many devils had tormented Francisca, especially at night when they 'bit her furiously on her arms and hands' in the presence of three witches, one of whom she recognized as the mice-sucker.

Any qualms that Sarmiento may have had about the genuineness of Francisca's diabolical locutions were substantially diminished when he discovered that Juana de los Reyes, another keen Franciscan devotee, had been found by the provincial of Michoacán, Fray Domingo de Ojeda, to be displaying remarkably similar symptoms. On his first visit to Juana's house, Fray Pablo Sarmiento explained that he had found her 'like a dead body' and 'emitting a most intolerable stench' such as that which 'comes out of a grave when it is open eight days after the body has been buried'. Admirably, the smell disappeared after a few 'conjurations', but Juana's body remained 'dumb-struck and stiff…as if it was made of wood or stone'. After Sarmiento ordered the devils in the name of God to let Juana speak she sat up slowly and a devil, speaking through her, revealed that the mice-sucker, whom he called 'my lady', had sent him into the demoniac's body because she had felt jealous of Juana's nice feet and wished to harm her. Anxious to attend Juana with the same remedies that had brought Francisca some consolation, Fray Pablo gave the victim 'two or three holy drinks', after which Juana expelled 'visibly and patently, three avocado stones…and while nearly choked by vomit, she pointed to the inside of her mouth and pulled out a toad by the leg, throwing it on her bed'. The toad, which was unnaturally large, was quickly killed by Juana's father. Sarmiento then diligently burnt it in 'holy fire', whereupon the toad emitted an 'indescribably unpleasant smell'. Stranger still, after half an hour of 'very strong flames' the toad still retained its former shape. Naturally alarmed, Sarmiento took courage and 'pulverised' it with a club. After this he noticed that Juana had recovered 'slightly'.[39] But again his triumph was short-lived. Juana's ailments soon grew worse and strange things kept emerging from her body and now more frequently from her 'intimate parts'. One day an iron spindle; the next a paper bag with twenty pins; from her lungs a bundle of black wool which suffocated her. Devils entered and left her body by their hundreds and announced their next move in merry anticipation. The puzzled Franciscans worked fervently every evening for up to eight hours in their attempts to drive out the devils, but their efforts were only temporarily efficacious. The devils often refused to obey, arguing that they were incapable of complying with the orders of the exorcists until the witches'

---

39 A.G.N., Inq., 527.8, fols 505r.–507v.

wishes were fulfilled and promising that the number of possessions would continue to increase daily.[40]

The battle must at times have seemed hopeless. But the Franciscans were not easy to dissuade. From the midst of all their difficulties they could point to a number of important triumphs. The way in which they had expelled many devils and constrained others to explain what they were doing was proof that God, through his ministers, was actively engaged in keeping the devils at bay. On one occasion, after one of the devils had declared that Juana's torments would only subside after she made a writ of slavery to Satan, Juana replied that she preferred to suffer her martyrdom patiently. Indeed, it had been precisely her reluctance to 'do anything without the approval of Fr Sarmiento' that had persuaded the devils, in desperation, to appear to her in the shape of Sarmiento himself. Even then they had failed in their attempt to make their victim sign the contract. As a last resort, the mice-sucker had tried to poison Juana with an apple, but Sarmiento had miraculously arrived just in time to 'conjure' her and save her life. He then solemnly proceeded, in the name of God, to force the devils to confess that it had been their impotence against the supernatural resources of the Church that had led the mice-sucker to resort to poison. Moreover, when a few days later the mice-sucker had succeeded in poisoning Juana again, this time with the express help of the devils, another Franciscan, Fray Mateo Bonilla, had again forced one of the devils to confess that Juana had been saved by the miraculous intervention of her patron, the Archangel St Raphael, who had made her vomit the poison. 'And in order that you may believe this', the devil continued, 'I shall bring you the piece of wool where the poison was administered'; whereupon the devil 'descended into the creature's stomach and returned to the mouth with the promised proof'.[41]

Despite the Franciscans' good reasons to be optimistic, a puzzling question still awaited a satisfactory answer: Why had God allowed these things to happen in the first place and why was he allowing them to increase in number? It was of course accepted doctrine that a divine predilection was not incompatible with a divinely permitted possession. But this was by no means the only explanation. Authorized manuals such as the *Malleus Maleficarum* stated that although people could 'sometimes be possessed for their own greater advantage', they were more often possessed 'sometimes for a slight sin of another, sometimes for their own venial sin, sometimes for another's heavy sin, and sometimes for their own heavy sin'.[42] In the context of accepted doctrine, therefore, it could not be seen as an act of impiety

---

40 A.G.N., Inq., 539.26, fols 468v–474r. On Juana de los Reyes see also Solange Alberro's vivid account in *Inquisición y sociedad en México 1571–1700* (Mexico City, 1988), pp. 516–17.
41 A.G.N., Inq., 527.8, fols 508v–509v.
42 *Malleus Maleficarum*, part II, qu. 1, ch. 10. Eng. trans. *The Malleus Maleficarum of Heinrich Kramer and James Sprenger*, trans. and ed. Rev. Montague Summers (New York, 1971). p. 129.

or incredulity to feel somewhat sceptical about what the commissary of the Inquisition in Querétaro, José de Frías, called the 'conjuring tricks' of the Franciscans which 'had gone beyond a mere disturbance or scandal' and had been 'filled with plenty of nonsense'. In this, the municipal magistrate of Querétaro, José Pozuelo, clearly concurred. 'While I accept', he wrote to the inquisitors in a letter of 5 October 1691,

> and venerate the most high permission of Our Lord in such punishments and tests of souls, nevertheless, in the present case (with the exception of the fathers of St Francis) there has as yet been no recognition by any person worthy of respect of any extraordinary sign or effect. It follows, therefore, that it is not the indwelling of the devil that is the cause of the problem, but rather the effects of some spell or frenzy.

On the other hand, he continued, it was well known that one of the women who had claimed to be possessed had confessed during an illness, and sworn it as a Christian, that it had all been a lie. Yet everyone in Querétaro was still 'disturbed and scandalized' by what the Franciscans were preaching from the pulpit. 'Only God knows whether they are possessed or not,' continued the magistrate,

> all I know is that the Church's relics and sacred objects are being abused...[and therefore] I ask that a dispassionate person be sent to examine the matter, so that your lordships may prescribe a convenient remedy and with the sickle of your holy zeal mow the darnel that the enemy seeks to plant amidst the Christian wheat.[43]

The matter was even more worrying because it was likely to be believed by many. As the Carmelite Manuel de Jesús María wrote to the inquisitors on 13 November 1691,

> the city of Querétaro is undergoing a most painful tribulation.... Men are disconsolate, women are afflicted and souls are everywhere riddled with doubt. The holy religious orders are nearing a very grave confrontation which is emerging from the disunity and the differences of opinion over the recent happenings. Already there are signs of disturbances and controversies from which very harmful scandals can ensue.

The arguments with which the Franciscans were 'trying to put fear into the minds of the people', he continued, were 'fundamentally weak and of little consequence'. The number of the possessed had grown so large that it had surpassed all possible credulity. Indeed, never since the creation had God

---

43   Letter of José de Frías to the Inquisition, 5 Oct. 1691, A.G.N., Inq. 527.8, fols 465r–v.

been known to punish sinners 'by handing over his creatures to the devil in the manner of a plague'. Moreover, none of the extraordinary things that the Franciscans claimed that the alleged demoniacs were doing were 'beyond natural powers', and it was widely rumoured that many of these women were either drunk or mad and that they merely pretended to be possessed in order to hide the real reason for their refusals to receive communion, that is, their fear of committing sacrilege by receiving the sacrament in a state of mortal sin.[44]

For their part, the Franciscans were concerned with proving the innocence and genuineness of their devotees. It was thus fortunate for them that at this time two more devils had been discovered inside the body of the young girl Caterina de las Casas, who had apparently been taken through the air to a hill far away from Querétaro where the witches had tried to persuade her to make a written pact with Satan that would enable her to visit Spain and Rome whenever she wished. Since Caterina was barely ten years old, her case could be used as evidence that the demoniacs were innocent and holy people. Sarmiento himself had already taken good care to offer his personal assistance to the girl and, after the customary exorcisms, a devil was forced to declare that, since 'in older women such happenings can easily be explained away as madness or melancholy, and thus they die without remedy', Caterina's possession had been allowed by God specifically 'in order that the contagion may be discovered, remedied and halted'.[45]

The sceptics, however, would not budge. In a subsequent and more carefully argued letter, dated 3 January 1692, Fray Manuel de Jesús María wrote to the inquisitors that the Franciscans were stubbornly implementing practices that they had learnt in Spain under very different circumstances. Thus, 'without any knowledge of the people or of their temperament, goodness and kindness of heart', they had attempted to turn them into saints overnight. The result was that many 'weak souls' had convinced themselves of a compulsory need to attend the Franciscan mission, which they did to the detriment of the wellbeing of their households and against the will and better judgement of their husbands, 'wasting long hours in the confessional' and encouraging an improper familiarity between penitents and confessors. In this misguided state of exhilaration, he explained, it was foreseeable that many of these women should develop 'strange illnesses' which were simply the result of 'inappropriate' or 'unwise' penances given by over-zealous and over-scrupulous confessors. The friars had thus 'engendered very serious scruples and very dangerous inclinations' among their parishioners, even persuading some of them that it was a mortal sin to wear fashionable clothes, 'with no distinction of the ends and aims of each one of them or of their particular states of life'. Moreover, despite their initial enthusiasm it

---

44   A.G.N., Inq., 527.8, fol. 479v–480v.
45   A.G.N., Inq., 527.8, fols 511v–512r.

was well known that many of the Franciscans' newly acquired 'saints' had abandoned their coarse habits only a few days after they had so eagerly accepted them. Others were often seen around the town looking 'light in the head' or with mad expressions on their faces. To anyone with some experience in the spiritual life, explained Fray Manuel, it was obvious that the spirituality of the alleged demoniacs was more of a 'charade' and that all their 'demonic chimeras' were spurious attempts to give their mediocre and often sinful lives the appearance of holiness.[46]

Fray Manuel had good reasons for his confident diagnosis. For he was voicing these remarks the day after a suspicious development in the diabolical possession of Juana de los Reyes had brought a dramatic setback to the claims of the Franciscans, only serving to confirm the scepticism of the other religious orders. During the last days of 1691 Juana's demonic attacks were approaching a dangerous climax. On 1 January 1692 she was on the verge of death. Four hundred devils were said to inhabit her body, although two hundred of them had announced their imminent and simultaneous departure. Presently she felt the most disturbing convulsions: she stopped breathing until her whole body turned black, and in the middle of the crisis she allegedly expelled twenty needles wrapped in a blue paper bag from her 'intimate parts'. Having lost hope, the Franciscans gave her the last rites and prepared her for death. But the next morning things were back to normal. Even the growth in her stomach had disappeared. It was no miracle: she had given birth to a child.[47]

In the intellectual climate of the late seventeenth century it should perhaps come as no surprise that the Franciscans seemed undeterred by this momentous event. Although understandably alarmed, Fray Pablo Sarmiento was quick to find an explanation that would save Juana's saintly reputation. It was, after all, accepted doctrine that

> although at first sight…it is not in accordance with the Catholic faith to maintain that children can be begotten by devils…it may be argued that devils take their part in this generation not as the essential cause, but as a secondary or artificial cause, since they busy themselves by interfering with the process of normal copulation and conception by obtaining human semen and themselves transferring it.[48]

Such a possibility must have been common knowledge to the Franciscans. For even before the news of the birth had reached Sarmiento, his assistant, Fray Mateo Bonilla, had already forced a devil to confess that the preg-

---

46 A.G.N., Inq., 527.8, fols 580r–583r.
47 A.G.N., Inq., 539.26, fols 473r–474r; 527.8, fol. 512v. See also Alberro, *Inquisición y sociedad*, pp. 516–17.
48 *Malleus Maleficarum*, part I, qu. 3, Eng. trans. pp. 21–2.

nancy had been a diabolical trick, since one of the devils had himself administered the semen through the mouth of the victim four months before the birth![49] With such evidence Bonilla felt justified to reply to the sceptics that

> it is as much a matter of faith to believe that the said women…are possessed by the devil as it is to believe in the Most Holy Sacrament of the altar, or…that the Most Holy Sacrament was really present in the host, or that they [the women] were as much possessed by the devil as the Most Holy Sacrament was present in the altar.[50]

For his part, Sarmiento continued to defend the honour and virtue of Juana de los Reyes and her family, arguing that God had allowed the devils to possess her in order to test her virtue.

But such claims now failed to carry much conviction. The weight of the evidence seemed rather to support the views of Fray Manuel de Jesús María, whose carefully argued claims reached the Inquisition at the same time as a complaint by the prior provincial of the Dominicans, Fray Andrés del Rosario. With obvious impatience, Fray Andrés stated that the birth had brought to light the bad faith and malice of 'these women' and that it was a very serious and worrying matter that such 'scandals of wenches' should not only be believed but also positively encouraged by important prelates such as the guardian of the College of Querétaro and his assistants. Everybody had been able to witness how these impertinent friars would use any excuse to put their 'conjurations' into practice. Once they had insisted on 'conjuring' a man who was merely ill with tumours and had only forced him to say a great deal of nonsense, all of which he denied before he died. All the Franciscans had achieved in this case was to convince the poor man's mother that Sarmiento had killed her son with a purge. Moreover, it seemed very odd that the Franciscans constantly changed their minds about the causes of the illnesses: at one time they claimed that the women were possessed, at another that they were 'obsessed' or 'extremely persecuted'. Then they claimed that the devils had announced that they would leave the bodies of the victims at a specific day and time, and when the demoniacs showed no sign of recovery they argued either that the devils had refused to leave, for various reasons, or that they had been replaced by a new set of devils. And as to Juana's pregnancy, even if one accepted the possibility, defended by some theologians, that the devil could cause such things through the operation of incubi, it had merely brought to light what most people suspected: that Juana was a liar and a sacrilegious sinner.[51] For his

49   A.G.N., Inq., 527.8, fols 481r–482r.
50   A.G.N., Inq., 523.3, fol. 340r.
51   A.G.N., Inq., 527.8, fols 522r–526r.

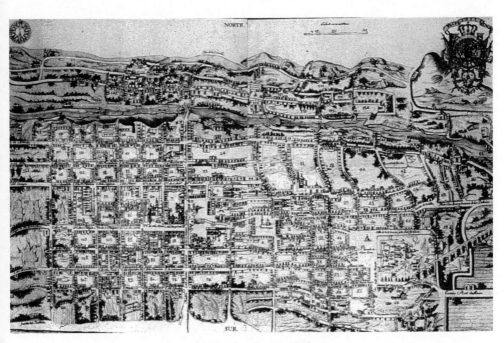

Plate 24. Querétaro, *c.*1750

part, Fray Manuel, whose patience could not be tried much longer, affirmed that the pregnancy and birth had been perfectly natural, and that the new claims of the Franciscans would only result in 'new errors and new non-sense'. It was now known, for instance, that another of the alleged demoniacs was pregnant. Would people be prepared to believe the new Franciscan interpretation of the facts, no doubt revealed to them by some humbled demon during an exorcism, that a devil had taken the foetus out of a woman's womb and introduced it into the womb of the demoniac? In an uncharacteristic mood of indignation, Fray Manuel this time went so far as to suggest that the Franciscans themselves might be implicated in the preg-nancies, for it was well known that during the 'conjuring tricks' the alleged demoniacs were frequently touched on 'the face, the breasts and other less decent parts'.[52]

When the time came for the inquisitors to intervene their action was swift and decisive. After forbidding any further mention of the possessions or any further practice of exorcism in an edict of 18 January 1692, they formally accused Francisca Mejía, Juana de los Reyes and Caterina de las Casas, together with other alleged demoniacs, of pretending to be pos-sessed as a mere pretext to blaspheme and to utter heretical remarks, thus causing great and unnecessary scandals. On the same day Fray Mateo

52 A.G.N., Inq., 527.8, fol. 482r–v.

Bonilla was arrested for his 'rash and heretical propositions', and Sarmiento and his assistants were severely reprimanded for 'sowing discord, sedition and disquiet,...[and] encouraging judgements which are contrary to honesty and good custom'.[53]

In this way, one of the most exhilarating cases of diabolism in New Spain was brought to a cool, calculated and somewhat disappointing end by the direct and sceptical intervention of an institution that was better known for its credulous concern in such cases.

53   A.G.N., Inq., 527.8, fols 528r–530r.

5

Crisis and Decline

THE BIZARRE STORY of the demoniacs of Querétaro is one of the first known cases in the archives of the Mexican Inquisition in which diabolism was so blatantly dismissed. Hitherto, the inquisitors had shown a marked and often obsessive interest in such activities even when, as was often the case, the accused themselves seemed unconvinced of their guilt. As early as 1556, for instance, María de Ocampo, after 'spontaneously' accusing herself of having attempted a pact with the devil in a moment of depression and after seeking the mercy of God and the 'salutary penance' of the Inquisition, was imprisoned, questioned and forced into fantastically vivid and inconsistent descriptions of her various sexual intimacies with Satan.[1] As we saw in chapter 3, comparable rigours were deployed in 1598 against the unfortunate mestizo Juan Luis, when the inquisitors delved meticulously into every detail of the prisoner's declarations, seeking to establish whether his actions were part of a more widespread diabolism where Satan was deemed to be at least as powerful as God and to demand his own prayers, rites and ceremonies.[2] In 1630 Luis de Ribera was no more successful in persuading the inquisitors that he had never 'seen the devil visibly' or 'communicated with him in any way' and that he was unable to give them the description of his physiognomy that they so badly seemed to need.[3] And the same concern still seemed to haunt the inquisitors only three decades before the incidents of Querétaro, when in 1666 they ordered a master of surgery to carry out a detailed search over the body of Manuel de Tovar Olvera in the hope of finding some mark or sign that might serve as proof of a suspected diabolical compact.[4]

It might seem incongruous, then, that within the space of one generation

---

1   Archivo General de la Nación, Mexico City, Ramo Inquisición (hereafter A.G.N., Inq.), tomo 31, exp. 1 (hereafter 31.1), fols 1r–392v.
2   A.G.N., Inq., 147.6, fols 10r–29r.
3   A.G.N., Inq., 366.41, fol. 416v.
4   A.G.N., Inq., 568.1, fol. 90r.

the situation should have been practically reversed. For in the case of Querétaro it was now the victims and the local friars who sought to convince the inquisitors of the reality of diabolism. And Querétaro was not an isolated incident. By the end of the seventeenth century it had become the rule that those who had made a pact with the devil and repented were finding it increasingly difficult to persuade the inquisitors of the truth of their claims and of their need for 'suitable' and 'salutary' penances. The tendency can be observed only five years after the events of Querétaro, when the inquisitors showed a surprising leniency towards Gregoria Rosa de Ubeda, a twenty-seven-year-old spinster 'of virginal repute', who claimed to have made a pact with the devil in order to have 'carnal acts' with him while kissing 'his indecent parts' and sucking babies 'through their intestines and through their feet', and to have adored him on her knees with full intellectual conviction and with full 'affection and veneration' on at least three occasions. It is not hard to imagine the sort of reaction that this kind of evidence would have provoked two or three decades earlier, but at the end of the seventeenth century the Holy Tribunal seemed indifferent to it. After a few conventional and somewhat rushed questions the inquisitors concluded that Gregoria was full of 'mad fantasies' peculiar to the unfortunate members of 'the fragile sex', and that she should be returned to her confessor with the suggestion that she should say the *Pater noster,* the *Ave Maria,* the *Credo* and the *Salve Regina* every morning for a year.[5]

An even more blatant indifference became apparent two decades later in the case of María Francisca Mendivil and Petra Rita who, according to a letter written to the inquisitors by their confessor in 1729, had

> never properly received the sacrament of penance because, ever since they had the use of reason, they had offered themselves to the devil, making many written pacts with him and signing them with their own blood so that they could be his slaves and cohabit with him, especially with Asmodeus, from whom they had procured the ability to have instant copulations with however many men they desired.... They persecuted God with formal hate, squashing, beating, burning and whipping his most holy body in the Eucharist and hiding it in the foulest of places.... They had prevented innumerable babies from being baptized with the specific purpose of destroying the Holy Catholic Church....

Of all these things they had repented and were seeking for help to fetch the hosts and take them out of the foul places where they had put them, and to baptize all the babies that they had offered to the devil. But the inquisitors did not even bother to pursue the case, and all the letters and testimonies

5   A.G.N., Inq., 449.10, fols 79r–81r.

were simply filed with annotations on the margin wherever they pointed to any inconsistency or contradiction.[6]

In some respects, the marked change in the inquisitors' approach might seem straightforward. After all, it was precisely during these years that the witch-hunts had begun to subside in Europe and it might be argued that the developments that can be observed in Mexico were a mere reflection of contemporary European events. Once this is accepted, any explanation of the inquisitors' change of attitude will tend to follow a predictable pattern. The case of Querétaro, it might well be argued, was a normal incident of witchcraft accusations resulting from local rivalries and envies which, if left to itself, would most probably have gone very largely unnoticed. It thus seemed extraordinary only to the educated, who could distinguish between two conflicting views: on the one hand there was the 'traditional' position of the Franciscans who managed to raise the case from its otherwise pedestrian level to the higher ranks of learned early modern demonology; on the other, there was the more 'modern' and 'sceptical' position of the inquisitors who quietly realized that new scientific paradigms had rendered the idea of demonic intervention in nature inherently absurd. Where the prosecutions had reflected the turgid scholastic Aristotelianism of the educated, their decline could be seen as the direct consequence of the impact of the materialism of Hobbes, Descartes and Locke and its rejection of the concept of incorporeal substances, and, more importantly, of Newton's application of the law of gravity to the movement of the heavenly bodies, which justified Galileo's belief in the power of mathematics to solve the mysteries of the universe by proving that the same physical laws were universally applicable. After Newton, the Aristotelian notion that heavenly bodies were moved by conscious spiritual forces that derived their motion from God, conceived here as the Prime Mover, was replaced by a mechanical conception of the world consisting of material bodies situated in absolute space and moved by physical laws. Not only were spiritual forces thus excluded from human experience by the new materialist philosophy, but their traditional control of nature was equally denied by the new science. God was no longer a providential being, nor even the immanent principle of nature, as the neo-Platonists would have it; rather, he was a sublime mechanic, who had constructed the cosmic clock and left it to follow its own laws.[7] If even God would not interfere in nature, what could the devil do?

However logical, an explanation along these lines is difficult to substantiate with the evidence available for New Spain. Even if we assumed that among Mexican scientific circles the 'New Philosophy' followed a similar

6   A.G.N., Inq., 920.18, fols 148r–182v.
7   For an explanation of the decline of witchcraft along these lines see Keith Thomas, *Religion and the Decline of Magic* (Harmondsworth, 1978 edn), pp. 681–3. The best account of the process is still A. N. Whitehead, *Science and the Modern World* (Cambridge, 1953 edn).

trajectory to the one observed in Europe,[8] there is no convincing evidence to suggest that inquisitorial scepticism was the result of the influence of mechanical philosophy. That some influence might have filtered down to the inquisitors from scientific circles would be hard to deny, given the large number of 'qualifications' and 'expurgations' by inquisitors of allegedly dubious philosophical and scientific works. But inquisitorial statements against traditional Aristotelian explanations are not only unknown, they were positively discouraged. Indeed, any attempt to divorce science from religious and philosophical speculations about the nature of matter and the universe would cause great unease, since it was more or less generally accepted that approved scientific theory should precede scientific practice and that scientific knowledge could not derive from the particular but should be directed by God-given laws.[9]

Conversely, there is substantial evidence against the suggestion that the Franciscan position was traditional. As I shall try to demonstrate, a careful analysis of that position at once reveals elements which were not only new, but actually contrary to the traditional Christian view of the devil. Take, for example, the way in which Fray Pablo Sarmiento, soon after the birth of Juana de los Reyes's child, eagerly welcomed the 'discovery' that two more devils were inside the body of the young girl Caterina de las Casas. As we have seen, the incident was especially significant because one of the devils had declared that their presence inside a young and innocent girl was a 'great favour' of God that would persuade the growing number of sceptics to accept the Franciscan claims. And indeed, Caterina's devil was only repeating the same statements that the devils of Juana de los Reyes had been allegedly asserting for some time. One of them had even stated that the reason for the possessions was that 'the way in which so many people are being converted to God' could no longer be tolerated. Indeed, he continued,

these fathers [the Franciscans] have launched so many wars upon us with their sermons and snatched so many souls from our hands that, unable to endure it any longer, we have revealed ourselves...by order and permission of God. This represents a great kindness on his part, because otherwise we would never have been able to reveal ourselves and these poor creatures would have suffered unto death....These events will therefore result in great profits for many and in many torments for myself and my companions.[10]

8   This claim is made by Elías Trabulse, *Historia de la ciencia en México*, 4 vols (Mexico City, 1983–5), i, pp. 21–7.
9   For the partial reception of the 'New Philosophy' in Spain see Anthony Pagden, 'The Reception of the "New Philosophy" in Eighteenth-Century Spain', *Journal of the Warburg and Courtauld Institutes*, LI (1988), pp. 126–40; and, more recently, I. L. McClelland, *Ideological Hesitancy in Spain 1700–1750* (Liverpool, 1991), especially pp. 18–25.
10   A.G.N., Inq., 527.8, fol. 508r.

And in similar vein, after one of the mice-sucker's attempts to poison Juana, Sarmiento reported that the devil had said to him:

> Know, O priest of God, that these bad Christians [the witches], seeing that you have annulled the virtue of their malefice so completely with your powerful conjurations, so that even we are powerless to assist them (since through the Church's conjurations we are constantly being expelled from the body of the creature by God's virtue),...they have opted to try to kill this creature with poison.[11]

There is of course much that is commonplace in these statements, but their style and inspiration can hardly be classed as traditional. For, while it is true that demonic possessions could be seen as having been permitted by God for some ultimate greater good, the actual demonic actions involved in them were traditionally seen as intrinsically evil and in no way willed by God. Sarmiento's devils, by contrast, seemed to have been relegated to their primeval, Old Testament role of messengers. Far from being God's opponents, they had become docile pawns in a kind of cosmic battle where God would inevitably win.

On the other hand, Satan was still paradoxically seen as a terrifically evil force capable of destroying God's works but for the brave resistance of Christ's Church and her army of exorcists. The Franciscans were therefore caught in the difficult predicament of having to deal with a devil who was simultaneously a docile messenger of God and the cause of great suffering and pain. His power had grown so immense that it threatened the very concept of God's omnipotence. The way they saw out of this difficulty was to stress the inviolability of divine omnipotence by making the devil completely subservient to God. This was sound theology when the devil was perceived to be under God's control, but when he was allowed so much freedom and actually encouraged to act by God himself, the devil's subservience amounted to turning God into a capricious tyrant. This was hardly traditional theology.

It might of course be objected that the Franciscans were voicing these opinions on the day that Juana de los Reyes gave birth and that their urge to defend her innocence led them into rash assertions which they would not have made otherwise. But there is conclusive evidence that similar opinions were being voiced well before the birth. On 11 December 1691, for instance, a letter was sent to the Inquisition by the Franciscan José Díez, an 'unaffected..., sincere and practical man' who would eventually be elected guardian of the College of Santa Cruz in 1703.[12] In a short letter he

---

11 A.G.N., Inq., 527.8, fol. 509r.
12 Lino Gómez Canedo, Introduction to Espinosa's *Crónica Apostólica y Seráfica de todos los colegios de Propaganda Fide de esta Nueva España*, ed. L. Gómez Canedo (Washington, D. C., 1964), p. xxxi.

expressed doubts about the possessions, but thought it safer to give the devils the benefit of the doubt, especially after witnessing some extraordinary signs. While hearing the confession of Francisca de la Serna (another keen Franciscan devotee), he had heard her bones 'creaking so loudly' and 'causing her so much agony and distress' that he decided to exorcize her. Noticing a marked improvement and eager to disperse his doubts, he made the following experiment:

> I painted the image of Lucifer following the dispositions of the manuals and threw it in a filthy place. Then, on a subsequent evening, during the exorcisms, I asked him: '...O you miserable one! Where did I put you last night?' He replied angrily, naming the place, which I do not here repeat because of the respect that I owe to the Holy Tribunal.[13]

Although Díez ended his letter with a plea to the Inquisition to 'solve his predicament', he then included a text which he claimed to be a literal transcription of the 'locutions of a devil in the mouth of a creature'. It is by far the strongest case that a devil ever made to confirm the Franciscan interpretation of the events.[14]

> I Lucifer, Prince of Hell, swear to Almighty God and to this Holy Cross that I hold in the left hand of this creature and to this other that I make with the right hand and to that Most Holy Cross in that reliquary, that it is the will of the Most High, my Creator and the Creator of the whole world, that I say what I am about to say for his greater glory. And if I should not tell the truth, I ask God to send me all the sorrows of all the damned and all those that the divine power can send me, and that the wrath of the Irate God descends upon me and punishes me like a perjurer.

After stating that a thousand devils had entered Francisca's body, he made a point of stressing that this should not be seen as a punishment; for it had been only after Francisca had asked God to do with her as he willed that God had decided to send the devils into her body in order to 'exercise her'.

In an unprecedented way, therefore, the role of the witches in the possessions had been made redundant. It was no longer the 'mice-sucker' and her cronies who had originally willed the possessions and God who had allowed them for an ultimate greater good, but God who had willed them in the first place, only using the witches as mere agents in the enactment of his will. In this way, the devil's actions had become the direct effect of God's express will, and the devils themselves had become essential instru-

13   A.G.N., Inq., 527.8, fols 488r–488v.
14   See A.G.N., Inq., 527.8, fols 490r–493r, for what follows.

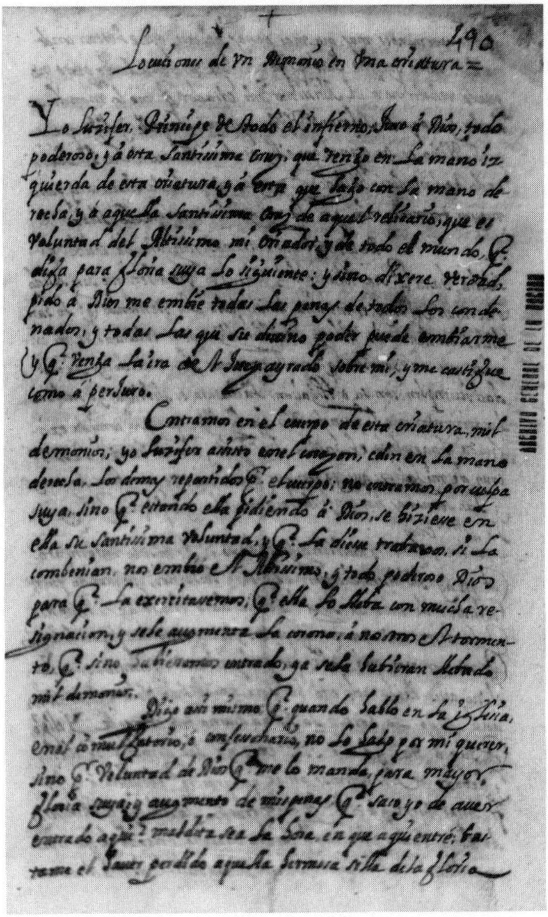
490

Locuciones de vn demonio en vna criatura =

Yo Luzifer, Príncipe de todo el infierno, Juro a Dios, todo poderoso, y a esta Santíssima Cruz, que tengo en la mano izquierda de esta criatura, y a esta que tengo con la mano derecha, y a aquella Santíssima Cruz de aquel relicario, que es Voluntad del Altíssimo mi Criador y de todo el mundo q. diga para gloria suya lo siguiente: y sino dixere verdad, pido a Dios me embíe todas las penas de todos los condenados, y todas las que su diuino poder puede embiarme y q. venga la ira de el Juez ayrado sobre mí, y me castigue como a perjuro.

Plate 25. First page of Fray José Díez's transcription of the 'locutions of a devil in the mouth of a creature'.

ments in Francisca's salvation. As they revealed in an illuminatingly paradoxical phrase, 'if we had not entered [her body] a thousand devils would by now have carried her away'.

Moreover, the devils' statements were not to be heard as their own opinions but as God's word: 'When I speak in the church or in the communion rail or in the confessional box', Lucifer declared, 'I do not do it because I want to, but because it is the will of God that forces me to speak for his greater glory and for the aggravation of my torments'. Obeying God's will, he thus urged Díez to contradict the rumours that sought to dishonour Francisca de la Serna and Juana de los Reyes, even offering to endorse any testimonies: 'I do not mind if they call me the preacher devil,' he exclaimed, 'take me to the Holy Tribunal!' As God's faithful, if unwilling emissary, Lucifer then poured scorn on the 'vile' devils that made pacts with witches and contradicted God, refusing to accept that 'there is only one God'. For

Lucifer was no 'vile' devil: he did God's will. 'Hold no doubts that I am Lucifer,' he continued,

> God has put me here for the torment of these devils and for the justification of his cause. For God is very irritated with the world. You have made him very angry. How long is it since Lucifer came out of hell? God has now sent me so that you may realize that he is just. The more you refuse to give credit to these words, the greater your condemnation will be.

Lucifer was here no longer a proud spirit consumed by hate but a suffering and tormented victim of divine justice. Accordingly, he humbled himself in front of the Blessed Sacrament during the singing of the *Tantum ergo*, exclaiming: 'Oh miserable me! Oh wretched me! Oh downcast! I am compelled to stay inside this body for my greater torment. O Sovereign Lord...take me out of here and send another devil to carry out this task....' And in order to dispel any doubts about the truth of his declarations, he concluded: 'I am Lucifer, prince of all the devils and cause of all the damned, and in corroboration of everything I have said, I kiss these crosses.' 'Oh that the whole world had been present there.' wrote Díez,

> or at least the sacramental heretics, so that they would know the virtue of this divine sacrament, the reverence with which the devil spoke and took part in the ceremony, and the power with which the Sovereign Lord subjected him!

There was something inherently pitiful in this image of Lucifer which was quite foreign to the concept of the devil that had been developing since the late middle ages. Indeed, it had more in common with the devil of the medieval mystics, and yet there was nothing in it of the confident humour that characterized medieval spirituality. Where the devil of Julian of Norwich or even of Thomas More could be mocked and ridiculed, the devil of the Franciscans had to be carefully listened to and even obeyed. Such different approaches stemmed clearly from two quite different conceptions of the devil and the diabolic. While the medieval devil was a subordinate creature who was powerless without God, he was at the same time a free and independent agent who had made evil his own unforced choice; it was in this gratuitous and unrealistic choice that the intrinsic comicality of his position lay. By contrast, the devil of the Franciscans had lost his freedom and independence, and with them he had also implicitly lost all responsibility for his evil actions. He was merely a faithful messenger of a God who, in that context, seemed to have turned into an omnipotent and capricious tyrant. An evil God, in effect, even if faith required one to believe that his ultimate purpose was good.

*

The extreme development in the Franciscans' approach to diabolism might seem farfetched when we consider that it is still possible to offer an explanation of their attitude in terms of a local and primarily circumstantial political preoccupation. At this time, the Franciscans of *Propaganda Fide* were not only seeking to establish themselves as the spiritual leaders of the region, but they were also anxious to regain the preponderance that the Franciscan order had enjoyed there since their arrival in 1531, which had been progressively eclipsed by the growing importance of Jesuits, Dominicans and Augustinians.[15] As Solange Alberro has argued, it is in this essentially political climate that the best sense can be made of their obsessive insistence on the importance of the possessions.[16]

If, however, the political scene provides useful guidelines for understanding the position of the Franciscans, the actual theology that substantiated their peculiar demonology cannot be seen as a mere product of circumstance. Indeed, it is very unlikely that it could have been voiced so openly and emphatically, especially to the Inquisition, had it not been the expression of a more generally accepted 'orthodoxy'. The question, therefore, is not so much how the Franciscans developed their peculiar demonology to fit their particular circumstances, but rather, how they came to regard it as an orthodox opinion that could be openly and emphatically propagated.

The question is especially puzzling when seen in the context of the traditional view of the devil as both a creature of God and the cause of evil. For in that light the Franciscan position was clearly steeped in heresy and it would thus seem odd that the inquisitors did not take positive action to condemn it. When, however, the question is seen more specifically in the context of late seventeenth-century thought, it is possible to make more sense of both the boldness of the Franciscans in asserting their position and the diffidence of the inquisitors in condemning it. Much more than a heresy or an innovation, the demonology of the Franciscans was a clear reflection of the exaggerated Augustinianism that, as we have seen, had come to dominate Christian spirituality on both sides of the confessional front since the Reformation. The division of the natural and the supernatural, with its consequent distrust of human reason and values, tended to turn the divine attributes of goodness and justice into mere empty names. If divine justice was deemed incomprehensible to human intelligence and totally distinct from human justice, God's exercise of power could only appear as arbitrary, and his justice, like the justice of Thrasymachus in Plato's *Republic*, as the mere advantage of the stronger. Although this tendency to what R. A. Knox

15 Lino Gómez Canedo, *Sierra Gorda: Un típico enclave misional en el centro de México* (Pachuca, 1976), pp. 29–40.
16 Solange Alberro, *Inquisición y sociedad en México 1571–1700* (Mexico City, 1988), pp. 508–9.

once called 'ultrasupernaturalism'[17] is more often associated with the Protestant world, one only needs to remember the Jansenists and the Quietists to realize that the tendency was very much present among Catholics.[18] At the end of the seventeenth century the tendency was so widespread that Pierre Bayle could class it as characteristic of Christianity *tout court*. In his *Dictionnaire* (1695–7) Bayle stated that the division of the natural and the supernatural had, at best, reduced religiously based morality to a servile observance of capricious norms instituted by divine decree and changeable at any moment, while, at worst, it led men into positive wickedness by the imitation of God's arbitrary exercise of power. In this way, Bayle sharply highlighted the logic behind the ironical accusations of devil-worship that were often levelled against Calvinists and Jansenists. His critique was so subversive that the philosophical response it evoked in Leibniz's *Theodicy* was forced to forgo a positive argument in the style of Malebranche and to limit itself to the basic assertion that *if* God could not be justified by men, he could not be conclusively condemned either. Significantly, however, in his rejection of the claim that God was the direct cause of moral evil, Lebniz found no option but to reject the extreme Augustinian division of divine and human values which the nominalist undercurrent in early modern philosophy had brought about. In this he was not only the heir of the Cambridge Platonists, who had aimed to establish a priority of moral ideas over the divine will in order to defend the concept of divine justice and goodness; more significantly, he was also in fundamental agreement with the Thomist concordance between nature and grace.[19]

In the case of Querétaro, it is interesting to notice that Bayle's argument against Christian morality could have been applied perfectly well to the

17   R. A. Knox, *Enthusiasm: A Chapter in the History of Religion with Special Reference to the XVII and XVIII Centuries* (Oxford, 1950), p. 2
18   Ibid., pp. 176–421. 'Molinos's *Spiritual Guide*', writes Knox, 'was published in the same year (1675) as the *Pia Desideria* of Spenser, and the disturbances of St Médard began in 1728, the year before Wesley founded his Holy Club. Neither Catholics nor Protestants were to have a monopoly of embarrassment.' Ibid., p. 6.
19   I draw mainly on D. P. Walker, *The Decline of Hell: Seventeenth-Century Discussions of Eternal Torment* (London, 1964), pp. 53–7, 202–13. A summary of the more general preoccupation will be found in John McManners, *Death and the Enlightenment: Changing Attitudes to Death in Eighteenth-Century France* (Oxford, 1985), pp. 176–90. Leibniz's difficulties with contemporary Christian authorities on both sides of the confessional front over the question of nature and grace have recently been seen as one of the main obstacles that prevented him from becoming a Catholic. 'There are some philosophic opinions', he wrote to Ernst von Hessen Rheinfels, 'which...although they are not opposed to anything I know in holy scripture, tradition, or the definition of any council, may be disapproved and even censured sometimes by the school theologians, who imagine them contrary to the faith.' As R.C. Sleigh has shown, the philosophical opinions in question are those put forward in the *Discourse on Metaphysics* where they are applied to 'the questions of grace, the concourse of God and creatures, the cause of sin and the origin of evil'. See R.C. Sleigh, *Leibniz and Arnauld: A Commentary on their Correspondence* (New Haven and London, 1990), p. 21.

Franciscan position. After all, could not their insistence on the need to believe the devils and on God's direct responsibility for the possessions be seen as a form of devil-worship? It is of course true that the Franciscans, and even their opponents, would have been horrified at such a suggestion. The ease with which they seemed to accept God's arbitrary power derived rather from a characteristic asceticism which sought to replicate the passion and sufferings of Christ through intense personal mortification. Indeed, the paradoxical appearance of a Manichean evil God at the side of the God of Augustine was not something that the Franciscans would have been particularly disturbed by. Their central concern was not whether God's will was just or unjust, but rather whether it would allow them to undergo sufficient suffering for their sanctification and the salvation of those around them.

Yet, even those who did not share the extreme asceticism of the Franciscans still failed to provide a satisfactory counterargument. It was clear from the complaints of the Carmelite Manuel de Jesús María and the Dominican Andrés del Rosario – and it was common knowledge that their views were shared by the Jesuits and the Augustinians – that the claims of the Franciscans were unacceptable. But their complaints remained at the level of practical observations and the suggestion of heresy (let alone devil-worship) was never made.

This apparent incongruity was in fact a clear reflection of the contemporary intellectual predicament that we have analysed. It could be said that, like Bayle, the opponents of the Franciscans were aware of a basic contradiction in the idea of a powerful and independent devil who was at the same time compatible with God's omnipotence; but unlike Bayle, they feared that emphasis on such a contradiction would only serve to undermine the cause of orthodoxy. Similarly, like Leibniz, they saw the need to provide a defence of God's omnipotence in the context of the problem of evil; but unlike Leibniz, they could not reject the separation of the natural and the supernatural. In other words, the 'failure' of the opponents of the Franciscans to provide an adequate theological explanation for their doubts was not so much due to the strictly practical nature of their observations, but rather to the way in which their arguments were based on essentially the same premise that gave the Franciscan position its peculiar strength: namely, the nominalist-inspired separation of the natural and the supernatural.

The same logic could be applied to the attitude of the Inquisition. On the one hand, the inquisitors were becoming aware that, since most accusations concerning demonic activity were easy to make and difficult to disprove, they were often likely to be motivated by malice or imposture. If such accusations were encouraged, therefore, they would have the counterproductive effect of collapsing under their own weight and of promoting an idea of the demonic that seemed to put into question the very omnipotence of God. On the other hand, the alternative position that the Franciscans were advocating only offered the still more unpleasant prospect of a seem-

ingly unjust God who used the devil in the way that a tyrant might employ
a cruel chief of police. Both positions were unacceptable, and yet there
seemed to be no satisfactory solution to either of them.

In this context it is more helpful to see the change of attitude among
inquisitors as a response to this predicament rather than as a reflection of
current intellectual trends. For although their new approach tended to play
down the role of the devil, it was nowhere accompanied by a new conception of the demonic itself. Diabolism was played down or ignored not
because it was too credulous but, on the contrary, because it might lead to
incredulity. The clearest proof cited by the inquisitors against Juana de los
Reyes's devil was that she had stupidly portrayed him as weak, or ignorant
or illogical. Her 'iniquitous fictions and hypocrisies' and her 'depraved exercises' could be deduced from the way in which she had persuaded the
candid Franciscans that it was the devil inside her who had declared that
she was possessed 'through maleficium or fascination', 'as if the devil was so
ignorant', the inquisitors added, 'that he did not know only too well the
difference that exists between the two'. Further evidence of her 'fictions and
fabrications' was provided by her claim that the Archangel Raphael in person had scared the devil out of her body, but that the same devil had
returned to possess her half an hour later; for the devil had never been
known to go in and out of human bodies with such ease. Even less had he
been known to swear by God and the holy cross with such religious fervour, or to feel sorry for his sins, or to ask God to lessen his torments in
hell, as he had allegedly done, following the instructions of one of the
exorcists who, in turn, had offered to pray for him![20]

Clearly, as far as the inquisitors were concerned, the danger of the demoniacs' remarks did not lie in the power that they gave to Satan over their
bodies, but in the way in which they threatened to turn the traditional concept of the devil into an incredible and ridiculous idea, and it is in this
defensive spirit, rather than in a climate of precocious intellectual scepticism, that the best sense can be made of the new inquisitorial contempt for
popular diabolism.

In the case of the demoniacs of Querétaro, the inquisitors found it easier
and more expedient to shift the problem from the intellectual on to the more
manageable popular level. Rather than attack the Franciscans, they chose to
blame the 'fantasies' and 'hypocrisies' of ignorant and sanctimonious women for whatever they found to be contrary to the traditional concept of
the devil. Their decision to concentrate on popular ignorance and to avoid
the more intellectual aspects of the problem was suitably prudent; for an
attack against the Franciscan position might have provoked a response; and the
inquisitors knew that, behind their apparent inconsistencies, the Franciscans
were making a point that was as valid as it was disturbing, and best left alone.

*

20   A.G.N., Inq., 538.4, fols 581r–v, 585v, 590v–594v.

The case of Querétaro can be seen as a catalyst in the inquisitorial change of attitude towards cases of diabolism that became the rule from the last years of the seventeenth century onwards. Until then, a willingness to investigate and to deploy a certain meticulousness could still be detected. Even in the case of Juana de los Reyes, the inquisitors were interested in establishing whether the baby had done anything unusual at birth, or spoken during the baptism, or whether he had any marks or signs that might point to a demonic origin.[21] But their mood had clearly changed. Whereas a generation before they would have been at pains to find evidence to confirm that demonic activities were real, by the 1690s they had come to realize that, if the concept of the devil was to retain its credibility, the best they could hope for was that no such evidence would be found.

As we have seen, this new attitude was reinforced in the ensuing decades, becoming constant and recurring even in cases where the traditional concept of the devil was hardly threatened. When, in 1704, the mulatto Baltazar de Monroy claimed to have talked with the devil and to be a witch, the commissary of the Inquisition, Pedro López de Ramales, stated with confidence that 'such vices and superstitions are very widespread among the vulgar folk'.[22] And a few years later the Indian Tomás de Aquino was sentenced by the Inquisition to twenty-five lashes for daring to mislead a Franciscan who thought he might be possessed by the devil.[23] By the 1720s the change of attitude was fairly well established. When, in 1723, the chaplain of Santa Bárbara in San José del Parral wrote to the inquisitors about some rumours concerning Antonio Rodríguez, allegedly a Jew who was believed to have the devil 'locked in his pantry', he received a letter asking him to refrain from disturbing the Holy Tribunal with 'matters of no substance'.[24] The same 'lack of substance' was found in 1727 in the case of the mestiza Maritata, who was believed to have made a pact with the devil to 'regain an illicit friendship'.[25] That same year the Mercedarian friar Miguel de Aroche had to wait several months for a reply to a letter he had written to the Inquisition concerning a man who had 'indulged in all manner of superstitions involving demonic pact' since the age of nine. The reply of the inquisitors stated that

> to believe such things is not something that one should do with undue promptness. Instead, it is advisable to tread with great caution and languid steps; for people of such breeding are naturally inclined to lie, sometimes doing it willingly in order to deceive, and more often simply misled by their wild imagination.[26]

21   A.G.N., Inq., 538.4, fol. 516r.
22   A.G.N., Inq., 727.18, fol. 503r.
23   A.G.N., Inq., 760.22, fols 241r–261v; 760.23, fols 265r–269v.
24   A.G.N., Inq., 803.54, fols 510r, 511v, 519r.
25   A.G.N., Inq., 817.30, fols 520r–525r.
26   A.G.N., Inq., 788.25, fols 536r–543v, 549r.

By the 1730s the inquisitors seemed to have abandoned even the courtesy of replying. An extant letter from a certain Cristóbal de Cañas in 1735 reveals that they had not acknowledged his previous reports about some people involved in demonic pacts. Despite Cañas's insistence that the practice was very widespread and popular and that it seemed urgent to do something about it, his letter was quickly read and carefully filed, and he was again kept waiting indefinitely for a reply.[27] Even those scattered cases thought worthy of attention by the local commissaries of the Inquisition themselves, were treated with surprising indifference. In 1739, for instance, Felipa de Alcaraz confessed 'spontaneously and in danger of death', and repeatedly 'swearing and ratifying' that her declaration was true, that she had for many years been involved in diabolical practices involving sacrilege, blasphemy, sodomy and 'Satanic and Judaic' excursions in and around Oaxaca. Although he was conscious of the inquisitorial reticence to deal with such cases, the commissary of Oaxaca, Jerónimo Morales, wrote to his superiors in Mexico City stating that the urgency and circumstances of the case lent it 'special attributes to accord it credibility'. Yet the inquisitors merely instructed Morales to find another confessor for Felipa, taking special care

> to choose a learned and prudent man, who is not inclined to be too candid or too credulous, and also one who is not bogged down by his daily duties.... For these things are full of deceit and in this particular business one is likely to find plenty of fraud, treachery, imposture and dishonesty.

It is true that Morales's plea did not go completely unheeded. But the interest of the inquisitors in the case was limited to raising objections and to pointing to any lack of verisimilitude in Felipa's declarations. Her assertion that she had offered herself to the devil as one of his concubines in hell after she died was absurd, for the nature of demonic temptation was limited to worldly attractions and a pledge to comply with a promised role beyond the grave went against the possibility of repentance, something which the devil could not possibly enforce. Felipa's confessions were thus more likely to be the product of those 'fantasies and hallucinations' that were so characteristic of the rabble.[28]

The most illustrative case of the growing inquisitorial contempt for cases of diabolism was reported in 1748 by the judge and vicar-general of the archbishopric of Mexico, Dr Francisco Javier Gómez de Cervantes. It concerned the mestiza Josefa de Saldaña who had allegedly been bewitched by her ex-lover, Juan de Cadena, with the result that Josefa was now possessed

27   A.G.N., Inq., 858 (unnumbered), fol. 499r.
28   A.G.N., Inq., 876.41, fols 226r–228v, 235r–242r, 247v–248r, 257r–276r.

by the devil. In support of this allegation, Gómez de Cervantes provided several testimonies of witnesses who had heard Cadena say that he would make a pact with the devil if Josefa brought an end to their affair. Some time afterwards Josefa had become ill. After the failed attempts of many doctors to cure her, she had asked the chaplain of the hospital to exorcize her, a decision that not only made her feel better, but also caused her to expel many 'foul things' such as mice, snakes, frogs, scorpions, worms and even the occasional bird. Probably aware of the reticence that had come to dominate the Inquisition in such cases, Gómez de Cervantes took care to include a detailed report by Apolinario Antonio de Gálvez, master of surgery, where he gave an account of his many failed attempts to cure Josefa while praising the wisdom of her decision to 'resort to the best healer of malicious deeds, the Holy Church; for it now seems clear that her ailments result from malefice and have not been caused by natural humours'. In addition, Gómez de Cervantes included a letter of Nicolás Fernando de Tapia, Josefa's protector, where he states that at first he had attributed her symptoms to the common causes of 'passion and hysteria', or to the kind of 'anger, hate, rancour and vengefulness' that could lead to 'delirium, dementia, apoplexy, hypochondria or obsession'. But after he had spoken with Josefa she had

> uttered a number of blasphemies that the will, wit and lip are as scared to pronounce as the pen is tremulous to write down. The least of them is that when the news of the exorcisms...had reached the prisoner [Cadena had now been sent to the Inquisition gaol by Gómez de Cervantes] he had said that she would never get better like that...that in this particular malefice the devil was more powerful than God, that God would not be God otherwise, and that as long as the wills of agent and patient were not united she would not achieve anything.

It was then that Tapia had decided to study 'some manuals of exorcism' and to persuade the exorcist to address the spirit in Latin. The devil had then 'gone up to Josefa's tongue' and confessed, in Spanish, that the victim had been bewitched by Juan de Cadena after signing a demonic pact with his own blood. Asked why he did not speak Latin the devil had explained that, although he spoke Latin well, he would not be allowed to speak it until he was put face to face with Cadena, having previously sworn, 'in the name of Our Saviour's cross', that what had happened had been 'commanded by the Most High for his greater honour and glory'.[29]

The parallels with the case of Querétaro are immediately striking, and it is hardly surprising that the first step taken by the inquisitors was to prohibit any further exorcisms 'under pain of major excommunication'; for 'the

29   A.G.N., Inq., 827.24, fols 354r–376r.

necessary grounds' to justify such 'grave matter' were absent, whereas the 'too ready inclination and prompt credulity that these priests have shown towards such implausible cases' was easily attestable.[30] What gives an added interest to this case is that this time the inquisitorial prohibition provoked a confident response against the Inquisition's reluctance to intervene. In a long and carefully argued letter, Nicolás Fernando de Tapia and Bachiller Juan de Cordero stated that, while they had at no time affirmed that Josefa was possessed by the devil, all the facts pointed to such a possibility. Consequently, the 'qualification of the Holy Tribunal' was no light matter:

> Since it is clear that the whole affair can, then and now, be reduced to the factual evidence…(which only those…who have been contaminated by common errors have chosen to ignore), it is our firm belief that, by a lofty and incomprehensible judgement of God, this case and its circumstances have been allowed with such purpose that, when confronted with Your Illustrious Lordship's qualification of the factual evidence (which is demanded by virtue of your state), the common errors and incredulity that have been recently introduced may be dispersed…[thus] helping to ameliorate the disdain that in these cases the vulgar and ignorant are apt to express towards the ecclesiastical remedies…causing no small damage to the faith…and exposing the vulgar and ignorant to innumerable errors.

Tapia and Cordero's main target was the 'vulgar and ignorant incredulity' of those who sought to explain everything as the result of a natural cause. It was true that strange ailments that caused the body to expel 'foul things like snakes and frogs' could, according to authorized writers like Fathers Torresillas and Nieremberg, sometimes be explained by natural causes like the 'corruption of humours'. But it was totally unjustifiable to prohibit the practice of exorcism on this account. The 'authorized teachings of the Roman Ritual, Remigius, Luis de la Concepción, the *Flagellum Daemonum* and the *Malleus Maleficarum*' specifically stated that the devil was perfectly capable of causing such phenomena by 'either forming them out of aerial bodies' or by 'impressing such phantoms on, or proposing them to, the imagination by directly exciting the humours'. Equally dangerous was the 'vulgar error' of those who tried to turn the apparent inability of the devil to speak Latin into the 'Achilles tendon of their incredulity'; for, as Remigius clearly stated, the devil rarely spoke in Latin through rustic or ignorant people, refusing to do so 'either so as better to dissemble his influence and duplicity, or because the rustic tongues are not well suited for it'. Indeed, in a well-known sermon St Vincent Ferrer had recounted how a devil inside the body of a peasant had said with great difficulty: 'Non pos-

30   A.G.N., Inq., 827.24, fol. 376v.

sum domare linguam huius rustici.' It was thus a 'dangerous…vulgar and common' practice to explain everything in the light of a naturalist reductionism which, although adequate in some cases of 'epilepsy, apoplexy, *uteri profocatione* [*sic*], and others', went, for the most part, clearly against the established authorities and the teachings of the Church.[31]

The very directness of their remarks points to Cordero and Tapia's confidence that the Inquisition would be hard pressed to refute their arguments. In their capacity as university graduates in canon law, and in the context of the support they had received from Gómez de Cervantes himself, they had good reason for holding such confidence. Their criticism of the inquisitorial reticence in cases of diabolism was in fact based on precisely the same intellectual tradition that the inquisitors were at pains to protect from ridicule. Indeed, had there been any major disagreement between them, it would be logical to expect the inquisitors to have replied to the objections. But instead, following the example of their predecessors in the case of Querétaro, they simply ignored the complaint and left Juan de Cadena in freedom without further ado.[32]

*

The defensiveness of the Inquisition was not simply a negative strategy. It rested on a much more widely held and deeply rooted way of understanding reality, one that underlay and made possible a serious belief in magic. As Charles Taylor has explained, the pre-mechanical cosmic order was believed to be a 'meaningful order' or one involving an 'ontic logos', where physical objects took their particular forms in order to exhibit an order of ideas or archetypes. The order of nature exemplified Reason and Goodness, in their Platonic sense, which in their Christian theological variant were equivalent to the wisdom of God. 'In other words,' Taylor continues, 'what we would consider today as the perfections of *description* or *representation*, of an order of perspicuous presentation, were considered perfections of *being*.' The world order thus conformed to a pattern of 'rational self-manifestation' where, according to Lovejoy's 'principle of plenitude', 'all possible niches are occupied'.[33]

This Platonic-influenced conception of the universe had proved extremely useful to the Tridentine efforts to restore Catholic liturgy and ritual in the context of a response to Protestantism. The stress laid by the Counter-Reformation on peculiarly anti-Protestant practices such as the cult of the saints, the veneration of relics and images and the belief in the efficacy of sacraments and sacramentals implied a firm belief in the notion that

---

31   A.G.N., Inq., 827.24, fols 384v–393v. Unfortunately, the letter is incomplete.
32   A.G.N., Inq., 827.24, fols 395r–397r.
33   *Sources of the Self: The Making of the Modern Identity* (Cambridge, 1992 edn), pp. 160–1.

certain powers have their seat in certain substances or speech acts. This notion that a power inhabits the object itself, moreover, was not understood as the result of the causal properties of the object, but rather in the same way as in a pre-Cartesian mental world the soul was believed to inhabit the body and to animate it, or in which a significance inhabited its expression.[34]

This deployment by the Tridentine Church of what might anachronistically call 'white magic', made it imperative to provide a clear definition of its counterpart, black or demonic magic. Implicit in this was the need to provide a fierce attack upon diabolism.[35] This became a recurring theme in the thought and work of those authors who found an echo in New Spain in Carlos de Sigüenza y Góngora and Sor Juana Inés de la Cruz[36] and whose best representative was the Austrian Jesuit Athanasius Kircher. In Kircher's work, particularly his *magnum opus, Oedipus Aegypticus* (1652–4), the inescapable significance of the belief in magic and the consequent danger of diabolism is immediately apparent. The need to 'extirpate those false arts which, sown by the devil, have spread their roots into our own times', he wrote, required the 'revelation, by true interpretation, of the secrets of the hieroglyphic doctrines'. Thus Kircher highlighted the sharp rift that separated the common resort to amulets and similar superstitious practices, from the true spiritual healing derived from Adam and taught by Hermes Trismegistus, which rested in natural sympathies and antipathies and was confirmed in prayer. In his attempt to provide a solid base for Hermeticism within Catholic doctrine, Kircher argued that the Egyptians had bequeathed a double occultism to humanity: the occultism descended from Ham on the one hand, consisting of the diabolical practices of astrology, divination, superstition and idolatry, and the occultism descended from Adam on the other, brought to light by the sacramental insight of Hermes into the divine properties, the Trinity, the origins of creation, angels and demons which, when suitably insulated from the depravities of the profane, formed the foundation of all philosophical and theological thinking, what he called the 'Theosophia Metaphysica'.[37]

Formidable as Kircher's intellectual achievement may appear to the historian, at the time it provoked neither controversy nor even much comment. His theories, like those of his equally neglected contemporary Emmanuel Maignan, preserved an essentially organicist method of proceeding from

34   Ibid., p. 191.

35   R. J. W. Evans, *The Making of the Habsburg Monarchy 1550–1700: An Interpretation* (Oxford, 1979), p. 345.

36   On these see Irving Leonard, *Don Carlos de Sigüenza y Góngora: A Mexican Savant of the Seventeenth Century* (Berkeley, Calif., 1929) and Octavio Paz, *Sor Juana: Her Life and her Work* (London, 1988). More generally, D. A. Brading, *The First America: The Spanish Monarchy, Creole Patriots and the Liberal State 1492–1867* (Cambridge, 1991), ch. 17.

37   Evans, *Habsburg Monarchy*, pp. 433–40. On Kircher see Jocelyn Godwin, *Athanasius Kircher: A Renaissance Man and the Quest for Lost Knowledge* (London, 1979).

being to thinking, and this placed the whole doctrine they sought to defend outside the scope of the distinction of spiritualism and materialism that the Cartesian method of proceeding from consciousness towards the outside world had begun to force upon late seventeenth-century thought.[38]

It is true that the Cartesian notion that self-mastery consists in the capacity of reason to shape human life was reminiscent of the Stoic notion of *autarkeia* as well as of the Augustinian doctrine of the perversity of the human will. But whereas both the Stoics and St Augustine still described the fullness of perfection in terms of the acquisition of insight into 'the order of things' or 'the good', Descartes, by contrast, stressed that true insight entailed the emptiness of all ancient conceptions of order; the mind, in other words, should be utterly separate from a mechanistic world of matter which was emphatically not a medium of thought or meaning.[39]

In the post-Cartesian world, therefore, the cosmos could no longer be seen as the embodiment of a meaningful order which was capable of defining the good for humanity. Likewise, the primacy of reason was no longer that of a dominant vision but rather that of a directing agency seeking the subordination of an essentially functional domain. For Descartes reason rules the passions by turning them into instruments. Thus the former notion that the ultimate criterion of rationality was conformity with 'the good', which entailed that the disposition of things could constitute the measure of rationality, was in effect neutralized. As Taylor has put it, 'rationality is no longer defined substantively, in terms of the order of being, but rather procedurally, in terms of the standards by which we construct orders in science and life'; it is now 'an internal property of subjective thinking', it has 'moved from substance to procedure, from found to constructed orders'.[40]

It is difficult for us to appreciate the radical novelty that the Cartesian system posed to contemporaries. Descartes's insistence that his readers should spend a whole month considering the first *Meditation* points to his awareness of the difficulties of grasping the mind/body dualism that his sceptical methodology entailed. The claim that the human mind could be seen as a mirror capable of reflecting a law-governed nature and that the role of philosophy was to brighten that mirror so as to produce accurate images would ultimately promote an empirical rationalism into the place formerly occupied by theology. To those thinkers concerned with orthodoxy and the preservation of order (an overwhelming majority in the Hispanic world) scepticism and the insistence on the primacy of the self as the object of knowledge were not merely heretical but fundamentally erro-

---

38   On Maignan see J. S. Spink, *French Free Thought from Gassendi to Voltaire* (London, 1960), pp. 77–84. His association with Kircher is discussed in P. J. S. Whitmore, *The Order of Minims in Seventeenth-Century France* (The Hague, 1967), p. 165.

39   See, for example, Descartes's letter to Chanut, 15 June 1646, *Descartes: Philosophical Letters*, trans. Anthony Kenny (Oxford, 1970).

40   *Sources of the Self*, p. 156.

neous. Even the well-known sympathizer of the New Philosophy in Spain, the Benedictine encyclopaedist Benito Jerónimo Feijóo, saw Cartesian dualism as counterintuitive and contrary to experience, for it demanded a complete reevaluation of traditional epistemology which ultimately reduced the realm of theology (hitherto accepted as the queen of sciences,' to which no argument, no disputation, no topic is alien', as Francisco de Vitoria had put it) solely to the relationship of God and his creation.[41]

Traditional opposition to the New Philosophy is thus no great surprise. With hindsight it is tempting to see it as a reactionary response by a cluster of thinkers sentimentally attached to a decaying cosmology threatened by a more powerful and coherent philosophy. 'Kircher and his friends', writes R. J. W. Evans, 'had piped a *danse macabre*, raising to life once more the skeletons of a decaying world order before the midnight hour.'[42] But in the contemporary context the crisis was not so much that of a mere clash between two distinct and competing systems of thought. Despite its dualistic claims, the Cartesian philosophy did not emerge from a cultural vacuum. Its impetus came from an anti-teleological morality which found its source in the nominalist revolt against Aristotelian naturalism and the threat it seemed to pose to the sovereignty of God.[43] Ultimately, a mechanistic universe was the only one compatible with this voluntaristic understanding of divine sovereignty. Descartes himself laid special emphasis upon the notion that what he understood as the 'eternal verities', such as the axioms of mathematics, were made by divine fiat.[44]

As we have seen, this voluntarist tendency not only was at the root of early modern demonology but it also underlay the work of those philosophers and theologians who had most reason to feel threatened by Cartesianism. The explicit rejection of hylomorphism in Descartes was already implicit in the metaphysics of Suárez, and the whole of early modern scholasticism was characterized by an eclectic effort to reconcile the different traditions in medieval thought that left no room for the Thomistic doctrine of the concordance between nature and grace. There was an insoluble tension, therefore, in the unease caused by Cartesian scepticism. If it was true that it threatened to divorce science from theological preoccupations about the nature of matter and the universe, it was also true that this was the direction that orthodox theology had been taking implicitly. The effects of the tendency were most clearly visible in spirituality and in the extreme forms that late seventeenth-century diabolism had reached. Most orthodox thinkers realized that there was a problem here but, as we have seen in the case of Querétaro, they failed to provide an explanation along

41 Pagden, 'The Reception of the "New Philosophy"', pp. 126–7.
42 Evans, *Habsburg Monarchy*, p. 442.
43 See above, pp. 21–3.
44 Letter to Mersenne (15 April 1630) *Œuvres de Descartes*, ed. Charles Adam and Paul Tannery (Paris, 1973), i, p. 145.

the lines of Leibniz. Seeing the nominalist-inspired separation of divine and human values as an expression of orthodoxy, they found themselves unable to fall back upon the Aristotelian theory of knowledge which, as interpreted by Aquinas, alone would have made possible a recognition of the independence of the natural world without separating it from the supernatural realm. In other words, the hegemony of nominalist hyper-Augustinianism in early modern thought gave the orthodox distrust of the 'vulgar superstitions of the rabble' exactly the same basis as its distrust of the 'vulgar errors of the sceptics'. Just as the inquisitors' attacks upon Franciscan credulity were nowhere accompanied by a criticism of their theological claims, so too the conservative attacks upon Cartesian scepticism never developed a coherent criticism of its philosophical bases.

To see the triumph of the New Philosophy over Aristotelian scholasticism in terms of a clash between two competing systems of thought can thus be very misleading. For, despite the defensive claims of the conservatives, the 'Aristotelianism' that came under the attack of the sceptics had itself implicitly encouraged the same philosophical premises that denied it credibility. In the Hispanic world the crisis became more acute during the closing years of Habsburg rule, when an increasingly powerful group known somewhat contemptuously as *los afrancesados* had begun to stress that the only way to rejuvenate Spanish intellectual life was through the importation of French culture. The conservative and increasingly uncritical response that this new presence provoked among the more patriotic defenders of the old order can be seen in the fate that befell Diego Mateo Zapata, one of the founders and most distinguished members of the Regia Sociedad in Spain and the creator of an eclectic programme aimed at finding a place for Cartesian metaphysics and Gassendist physics within the formal Aristotelian academic structure. Despite being the personal physician to the Duke of Medinaceli and to Cardinals Borja and Portocarrero, Zapata was tried and condemned as a crypto-Jew by the Inquisition in 1725 and banished from Madrid.[45] It is true that his writings enjoyed considerable popularity among the more enlightened members of the nobility and that they were even taken up at a more formal academic level by mathematicians like Tomás Vicente Tosca and Juan Bautista Corachán, Félix Falco de Belaochaga and Baltazar Iñigo, upon whose work the famous Valencian Gregorio Mayáns could still build in the 1740s.[46] But the essentially eclectic nature of the programme, welcoming Cartesian dualism in methodology and psychology on the one hand while remaining submissive and obedient to the authority of the Church in all matters pertaining to theology and ethics on the other, rendered it fundamentally incapable of achieving an

45 Pagden, 'The Reception of the "New Philosophy"', pp. 134–5. The records of the case are in Biblioteca Nacional de Madrid, MS 10.938, fols 173ff.
46 On this see Antonio Mestre, *El mundo intelectual de Mayáns* (Valencia, 1978).

enduring philosophical synthesis in which scholasticism could survive. The result was that whenever those thinkers who were sympathetic to the new learning came to a religious turn in any argument they ceased to be open-minded, 'not so much', as I. L McClelland has written, 'out of loyalty as out of habit'.[47] Mayáns himself found Montesquieu 'more diabolical than Machiavelli' and Voltaire 'one of the greatest atheists alive today'.[48] Similarly, across the ocean in New Spain the enlightened cleric Juan Benito Díaz de Gamarra, whose university text *Elementa Recentioris Philosophiae* (1774) included the study of Newton, Franklin, Mariotte and Boyle, displayed an extreme conservatism in his inquisitorial censures.[49]

Thus traditional scholasticism, having found itself incapable of providing an answer to the new scepticism, resorted to an uncritical and positively servile appeal to established wisdom. As the Spanish Carmelite Domingo de Santa Teresa stated, no matter what their merit or interest, the arguments of the new philosophers had all been refuted *a priori* 'by the authority of Aristotle and St Thomas and Scotus, and all the other doctors and theologians who thought the contrary'.[50] 'The sciences', wrote the influential Spanish physician Bernardo López de Araujo, who thought that the microscope distorted the truth by making objects larger than they really are, 'are not founded upon experiments, which are fallible in many ways, but rather upon the general principles that can be apprehended by the light of reason.'[51] Similarly in New Spain, the bulk of those who felt attracted by the New Philosophy were forced to keep a low profile by the increasingly intolerant conservatism that came to reject all the works of the Enlightenment as 'the pestiferous expectorations of Satan', works that were impossible to read 'without shedding copious tears...on seeing the blindness that has overcome the human intellect as the result of the corruption of customs'.[52] Even Feijóo, who had carefully stressed the dangers of separating theology from epistemology and natural science,[53] was seen with distrust. The rector of the University of Mexico, Juan José de Eguiara y Eguren, referred to him as

a doctor who, despite being as Catholic as he is erudite, has callously and insensitively encouraged the abandonment of scholastic theology through the establishment of a modern, mechanical and entirely profane

47   McClelland, *Ideological Hesitancy*, p. 60.
48   Quoted by Pagden, 'The Reception of the "New Philosophy"', p. 138.
49   Monelisa Lina Pérez-Marchand, *Dos etapas ideológicas del siglo XVIII en México a través de los papeles de la Inquisición* (Mexico City, 1945), p. 112. On Gamarra see Elías Trabulse, *El Círculo Roto* (Mexico City, 1982), pp. 101–3.
50   Quoted by Pagden, 'The Reception of the "New Philosophy"', p. 133.
51   Bernardo López de Araujo, *Centinela médico-aristotélico contra scépticos* (Madrid, 1725), p. 336.
52   A.G.N., Inq., 1126, fols 211r–v; 1169, fol. 4v.
53   The natural philosopher, wrote Feijóo, 'must not lose sight of faith any more than the navigator can ignore the position of the pole star'. See Pagden, 'The Reception of the "New Philosophy"', p. 139.

philosophy.... Although he and his followers are very distant from the sects of the heretics... they do not guard against the shadow that shelters their intentions, thereby allowing our theologians to be held in scornful contempt.[54]

Even more characteristic was Francisco Ignacio Cigala's claim that modern physics was false and intrinsically contrary to religious truth because it had been founded by a heretic who wished to disarm the Church of Rome of scholastic theology. And Cigala's contemporary, José Mariano de Vallarta y Palma, deployed a 'natural scepticism' against anything contrary to orthodoxy and tradition that won him the reputation of 'a Catholic Pyrrhon or Pierre Bayle'.[55]

In their defensiveness, however, the traditionalists need not so much have feared the new sceptical philosophy as the new critical temper that had been brewing within the Hispanic world itself and which would ultimately prove much more harmful to their cause. If there was any French influence in the Hispanic world in the first half of the eighteenth century it was not to be found in Descartes and Voltaire, but rather in Bossuet and Fleury and the tradition of Gallican regalism which had found reinforcement in canon law from the works of Espen and Febronius and their defence of national hierarchies and Church councils against the monarchical claims of the papacy.[56] As we saw at the end of chapter 2, the new movement favoured clerics of a Jansenist persuasion (thus called not because of any close adherence to the spirit of Port Royal, but because of their fierce opposition to the Jesuits) who preferred the study of the Church Fathers and scripture to scholasticism and who sought to replace the rhetoric and mysticism of Baroque spirituality with a simple, interior piety based on good works. As David Brading has written,

> Spanish Jansenism formed a broad movement of reform and renewal, a current of opinion rather than a party, in which there figured zealots, moderates and place-men, united only by a repudiation of the spiritual and intellectual culture of Baroque, post-Tridentine Catholicism.[57]

It is perhaps a fitting irony that the ideas of the Enlightenment should have first penetrated the Catholic world in the guise of Jansenism, just as

54 Eguiara y Eguren to Feijóo, in Francisco Ignacio Cigala, *Cartas al Ilustrísimo y Reverendísimo Maestro Fray Benito Gerónimo Feijóo, que le escribía sobre el 'Teatro Crítico Universal'* (Mexico City, 1760), 2nd letter (unfoliated).
55 On this see Pablo González Casanova, *El misoneísmo y la modernidad cristiana en el siglo XVIII* (Mexico City, 1948), pp. 126—35.
56 On this see Owen Chadwick, *The Popes and European Revolutions* (Oxford, 1981), pp. 392–424.
57 Brading, *The First America*, p. 500.

they had first made an impact upon Protestant circles via the legacy of the Puritans and the fervour of the Pietists.[58] The movement's programme for moral reform was fundamentally alien to the concept of society upon which the Catholic monarchy had been founded and it tended to encourage a more conscious rejection of popular practices deemed superstitious. Much more than the defensive indifference that we detected among inquisitors, the Jansenist reformers made no secret of their contempt and distaste for the 'vulgar'. But by 'vulgar' was now meant not the 'ignorance' of the sceptics that had provided the target for Cordero and Tapia and which was still reminiscent of Kircher's claim that 'the world is founded upon principles far more intricate and indiscernible than either the naive minds of past ages or the *vulgar* philosophers of the present would have us believe'.[59] The 'vulgar' were now those of whom Hume had written in his *Natural History of Religion*, that is, 'all mankind, a few excepted...[who] never elevate their contemplation to the heavens'.[60]

The triumph of this Jansenist bourgeois anticlericalism, which prepared the way for the downfall of the Jesuits, marks the end of our journey. With a single stroke, the expulsion of the Jesuits in 1767 removed the most dynamic group of missionaries and it deprived the whole of the Hispanic world of the one religious order that had shown itself capable of meeting the Enlightenment upon grounds still capable of preserving a traditional vision of the world. Moreover, the new reforming movement did not introduce any coherent programme that could take the place of the old order. Having succeeded in dividing and weakening the forces of tradition, Jansenism became a lost cause, soon finding itself the victim of the forces it had helped to unleash. It is no accident that the last decades of the eighteenth century should have witnessed a reversal of the dwindling inquisitorial interest in cases of superstition and a marked increase in long and meticulous cases involving demonic pacts and invocations.

But this was no longer the devil that has formed the subject of this book, but a very different, pseudo-aristocratic spirit who had grown ashamed of the 'vulgar' and who now sought to seduce the literate into unbelief.[61] Thus he developed his more modern and politically useful role. Deployed primarily to justify a growing political weakness, the late colonial devil bore little resemblance to his more theological Baroque ancestor and, ironically, came to foreshadow the later, secularized myth that sought to explain the destruction of Christendom by a liberal conspiracy of Freemasons and Jews.

58   See, for example, Isaiah Berlin, *The Magus of the North: J. G. Haman and the Origins of Modern Irrationalism*, ed. H. Hardy (London, 1993), pp.5–6, 13–14.
59   Athanasius Kircher, *Iter Exstaticum Coeleste* (Wurzburg, 1660), p. 15 (my emphasis).
60   Quoted by Peter Brown, *The Cult of the Saints: Its Rise and Function in Latin Christianity* (London, 1981), pp. 13–14.
61   Some illustrative cases are in A.G.N., Inq., 1019.9; 1282.22; 1294.1; 1304.6; 1428.1; and A.G.N., Lote Riva Palacio, 32.2.

Epilogue

> What is sinister, deep…is not obvious just from learning the history of
> the external action, but *we* insert it from an experience in ourselves.
> Ludwig Wittgenstein, *Remarks on Frazer's Golden Bough*, p. 16

BY ALL ACCOUNTS the publication, in 1780–81, of Francisco Javier
Clavigero's *Historia Antigua de México*, in Cesena, Italy, marks a watershed in
the historiography of pre-Columbian Mexico. Until then, historians had
found it difficult to see through the conflicting and often contradictory
mass of information bequeathed by sixteenth-century missionaries and
chroniclers. As Alexander von Humboldt would write in the early nineteenth century, before Clavigero 'it seemed to be the duty of a philosopher
to deny what had been observed by the missionaries'.[1] But the sober neo-
classical style of the exiled Mexican Jesuit soon earned him a wide
appreciative audience in Europe, which included Edward Gibbon,[2] and the
Historia Antigua, unquestionably the most popular and influential account of
ancient Mexico since Acosta's *Historia natural y moral*, ably succeeded in lib-
erating the Mesoamerican past from its mysterious exoticism.[3]

Perhaps Clavigero's single most important achievement was to exorcize
the devil from his *patria's* past, to liberate the pre-Hispanic world from the
nagging interpretative burden of Acosta and Torquemada. For in sharp contrast to all previous accounts of ancient Mexico, the *Historia Antigua* adopted
an unmistakably secular historical approach. Given that men were both
rational and free, Clavigero emphasized, any explanation of human affairs
in terms of non-human agencies was fundamentally inadequate. No matter

1 *Vues des cordillères et monumens des peuples indigènes de l'Amérique* (Paris, 1810), p. ii.
2 See *The English Essays of Edward Gibbon*, ed. P. B. Craddock (Oxford, 1972), p. 318.
3 Clavigero has not been served well by historians. The most complete study is Charles E.
Ronan, *Francisco Javier Clavigero S.J. (1731–1787), figure of the Mexican Enlightenment: His life and
works* (Rome and Chicago, 1977); I am also indebted to the shorter studies by Luis Villoro, *Los
grandes momentos del indigenismo en México* (Mexico City, 1987 edn), pp. 95–125; Anthony
Pagden, *Spanish Imperialism and the Political Imagination: Studies in European and Spanish American
Social and Political Theory 1513–1830* (New Haven and London, 1990) pp. 97–116; and Elías
Trabulse, 'Clavigero, historiador de la ilustración mexicana', in *Francisco Javier Clavigero en la
ilustración mexicana*, ed. Alfonso Martínez Rosales (Mexico City, 1988), pp. 41–57.

how perfidious and influential the devil was deemed to be, the use of supernatural agents as an explanation of human actions was, quite simply, 'not
pleasing to the century in which we live'.[4]

It is true that this insistence upon the need for an empirical method in
history was, to some extent, reminiscent of Acosta.[5] But Clavigero's
approach differed markedly from that of his coreligionist in the way in
which it carried its empiricism into the supernatural realm without any of
the qualms that had led Acosta so thoroughly to demonize Amerindian religions. Indeed, it was precisely on the basis of his analysis of the religion of
the ancient Mexicans that Clavigero most persistently pointed to the
advanced stage that Mesoamerican civilization had reached. Nor was this
merely a defensive strategy against the contemptuous onslaught that
Europeans like Buffon, de Pauw, Raynal and Robertson (against whom the
Historia Antigua was specifically written[6]) had launched against the New
World. For Clavigero himself made no special effort to sweeten his readers'
pill when describing the 'practices of the barbarous and execrable religious
system' of the ancient Mexicans, who in the history of the world had been
'unequalled in the abominable cruelties' engendered by their belief that 'the
copious blood shed by their victims would not suffice to quench the diabolical thirst of their gods'.[7] Neither did he make any special effort to deny the
widely held claim that Amerindian civilizations had been 'entirely consecrated' (Clavigero's own words) to Satan before the arrival of Christianity.[8]
All the same, Clavigero was careful to temper these claims by stressing the
overriding role of God, who 'watches lovingly over his creatures and never
allows those capital enemies of the human race so much freedom to harm'.[9]
If it was true that Satanism was inherent to the religious practices of the
ancient Mexicans, the same was true of every other pagan religion 'which
has its origin in the caprices or fears of men'.[10] Indeed, from a comparative
analysis of these, the religion of the Mexicans emerged in a favourable light:
although Clavigero conceded that human sacrifice and cannibalism were
more prevalent among them than elsewhere, in all other respects the reli-

4   Francisco Javier Clavigero, *Historia antigua de México*, 4 vols (Mexico City, 1945 edn), iv,
p. 44. This is the original Spanish version, from which the Italian translation was made to
secure publication. Thus the first edition appeared as *Storia antica del Messico* (Cesena, 1780–1).
5   See above, pp. 26–7.
6   Clavigero dismissed their works as typical of 'an age in which more errors have been
published than in any previous century, in which authors write with licence, lie without
shame, and in which no-one is reputed to be a philosopher who does not mock religion and
adopt the language of impiety'. Quoted in D. A. Brading, *The First America: The Spanish
Monarchy, Creole Patriots and the Liberal State 1492–1867* (Cambridge, 1991), p. 452.
7   *Historia antigua*, i, p. 238; ii, pp. 119, 129.
8   Ibid., ii, p. 41.
9   Ibid., i, p. 220.
10   Ibid., ii, p. 61

gion of the ancient Mexicans was 'less superstitious, less ridiculous and less indecent' than the pagan religions of the old world:[11]

> Americans, Greeks, Romans and Egyptians, all of them were superstitious and puerile in the practice of their religions; but as far as the obscenity of their rites was concerned, that of the Mexicans shows not a remnant of those abominations that were so common among the Romans and other cultivated nations of Antiquity.[12]

It was not Satanic intervention, but human ignorance and weakness that was to blame for religious error.

Clavigero's intent was clearly polemical and many of his arguments were in some ways reminiscent of those deployed by Bartolomé de las Casas two and a half centuries before. In the context of the European Enlightenment, however, Clavigero's position was far wider in its implications. A striking novelty in the Jesuit's approach is the way in which his interests were not so much dominated by universal human values as by human and cultural differences. It is in this that the real originality of his work lies. Although both Aristotle and Augustine remain central to his basic hypotheses, they more than once give way to Montesquieu in the *Historia Antigua*'s naturalistic account of the civilization of ancient Mexico. It was above all Montesquieu's wide-ranging sympathies and his insistence that – in the words of Isaiah Berlin – 'the substitution of general principles for the faculty of sensing individual differences is...the beginning of evil'[13] which opened Clavigero's eyes to the possibility of defending a vastly different culture by representing it as following its own path of development and fulfilling the needs of its people no less acceptably than the cultures of the Old World. Just as Montesquieu's Persians were neither superior nor inferior to the Parisians whom they described, but so dissimilar that what was accepted in one culture might seem perverse in another, so Clavigero's Aztecs appear in an epic and heroic light where their different customs and traditions can compare adequately with the highest virtues of the classical world. Yet it was emphatically not such comparisons with the classical world that gave ancient Mexico its cultural value, but its own autonomous norms, which could claim no contact with any culture of the Old World and which could only be understood in their own terms.

Nowhere did Clavigero stress this more clearly than in his naturalistic treatment of religion with its concomitant rejection of diabolical intervention. 'The system of natural religion', he wrote, 'depends above all upon the idea that one has about the divinity.'[14] Religion, in other words, does not,

11 Ibid., iv, p. 410.
12 Ibid., iv, p. 399.
13 *Against the Current: Essays in the History of Ideas*, ed. Henry Hardy (Oxford, 1981), p. 158.
14 *Historia antigua*, iv, p. 392.

Plate 26. Francisco Javier Clavigero.

indeed cannot, have a supernatural origin. Its characteristics do not derive from the object of worship, be it divine or diabolic, but from the human perception of that object, a perception which is itself a strictly natural activity. As Luis Villoro put it, Clavigero 'does not begin with a reality that is hidden behind the image that the Indian has formed of his god, but rather, takes the end product of his belief together with its human characteristics and, from it, attempts to understand the religious system'.[15]

This naturalistic explanation left no room for the supernatural. The devil was effectively excised, if not, as we have seen, from the general scheme of things, certainly from every particular event or act described in the *Historia Antigua.* 'The good historians of the sixteenth century,' Clavigero wrote in a well-known passage,

15   *Los grandes momentos,* p. 122.

and those who later have followed their example, had no doubt about the continuous and familiar dealings of the devil with all the idolatrous nations of the New World....But although it is true that the malice of these spirits is bent upon harming men as much as they can, and that sometimes they actually appear to them visibly in order to seduce them, and especially to those who have not yet entered the regenerated community of the Church, it is hard to believe that such representations should have occurred so often, or that the devil should have dealt so frankly with such nations.[16]

It was in the reasons he gave for his doubts, however, that Clavigero differed from Montesquieu and revealed a more ingrained traditionalism. For whereas the Frenchman had implicitly attacked both Bossuet and the sceptics by stressing that neither God nor chance rules the world,[17] the Jesuit never abandoned his belief in the overriding role of Providence in history. Indeed, it was Providence, and only Providence, that had been responsible for keeping the devil at bay. If the supernatural had no place in Clavigero's naturalistic account of the historical progress of humanity, this was clearly not because God had abandoned the 'clockwork' of the universe to his own rules after creation, but because men were free and rational agents.

In all this Clavigero seems to have emerged successfully from the agonizing doubts about theodicy that had filled the minds of Christian thinkers from the last years of the seventeenth century. But if in spirit he is closer to Montesquieu and the secular values of the Enlightenment, his philosophical assumptions are still very much those of the Mexican inquisitors and of Cordero and Tapia, with their humble deference to the established canons and the persistent separation of the natural and the supernatural. What gave Clavigero's arguments a more persuasive power was the increasing prestige that the study of history, and in particular cultural history, with its growing awareness of the differences rather than the similarities between different societies, ages and cultures, had come to acquire.[18] Already in the 1720s the French Jesuit Joseph-François Lafitau had stated that cultures were primarily systems of symbolic representation which provide the means of communication between people in different societies, and his descriptions and interpretations of specific cultural phenomena (myths, burial rites, games, warfare and so on) sought primarily to explain their symbolic function.[19]

16 *Historia antigua*, i, p. 220.
17 *Oeuvres complètes de Montesquieu*, ed. A. Masson, 3 vols (Paris, 1950–5), i, pp. 8–9, 412.
18 The genesis of this movement can be traced to the sixteenth-century school of universal historians in France – Pasquier, Le Roy, Le Caron, Vignier, La Popelinière and Bodin – followed in the seventeenth century by, among others, Boulainvilliers and Fénelon. See Berlin, *Against the Current*, pp. 86–7.
19 *Moeurs des sauvages américains comparées aux moeurs des premiers temps*, 2 vols (Paris, 1724), passim.

Like Clavigero, he is often admired for his comparatively 'modern' achieve-
ments. Yet, as Anthony Pagden has argued, Lafitau was 'only able to do
these things because his epistemologically very orthodox mind had been
provided with the right set of questions, questions which were
suggested…by a concern with the *social* rather than the *psychological* sources
of human behaviour'.[20] The same was true of Clavigero; and indeed, as
soon as we step back from these specific concerns, the 'modernism' of both
men dissolves. Just as one of Lafitau's central aims had been to prove the
truth of Christianity by highlighting the workings of Providence in the way
in which pagans had unwittingly imitated Christian rituals and beliefs, so,
too, Clavigero was unable to abandon Providence and, in ambivalent fashion, brought its workings to bear heavily upon the unavoidable fact of the
Spanish conquest, a fact which the Indians should accept, stoically, as a
punishment for their sins.[21]

Human beings, Clavigero maintained, are free and rational; but Providence always disposes. The notion that men can break out of this circle,
make their own laws, build upon rational foundations and be free to rule
their own destiny – the faith of the secular Enlightenment – was not
Clavigero's creed. His vision was much closer to that of the Neapolitan
philosopher Giambattista Vico (1668–1744), who successfully combined a
secular outlook in his interpretation of human cultures with a devout belief
in the role of Providence in history.[22] The deep significance of this attempt
for my theme will become apparent after a brief analysis of Vico's thought.

*

'The world of human society', Vico wrote, 'has certainly been made by
men, and its principles are therefore to be found within the modifications of
our own human mind.'[23] Religious myths, in this context, were not pic-
turesque inventions or lying fables, as the humanists and the rationalists in
turn maintained; nor were they confused memories of extraordinary men as
the Euhemerists believed. They were concrete and systematic ways of ex-

---

20 *The Fall of Natural Man: The American Indian and the Origins of Comparative Ethnology*
(Cambridge, 1982), pp. 3–4 (my emphasis).

21 *Historia antigua,* i, pp. 114ff., 130; iii, pp. 32–3, 314.

22 Any direct influence of Vico on Clavigero is impossible to prove, but it is now more or
less generally accepted that the work of the Neapolitan was far more influential among Italian
scholars in the second half of the eighteenth century than it used to be supposed; see, for
example, Arnaldo Momigliano, 'Vico's *Scienza nuova*', *History and Theory*, V: 1 (1966), and
Joseph Mali, *The Rehabilitation of Myth: Vico's 'New Science'* (Cambridge, 1992), p. 10; in any
case, Clavigero knew Vico's work through Lorenzo Boturini, who appropriated Vico's system
in his *Idea de una nueva historia general de la América septentrional*; on this see Alvaro Matute,
Lorenzo Boturini y el pensamiento histórico de Vico (Mexico City, 1976).

23 *The New Science,* ed. and trans. T. G. Bergin and M. H. Fisch (Ithaca, N. Y., 1948), paragraph 331. Subsequent references to *The New Science* will continue to be given by paragraph
number.

pression and of understanding reality: neither devils nor poetic constructs, but 'true histories of customs', 'civil histories of the first peoples, who were poets', 'the first science to be learnt'.[24] And although it was undeniable that many of these myths were incomprehensible and even offensive, Vico thought that their condemnation on such grounds was not merely arrogant but intellectually naive and superficial, for even the most horrendous abominations of the ancient religions had fulfilled the indispensable function of binding and healing the ruptures of society. This indeed, Vico emphasized, was what the word religion (*re-ligo*) actually meant.

What might seem ambivalent to the modern reader is that, far from any kind of reductionism, Vico saw this binding role of religion in human society as a clear proof of the presence of God's Providence acting as a supreme purpose which was concealed from individual human eyes but without which the course of history could not be adequately understood.[25] At the heart of this conception is to be found an underlying contrast between two distinct worlds: on the one hand, the external world of natural processes which are more or less impenetrable since human beings can only manipulate them within the strict limits set by Providence; and, on the other, the stream of history in which alone human beings can feel at home, for, despite its recurring mysteries, it is the world which their own creative spirit has 'made'.[26] In Vico's famous words,

> whoever reflects on this cannot but marvel that the philosophers should have bent all their energies to the study of the world of nature, which, since God made it, he alone knows; and that they should have neglected the study of the world of nations, or civil world, which, since men made it, men could come to know.[27]

As is well known, this was the core of Vico's brilliant response to the Cartesian depreciation of history as mere gossip. Yet, no matter how anti-Cartesian in intent, Vico's solution was no less sharply dualistic. Where Descartes had drawn a line between mind and matter, Vico redrew it between physics and metaphysics, between the real and the nominal. 'What, if any,' writes Isaiah Berlin, 'is the relation of Vico's undoubted Christian faith, his Catholic orthodoxy, to his anthropological, liguistic, historical naturalism, or of his teleology to his belief that to each order of culture belong its own peculiar modes of consciousness…?'[28]

24   Ibid., 352, 7, 51.
25   Ibid., 342.
26   See Isaiah Berlin, *Vico and Herder: Two Studies in the History of Ideas* (London, 1976), p. 123. Berlin here is paraphrasing Enzo Paci, *Ingens Sylva: Saggio sulla filosofia di G. B. Vico* (Verona, 1949).
27   *New Science*, 331.
28   *Against the Current*, p. 116.

Vico's own implicit answer to this ambivalence is to be found in his notion of *conatus*. What he meant by this concept is more or less accurately rendered as 'endeavour'; but it is also clear that *conatus* is an irrational force, a kind of inhibition that enables humans to resist a given thought or a given action, an ability that he attributes to the 'metaphysical' capacities of humanity. What Vico meant by this was not the capacity for philosophical abstraction but rather the ability to deploy mythical images in order to transcend basic physical impulses. The fundamental historical truths about the origins and development of all human institutions had to be sought in ancient and primitive myths, in common 'vulgar' traditions, in short, in 'all prejudices'. It was these that made possible 'common sense', by which he meant 'judgement without reflection, shared by an entire class...people... nation...or the entire human race'.[29]

Significantly, the purpose behind Vico's introduction of the notion of *conatus* was the urgent need that he saw to provide a link between the divine and the human realms. For it is precisely through *conatus* that, according to Vico, God's Providence in history draws human beings out of barbarism and nations out of bestiality. It was thus that Vico subtly questioned the current hyper-Augustinian separation of the natural and the supernatural that has been central to my argument. At a more strictly philosophical level, Vico's use of the notion of *conatus* was an attempt to solve the tension between the true and the certain, between the realms of *verum* (which is an attribute of God and as such pertains to the supernatural) and of *certum* (which refers to what remains to humans after the Fall and as such pertains to their natural capabilities).[30] Vico's notion of *conatus* can thus be seen as an attempt to answer the question whether humans are capable of 'living in' *verum* or whether God can stoop to 'live in' *certum*.[31]

Now although his response to both these claims was positive, it remained at the level of a practical historical knowledge, which, in Vico's words, 'should know God's providence in public moral institutions or civil customs by which the nations have come into being and maintain themselves in the world'.[32] At the level of metaphysics, by contrast, the issue was not only left unresolved by Vico, but the gulf between the divine and the human was emphatically reasserted. His outrage, for instance, at Hugo Grotius's suggestion that the natural law would guarantee the preservation of humanity, *even* if there was no God, is reminiscent of the nominalist rejection of St Thomas's position on nature and grace. Indeed, Vico was convinced that Aquinas's failure to separate adequately the divine and the

29   *New Science*, 141–2.
30   Vico, *On the Most Ancient Wisdom of the Italians* [1710], trans. L. M. Palmer (Ithaca, N.Y., 1988), pp. 46–76.
31   See Mark Lilla, *G. B. Vico: The Making of an Anti-Modern* (Cambridge, Mass., and London, 1993), p. 24.
32   *New Science*, 5.

human had led to an unsustainable attempt to rationalize nature which fool-ishly denied the role of Providence in history.[33] This conviction remained constant throughout his writings. It is perhaps most clearly stated in his approach to the challenge that modern scepticism posed to the traditional understanding of Providence as 'midway between the two extremes of Calvin and Pelagius',[34] and especially in his staunch refusal to follow Leibniz's attempt to demonstrate the 'harmony between the physical king-dom of nature and the moral kingdom of grace...[a] harmony [which] leads things to grace through the very paths of nature'.[35] Instead of Leibniz's 'harmony' Vico proposed the *constantia* of God's presence among humans,[36] upon which alone depend the reconciliation of the divine and the human and the concomitant refutation of modern scepticism.

There is thus an underlying ambivalence in Vico's thought. On the one hand, against the sceptics he wished to establish a reconciling link between the divine and the human in order to defend a notion of Providence that did not conflict with human free will; on the other, against the Thomists he insisted emphatically upon the radical separation of the natural and the supernatural. To some extent this ambivalence lends weight to the influen-tial view that Vico was in fact an atheistic Epicurean who felt compelled piously to disguise his modernity for fear of the Inquisition.[37] But it is far more likely that the ambiguity responded to a genuine tension in contem-porary thought which resulted from the orthodox pretensions of the nominalist-inspired separation of the divine and the human. In this context, Vico's naturalistic treatment of religion and his quiet but persistent exclu-sion of the devil from his account of the origin of pagan mythologies (which would be so closely echoed by Clavigero in due course), were not the result of some incipient scepticism about the truth of the Christian faith or of some radical form of cultural relativism. It is true that the Inquisition persecuted the 'atheists' of Naples from 1686 to 1693, a time when some of Vico's friends and colleagues were harshly treated. But just as we have seen in the case of New Spain, this seems to have been the last effort by the Holy Office to assert a confident traditionalism. In the last years of the seventeenth century it virtually withdrew from Naples and Neapolitan

33 *De universi juris uno principio et fine uno liber unus* [1720], in *Opere giuridiche*, ed. Paolo Cristofolini (Florence, 1974), ch. lxxv.
34 *The Autobiography of Giambattista Vico*, trans. M. H. Fisch and T. G. Bergin (Ithaca, N.Y., 1944), p. 119.
35 G. W. Leibniz, *The Principles of Philosophy, or the Monadology* [1714], in *Philosophical Essays*, trans. R. Ariew and D. Garber (Indianapolis and Cambridge, 1989), p. 224.
36 See *De constantia jurisprudentis liber alter* [1721], in *Opere giuridiche*, passim.
37 The most influential recent works supporting this view are Frederick Vaughan, *The Political Philosophy of Giambattista Vico: An Introduction to La Scienza Nuova* (The Hague, 1972) and Gino Bedani, *Vico Revisited: Orthodoxy, Naturalism and Science in the Scienza Nuova* (Oxford, 1989).

intellectuals were left in relative freedom to conduct scientific research and to discuss the works of the New Philosophy under the guise of *libertas philosophandi*.[38]

It seems likely that this change of attitude on the Inquisition's part responded essentially to the same kind of concern that we saw at work in New Spain at this time, where care was being taken to tone down traditional theological explanations – in particular those related to the question of diabolism – not in order to disparage them but in order to protect them. What Vico's approach again brought to light was that the only acceptable way to do this in the current intellectual climate was through an emphatic affirmation of the separation of the natural and the supernatural. For as we saw in chapter 5, it was precisely this inability to escape from the accepted orthodoxy of the gulf between divine and human values that eventually persuaded Christian thinkers of the need to play down diabolism in order to retain a credible image of the devil. Soon, however, it became almost impossible to escape from applying precisely the same treatment to the notion of God. As Michael Buckley has written, the intellectual history of the modern western world has shown that wherever 'an antinomy is posed between nature or human nature and God, the glory of one in conflict with the glory of the other, this alienation will eventually be resolved in favour of the natural and the human'.[39] It is small wonder that the modern appreciation of Vico's achievement should have concentrated almost exclusively on his secular modernity. For it is precisely upon the basis of the affirmation of the value of ordinary human life that the modern world has been progressively ridding itself of many of the metaphysical abstractions that in the past, to quote Richard Rorty, posed a 'temptation to look for an escape from time and chance'.[40] There is no denying the importance of this revaluation of the human. All the same, as Charles Taylor insists, it seems just as absurd to assert that the stripped-down secular outlook that such revaluation often encourages is not itself a 'mutilation' which 'involves stifling the response in us to some of the deepest and most powerful spiritual aspirations that humans have conceived'.[41]

This is not the place to enter the debate. My intention, by way of conclu-

38   D. Carpanetto and G. Ricuperati, *Italy in the Age of Reason* (London, 1987), pp. 78–137. The antagonism of many scholars in Naples (as well as throughout the Hispanic world) towards the mechanical sciences at this time was more due to the contradiction between the absolutist pretensions of mechanicism and its failure to provide convincing hypotheses to practical problems encountered by scientists in fields such as medicine, education and politics. See Paolo Casini, *Introduzione all'Illuminismo: Da Newton a Rousseau* (Bari, 1973) and Mali, *Rehabilitation of Myth*, p. 18.
39   *At the Origins of Modern Atheism* (New Haven and London, 1987), p. 363.
40   *Contingency, Irony and Solidarity* (Cambridge, 1989), p. xiii.
41   *Sources of the Self: The Making of the Modern Identity* (Cambridge, 1992 edn), p. 520; see also, more generally, his *The Ethics of Authenticity* (Cambridge, Mass., 1992).

sion, is to return to some of the central themes that have emerged from this study and to suggest a way of looking at them that may shed some light upon the predicament highlighted by Taylor.

*

My central aim has been to trace the emergence and development of the early modern notion of the devil in the particular setting of New Spain and to point to the almost inevitable way in which it collapsed under its own weight during the first half of the eighteenth century. At the same time, I have been equally concerned to disclose some of the perceptions of the demonic prevalent among the wider sectors of society, sectors largely unaffected by the philosophical developments that led to the rise and decline of early modern diabolism and which, as I showed in chapters 2 and 3, managed to retain an earlier, more malleable notion of the devil which was not merely internally coherent but at times even essential to their understanding of reality and human relations.

There is still a widely held assumption that these 'popular' notions were somehow remnants of an outmoded form of knowledge which would progressively disappear as science and reason advanced. Yet it is clear that demonic beliefs and practices have persisted into our own day and, albeit in a disjointed fashion, even retained their persuasive power. More significantly, the philosophical assumptions that made the secularist outlook so convincing have been weakened. Indeed, a striking irony in the secularist position is that its affirmation of the human in opposition to the divine is based on essentially the same assumptions that led to both the emergence and the decline of early modern diabolism; namely, the separation of the natural and the supernatural. The more coherent philosophical attempts to combat this dualism by denying metaphysics altogether[42] themselves fail to escape from it; for their main target is not the totality of the western metaphysical tradition, but only that aspect of it based on the same nominalist-inspired separation of the natural and the supernatural whose strictly secular development they claim as their own. Thus, by attacking the metaphysics at the root of this development the secularists ignore the existence of an equally important metaphysical tradition which never attempted a separation of the physical and the spiritual and whose best exponent, *pace* Vico, is that other great name associated with Naples: St Thomas Aquinas.

The early modern attempt to separate the human mind from the world in which it operates would have seemed as absurd to Aquinas as it did to Wittgenstein, for whom the human understanding of meanings was primarily a *perception* of meanings and thus emphatically not a matter of inferences from inner states of consciousness of which words and gestures are

---

42   E.g. Rorty, *Contingency*, passim.

mere effects.[43] Wittgenstein's emphasis on 'action' and on the importance of ordinary life came to constitute a devastating critique of the modern notion of a solitary disembodied consciousness. One of Wittgenstein's most persistent aims was to liberate the modern mind from the almost inescapable antipathy to bodiliness that has afflicted western cultures since the late medieval period. Hand in hand with this went Wittgenstein's emphasis upon the deep continuities that exist between the sensibilities of primitive and modern cultures and the consequent inadequacy of the wide-spread modern tendency to deal with religious beliefs and practices by taking them to rest upon mistaken hypotheses about the world.[44]

In such a context it seems possible to reiterate Vico's 'rehabilitation of myth' (to use the title of a recent study[45]) without the need to insist upon the separation of the natural and the supernatural. For religion is an expression of human nature well before it gives rise to speculations about the divine. Like all concepts, religious concepts are rooted in specific ways of responding and relating to the natural environment; likewise, the very notions of the divine or of the demonic depend upon very basic human instincts.[46] Aquinas said very much the same thing when, for instance, he argued that the soul needed the body essentially, not just accidentally, in order to know. As we saw in chapter 1, for Aquinas the soul was not a different, spiritual substance imprisoned inside the body but the 'form' of the body. Physicality was not, in this sense, an optional extra, but an essential element in the make-up of a human being. If human beings were substances different from the bodies on which they act, they would be an amalgam of different things rather than a unity, a view which, as Aquinas himself put it, 'seems not to fit the facts', for human beings are 'sensible and natural realities' and thus 'cannot be essentially immaterial'.[47]

It was this insistence by Aquinas upon the human body as an essential element in human life, and his conviction that being a human person is inseparable from being a bodily animal, that led to that anti-Aristotelian reaction in late medieval and early modern thought which is at the root of the most persistent modern conceptions about human nature and the human self. As we have seen, however, this reaction is largely based on a misunderstanding of Aquinas. For if, on the one hand, Aquinas's anti-dualism led him to stress the importance of physicality, on the other he equally held that human understanding and willing were not physical processes. Thus Aquinas's insistence that human beings are not an amalgam of two distinct things (body and soul) was not contradicted by the need he saw to

---

43   *Philosophical Investigations*, trans. G. E. M. Anscombe (Oxford, 1953), nos. 503–7.
44   See the interesting discussion in Fergus Kerr, *Theology after Wittgenstein* (Oxford, 1986), pp. 160–2.
45   Mali, *The Rehabilitation of Myth*.
46   Kerr, *Theology after Wittgenstein*, p. 183.
47   *Summa contra Gentiles*, 2. 57.

distinguish between bodily and non-bodily functions. 'The principle of understanding', he wrote, '...has its own activity in which the body plays no intrinsic role.' From this it followed that the human soul was 'something incorporeal and subsisting'.[48] This meant simply that the human soul subsists because humans have an intellectual life which cannot be reduced to the bodily. It did *not* mean that the soul subsisted as a self-contained entity *apart* from the body. Human beings have intellect and will by virtue of their souls; but it is not their souls which understand and will: *they* do.[49]

Thus Aquinas's theory of knowledge left no room for any direct human self-knowledge in which the object known is something incorporeal. Since human beings can only know things through the encounter with material objects, it follows that they can only come to self-knowledge in the process of living a bodily life. This, as we saw in chapter 1, is the cornerstone of Aquinas's formulation of the concordance between nature and grace, of the natural and the supernatural; and it is the same theory of knowledge that seems to lie at the core of Wittgenstein's criticism of the modern conception of the self as well as of his most original intuitions about religious belief and practice.

What these considerations make clear is that the philosophical tradition that led to the rise and decline of early modern diabolism can hardly be said to be characteristic of the whole of Christianity. It was characteristic of merely one aspect of it which became dominant and which collapsed under its own weight during the first half of the eighteenth century. It was thus an internal crisis in one particular sector of the Christian tradition, rather than the threat posed to the whole of it by modern secularism, that accounts for the demise of diabolism and the subsequent decline in religious belief and practice. The common identification of this early modern philosophical tradition with the whole of Christianity is itself symptomatic of the compelling prevalence of the separation of the natural and the supernatural in Christian thought. As we have seen, even its denunciation by modern secularism is itself deeply implicated in the same dualist premise. But perhaps the most regrettable effect of this trend has been the denigration of the more 'popular' expressions of Christian culture. For no matter how unsophisticated they might appear, it is clear that they managed to retain a view of the supernatural that is closer to Aquinas than to Acosta and therefore more in tune with the modern affirmation of ordinary life.

48 *Summa Theologiae*, Ia, 75.2
49 I draw on Brian Davies's excellent discussion in *The Thought of Thomas Aquinas* (Oxford, 1993), pp. 207–15. See also Anthony Kenny, *Aquinas on Mind* (London and New York, 1993) and his *The Metaphysics of Mind* (Oxford, 1989).

Bibliography of works cited

For ease of reference, no distinction has been made between primary and secondary sources

Acosta, José de, *De Procuranda Indorum Salute* (Cologne, 1596)
————, *Confesionario para los curas de indios* (Lima, 1588)
————, *Historia Natural y Moral de las Indias* ed. E. O'Gorman (Mexico City, 1962)
Aguilar, Francisco de, *Relación breve de la conquista de Nueva España*, ed. F. Gómez de Orozco (Mexico City, 1954)
Aguirre Beltrán, Gonzalo, *Medicina y Magia: El proceso de aculturación en la estructura colonial* (Mexico City, 1963)
————, *La población negra de México* (Mexico City, 1984 edn)
Alberro, Solange, *Inquisición y sociedad en México 1571–1700* (Mexico City, 1988)
Aquinas, St Thomas, *Summa Theologiae*, 61 vols, Blackfriars edn (London and New York, 1964–80)
————, *Summa contra Gentiles* (Rome, 1984)
————, *Quaestiones Disputatae de Veritate*, ed. R. M. Spiazzi (Turin, 1953)
Augustine of Hippo, St, *Concerning the City of God against the Pagans*, trans. H. Bettenson (Harmondsworth, 1972)

Bakewell, Peter, *Silver Mining and Society in Colonial Zacatecas 1546–1700* (Cambridge, 1971)
Balsalobre, Gonzalo de, *Relación auténtica de las idolatrías, supersticiones y vanas observaciones de los indios del obispado de Oaxaca*, in *Tratado de las idolatrías*, ed. F. del Passo y Troncoso, 2 vols (Mexico City, 1953)
Bandini, Angelo Maria, *Vita e lettere di Amerigo Vespucci* (Florence, 1745)
Baudot, Georges, *Utopía e Historia en México: Los primeros cronistas de la civilización mexicana 1520–1569* (Madrid, 1983)
Bayle, Constantino, *El culto del Santísimo en Indias* (Madrid, 1951)

Bedani, Gino, *Vico Revisited: Orthodoxy, Naturalism and Science in the Scienza Nuova* (Oxford, 1989)

Berlin, Isaiah, *Vico and Herder: Two Studies in the History of Ideas* (London, 1976)

——, *Against the Current: Essays in the History of Ideas*, ed. Henry Hardy (Oxford, 1981)

——, *The Magus of the North: J. G. Haman and the Origins of Modern Irrationalism*, ed. Henry Hardy (London, 1993)

Bernand, C. and Gruzinski, S., *De l'Idolâtrie: Une archéologie des sciences religieuses* (Paris, 1988)

Boone, Elizabeth H., *Incarnations of the Aztec Supernatural: The Image of Huitzilopochtli in Mexico and Europe*, Transactions of the American Philosophical Society, vol. 79 (Philadelphia, 1989)

Bossy, John, *Christianity in the West 1400–1700* (Oxford, 1985)

——, 'Moral Arithmetic: Seven Sins into Ten Commandments', in Edmund Leites, ed., *Conscience and Casuistry in Early Modern Europe* (Cambridge, 1988)

Boturini Benaducci, Lorenzo, *Idea de una nueva historia general de la América septentrional*, ed. Miguel León Portilla (Mexico City, 1974)

Brading, D. A., *Miners and Merchants in Bourbon Mexico 1763–1810* (Cambridge, 1971)

——, *Haciendas and Ranchos in the Mexican Bajío* (Cambridge, 1978)

——, 'Tridentine Catholicism and Enlightened Despotism in Bourbon Mexico', *Journal of Latin American Studies*, 15 (1983)

——, 'Images and Prophets: Indian Religion and the Spanish Conquest', in A. Ouweneel and S. Miller, eds, *The Indian Community in Colonial Mexico* (Amsterdam, 1990)

——, *The First America: The Spanish Monarchy, Creole Patriots and the Liberal State 1492–1867* (Cambridge, 1991)

Bregman, J., *Synesius of Cyrene: Philosopher-Bishop* (Berkeley, Calif., 1982)

Brooke, Rosalind and Christopher, *Popular Religion in the Middle Ages* (London, 1984)

Brown, Peter, 'Sorcery, Demons and the Rise of Christianity: from Late Antiquity into the Middle Ages', in idem, *Religion and Society in the Age of St Augustine* (London, 1972 edn)

——, *The Cult of the Saints: Its Rise and Function in Latin Christianity* (London, 1981)

——, *The Body and Society: Men, Women and Sexual Renunciation in Early Christianity* (London, 1990)

Brundage, B. C., *The Fifth Sun: Aztec Gods, Aztec World* (Austin, 1979)

Buckley, Michael J., *At the Origins of Modern Atheism* (New Haven and London, 1987)

Burgoa, Francisco de, *Palestra historial de virtudes y ejemplares apostólicos* (Mexico City, 1670)

Burkhart, L. M., *The Slippery Earth: Nahua-Christian Moral Dialogue in Sixteenth-Century Mexico* (Tucson, Ariz., 1989)

Cambridge History of Latin America, The, ed. Leslie Bethell, 10 vols (Cambridge 1984–92)

Carmagnani, Marcello, *El regreso de los dioses: El proceso de reconstitución de la identidad étnica en Oaxaca, siglos XVII y XVIII* (Mexico City, 1988)

Caro Baroja, Julio, *Vidas mágicas e Inquisición*, 2 vols (Madrid, 1967)

Carpanetto, D., and Ricuperati, G., *Italy in the Age of Reason* (London, 1987)

Casini, Paolo, *Introduzione all'Illuminismo: Da Newton a Rousseau* (Bari, 1973)

Caso, Antonio, *Los calendarios prehispánicos* (Mexico City, 1967)

Castañega, Martín de, *Tratado muy sotil y bien fundado de las supersticiones y hechicerías y varios conjuros y abusiones y otras cosas tocantes al caso y de la posibilidad y remedio dellas* (Longroño, 1529)

Chadwick, Owen, *The Popes and European Revolutions* (Oxford, 1981)

Chevalier, François, *La formación de los grandes latifundios en México* (Mexico City, 1956)

Christian, William A., *Local Religion in Sixteenth-Century Spain* (Princeton, N. J., 1981)

Cigala, Francisco Ignacio, *Cartas al Ilustrísimo y Reverendísimo Maestro Fray Benito Gerónimo Feijóo, que le escribía sobre el 'Teatro Crítico Universal'* (Mexico City, 1760)

Ciruelo, Pedro, *Tratado en el qual se reprueuan todas las supersticiones y hechicerías* (Barcelona, 1628)

Clark, Stuart, 'Protestant Demonology: Sin, Superstition and Society', in B. Ankarloo and G. Henningsen, eds, *Early Modern Witchcraft* (Oxford, 1990)

Clavigero, Francisco Javier, *Historia antigua de México*, 4 vols (Mexico City, 1945)

Clendinnen, Inga, 'Disciplining the Indians: Franciscan Ideology and Missionary Violence in Yucatán', *Past and Present*, no. 94 (Feb. 1982)

———, 'The Cost of Courage in Aztec Society', *Past and Present*, no. 107, (May 1985)

———, *Ambivalent Conquests: Maya and Spaniard in Yucatán 1517-1570* (Cambridge, 1987)

———, *Aztecs: An Interpretation* (Cambridge, 1991)

Códice Xolotl, ed. C. E. Dibble, 2 vols (Mexico City, 1980)

Cohn, Norman, *Europe's Inner Demons: An Enquiry inspired by the Great Witch Hunt* (London, 1975)

Colón, Cristóbal, *Textos y documentos completos*, ed. Consuelo Varela (Madrid, 1982)

Constitutions of the Society of Jesus, The, trans. G. E. Ganss, S. J. (St Louis, Missouri, 1970)

Copleston, F. C., *A History of Philosophy. Volume III: Ockham to Suárez*

(London and New York, 1953)

Cortés, Hernán, *Cartas de relación*, ed. M. Alcalá, 10th edn (Mexico City, 1978)

Davies, Brian, *The Thought of Thomas Aquinas* (Oxford, 1993 edn)

Dawson, Christopher, *Religion and Culture* (London, 1948)

————, *Religion and the Rise of Western Culture* (London, 1950)

————, *Mediaeval Essays* (London and New York, 1953)

Delumeau, Jean, *Catholicism between Luther and Voltaire: A New View of the Counter-Reformation*, ed. John Bossy (London, 1977)

Descartes, René, *Philosophical Letters*, trans. A. Kenny (Oxford, 1970)

————, *Oeuvres de Descartes*, ed. C. Adam and P. Tannery, vol. 1 (Paris, 1973)

Díaz del Castillo, Bernal, *Historia verdadera de la conquista de la Nueva España* (various edns)

Duffy, Eamon, *The Stripping of the Altars: Traditional Religion in England c1400–c1580* (New Haven and London, 1992)

Durán, Diego, *Historia de las Indias de Nueva España e islas de Tierra Firme*, 2 vols (Mexico City, 1967)

Elliot, John H., *The Old World and the New* (Cambridge, 1970)

————, *Imperial Spain* (Harmondsworth, 1970)

Escalona y Calatayud, Juan Joseph de, *Instrucción a la Perfecta Vida: Máximas para su logro a personas de todos Estados: Mandadas a escribir a un Clérigo Sacerdote, domiciliario del estado de Michoacán y sacadas a Luz para el Aprovechamiento de sus Ovejas* (Mexico City, 1737)

Escobar, Matías de, *América Thebaida, Vitas Patrum de los Religiosos ermitaños de N. P. San Agustín*, 2nd edn (Mexico City, 1924)

Espinosa, Isidro Félix de, *Chrónica Apostólica y Seráfica de todos los Colegios de Propaganda Fide de esta Nueva España*, ed. L. Gómez Canedo (Washington, D. C., 1964)

Evans, R. J. W., *The Making of the Habsburg Monarchy 1550–1700: An Interpretation* (Oxford, 1979)

Farriss, Nancy M., *Maya Society under Colonial Rule: The Collective Enterprise of Survival* (Princeton, N. J., 1984)

Feria, Pédro de, *Revelación sobre la reincidencia en sus idolatrías de los indios del obispado de Chiapa después de treinta años de cristianos* in *Tratado de las idolatrías*, ed. F. del Passo y Troncoso, 2 vols (Mexico City, 1953)

Fernández de Oviedo, Gonzalo, *Historia general y natural de las Indias*, ed. J. Pérez de Tudela Bueso, Biblioteca de Autores Españoles, 5 vols (Madrid, 1959)

Finnis, John, *Natural Law and Natural Rights* (Oxford, 1980)

Flint, Valerie, *The Rise of Magic* (Oxford, 1991)

Foucault, Michel, *Moi, Pierre Rivière, ayant égorgé ma mère, ma soeur et mon frère* (Paris, 1973)

———, *The History of Sexuality: An Introduction*, trans. R. Hurley (Harmondsworth, 1981)

Freud, Sigmund, *Standard edition of Complete Psychological Works*, vol. xix (London, 1961)

Gentilcore, David, *From Bishop to Witch: The System of the Sacred in Early Modern Terra d'Otranto* (Manchester and New York, 1992)

Gerbi, Antonello, *La natura delle Inde nuove* (Milan and Naples, 1975)

Ginzburg, Carlo, *The Night Battles: Witchcraft and Agrarian Cults in the Sixteenth and Seventeenth Centuries* (London 1983)

Girard, René, *Violence and the Sacred* (Baltimore, Md, 1977)

———, *Le Bouc Emissaire* (Paris, 1982)

Godwin, Jocelyn, *Athanasius Kircher: A Renaissance Man and the Quest for Lost Knowledge* (London, 1979)

Gómez Canedo, Lino, *Sierra Gorda: un típico enclave misional en el centro de México* (Pachuca, 1976)

Gonzalbo Aizpuru, Pilar, 'Del tercero al cuarto concilio provincial mexicano, 1585–1771', *Historia Mexicana* 35 (1), 1986

González Casanova, Pablo, *El misoneísmo y la modernidad cristiana en el siglo XVIII* (Mexico City, 1948)

González de Rosende, Antonio, *Vida del Ilustríssimo y Excelentíssimo señor Don Juan de Palafox y Mendoza* (Madrid, 1762)

Greenleaf, R. E., *Zumárraga and the Mexican Inquisition 1536–1543* (Washington, D. C., 1961)

Gruzinski, Serge 'Le filet déchiré: Sociétés indigènes, occidentalisation et domination dans le Mexique central, XVIe–XVIIIe siècles', 4 vols (Thèse de doctorat ès lettres, Paris, 1985)

———, *Man-Gods in the Mexican Highlands: Indian Power and Colonial Society 1520–1800* (Stanford, Calif., 1989)

Gruzinski, S. and Sallmann, J.-M., 'Une source d'ethnohistoire: les vies de "vénérables" dans l'Italie méridionale et le Mexique baroques', *Mélanges de l'école française de Rome*, vol.88 (1976)

Harl, K. W., 'Sacrifice and Pagan Belief in Fifth- and Sixth-Century Byzantium', *Past and Present*, no. 128 (Aug. 1990)

Hodgen, Margaret, *Early Anthropology in the Sixteenth and Seventeenth Centuries* (Philadelphia, 1964)

Humboldt, Alexander von, *Vues des Cordillères et monumens des peuples indigènes de l'Amérique* (Paris, 1810)

Hvidfeldt, Arild, *Teotl and Ixiptlatli: Some Central Concepts in Ancient Mexican Religion* (Copenhagen, 1958)

Israel, Jonathan, *Race, Class and Politics in Colonial Mexico 1610–1670* (Oxford, 1975)

———, *European Jewry in the Age of Mercantilism 1550–1750* (Oxford, 1985)

Ixtlilxóchitl, Fernando de Alva, *Obras históricas*, ed. E. O'Gorman, 2 vols (Mexico City, 1975)

Jones, Grant D., *Maya Resistance to Spanish Rule: Time and History on a Colonial Frontier* (Albuquerque, N. Mex, 1989)

Kamen, Henry, *The Phoenix and the Flame: Catalonia and the Counter-Reformation* (New Haven and London, 1993)

Kenny, Anthony, *The Legacy of Wittgenstein* (Oxford, 1984)

———, *The Metaphysics of Mind* (Oxford, 1989)

———, *Aquinas on Mind* (London and New York, 1993)

Kerr, Fergus, *Theology after Wittgenstein* (Oxford, 1986)

Kircher, Athanasius, *Iter Exstaticum Coeleste* (Wurzburg, 1660)

Knox, R. A., *Enthusiasm: A Chapter in the History of Religion with Special Reference to the XVII and XVIII Centuries* (Oxford, 1950)

Kolakowski, Leszek, *Cristianos sin iglesia: La conciencia religiosa y el vínculo confesional en el siglo XVII*, trans. F. Pérez Gutiérrez (Madrid, 1982)

Kramer, H., and Sprenger, J., *Malleus Maleficarum*, ed. and trans. Montague Summers (New York, 1971)

Lafitau, Joseph-François, *Moeurs des sauvages américains comparées aux moeurs des premiers temps*, 2 vols, (Paris, 1724)

Las Casas, Bartolomé de, *Apologética Historia Sumaria*, ed. E. O'Gorman, 2 vols (Mexico City, 1967)

———, *Apologética Historia*, ed. J. Pérez de Tudela Bueso, 2 vols, Biblioteca de Autores Españoles (Madrid, 1958)

Lea, H. C., *Materials towards a History of Witchcraft* (Philadelphia, 1939)

Le Goff, Jacques, 'Les mentalités: une histoire ambiguë', in idem, *Faire de l'histoire* (Paris, 1974)

Leibniz, Gottfried Wilhelm, *Philosophical Essays*, trans. R. Ariew and D. Garber (Indianapolis and Cambridge, 1989)

Leonard, Irving, *Don Carlos de Sigüenza y Góngora: A Mexican Savant of the Seventeenth Century* (Berkeley, Calif., 1929)

Le Roi Ladurie, Emmanuel, *Montaillou* (Harmondsworth, 1980)

Lettres spirituelles du P. Jean-Joseph Surin de la Compagnie de Jésus, ed. L. Midhel and F. Cavallera, 2 vols (Toulouse, 1926–8)

Lilla, Mark, *G. B. Vico: The Making of an Anti-Modern* (Cambridge, Mass., and London, 1993)

Llaguno, J. A., *La condición jurídica del Indio y el tercer concilio mexicano* (Mexico City, 1963)

Lockhart, James, *Nahuas and Spaniards: Postconquest Central Mexican History and Philology* (Stanford, Calif., 1991)

————, *The Nahuas after the Conquest: A Social and Cultural History of the Indians of Central Mexico, Sixteenth Through Eighteenth Centuries* (Stanford, Calif., 1992)

López de Araujo, Bernardo, *Centinela médico-aristotélico contra scépticos* (Madrid, 1725)

López de Gómara, Francisco, *Primera Parte de la Historia General de las Indias*, Biblioteca de Autores Españoles, vol. 22 (Madrid, 1852)

MacCormack, Sabine, "The Heart has its Reasons": Predicaments of Missionary Christianity in Early Colonial Peru', *Hispanic American Historical Review*, 65 (3) (Aug. 1985)

————, *Religion in the Andes: Vision and Imagination in Early Colonial Peru* (Princeton, N.J., 1991)

MacIntyre, Alasdair, *Whose Justice? Which Rationality?* (London, 1988)

————, *Three Rival Versions of Moral Enquiry* (London, 1990)

Magliabecchi: Libro de la vida que los indios antiguamente hacían, facsimile edn (Berkeley, Calif., 1903)

Mali, Joseph, *The Rehabilitation of Myth: Vico's 'New Science'* (Cambridge, 1992)

Matute, Alvaro, *Lorenzo Boturini y el pensamiento histórico de Vico*, ed. Miguel León Portilla (Mexico City, 1976)

McBride, G. M., *Land Systems of Mexico* (New York, 1923)

McClelland, I. L., *Ideological Hesitancy in Spain 1700–1750* (Liverpool, 1991)

McManners, John, *Death and the Enlightenment: Changing Attitudes to Death in Eighteenth-Century France* (Oxford, 1985)

Menghi, Girolamo, *Flagellum Daemonum: Exorcismos terribiles, potentissimos et efficaces* (Venice, 1587)

Mestre, Antonio, *El mundo intelectual de Mayáns* (Valencia, 1978)

Miqueroena, Agustín de, *Vida de la Venerable Madre Sor Michaela Josepha de la Purificación: Religiosa de velo y choro del observantíssimo convento de Señor San Joseph de Carmelitas Descalzas de la ciudad de Puebla del que fue cinco veces priora* (Mexico City, 1755)

The Mission to Asia. Narratives and Letters of the Franciscan Missionaries in Mongolia and China in the Thirteenth and Fourteenth Centuries, ed. C. Dawson (London, 1980)

Molinos, Miguel de, *Guida espiritual que desembaraza el alma y la conduce por el camino para alcanzar la perfecta contemplación y el rico tesoro de la interior paz* (Rome, 1675)

Momigliano, Arnaldo, 'Vico's *Scienza nuova*: Roman "bestioni" and Roman "eroi"', *History and Theory*, V:1 (1966)

Montesquieu, Charles Louis de Secondat, Baron de, *Oeuvres complètes de Montesquieu*, ed. A. Masson, 3 vols (Paris, 1950–5)

Mörner, Magnus, *Race Mixture in the History of Latin America* (Boston, 1967)

Motolinía, Toribio de, *Historia de los Indios de la Nueva España*, ed. E.
O'Gorman (Mexico City, 1973)
Muñoz Camargo, Diego, *Historia de Tlaxcala* (Mexico City, 1947)
————, *Descripción de la ciudad y provincia de Tlaxcala de las Indias y del Mar Océano*, ed. René Acuña (Mexico City, 1981)
Murray, Alexander, 'Missionaries and Magic in Dark-Age Europe', *Past and Present*, no. 136 (Aug. 1992)
Murray, Gilbert, *Five Stages of Greek Religion* (Oxford, 1925)

Nutini, Hugo G., 'Syncretism and Acculturation: The Historical
Development of the Cult of the Patron Saint in Tlaxcala, Mexico
(1519–1670)', *Ethnology*, 15, no. 3 (July 1976)
————, *Ritual Kinship*, 2 vols (Princeton, N. J., 1980–84)

Oberman, Heiko A., 'The Reorientation of the Fourteenth Century', in A.
Marieu and A. Paravicini Bagliani, eds, *Studi sul XIV secolo in memoria di Anneliese Maier* (Rome, 1981)
————, '*Via Antiqua* and *Via moderna*: Late Medieval Prolegomena to Early Reformation Thought', *Journal of the History of Ideas* (1987)
O'Gorman, Edmundo, *Destierro de sombras: Luz en el origen de la imagen y culto de Nuestra Señora de Guadalupe del Tepeyac* (Mexico City, 1986)

Paci, Enzo, *Ingens Sylva: Saggio sulla filosofia di G. B. Vico* (Verona, 1949)
Pagden, Anthony, *The Fall of Natural Man: The American Indian and the Origins of Comparative Ethnology* (Cambridge, 1982)
————, 'The Reception of the "New Philosophy" in Eighteenth-Century Spain', *Journal of the Warburg and Courtauld Institutes*, LI (1988)
————, *Spanish Imperialism and the Political Imagination: Studies in European and Spanish-American Social and Political Theory 1513–1830* (New Haven and London, 1990)
————, *European Encounters with the New World: From Renaissance to Romanticism* (New Haven and London, 1993)
Papeles de la Nueva España, ed. Francisco del Passo y Troncoso, 7 vols (Madrid, 1905–6)
Paz, Octavio, *Sor Juana: Her Life and Work* (London, 1988)
Peñalosa, Joaquín Antonio, *El Diablo en México* (Mexico City, 1970)
Pérez de Ribas, Andrés, *Historia de los triunfos de nuestra Santa Fe entre gentes de las más bárbaras y fieras del nuevo orbe* (Madrid, 1645)
Pérez-Marchand, Monelisa Lina, *Dos etapas ideológicas del siglo XVIII en México a través de los papeles de la Inquisición* (Mexico City, 1945)
Peters, Edward, *The Magician, the Witch and the Law* (Sussex, 1978)
Ponce, Pedro, *Breve relación de los dioses y ritos de la gentilidad* in *Tratado de las idolatrías*, ed. F. del Passo y Troncoso, 2 vols (Mexico City, 1953)
Powell, P. W., *Soldiers, Indians and Silver* (Berkeley, Calif., 1969)

Proceso inquisitorial del Cacique de Texcoco, ed. Luis González Obregón (Mexico City, 1910)

Procesos de indios idólatras y hechiceros, ed. Luis González Obregón (Mexico City, 1912)

Ravicz, M. Ekdahl, *Early Colonial Religious Drama in Mexico: From Tompantli to Golgotha* (Washington, D.C., 1970)

Reeves, Marjorie, *The Influence of Prophecy in the Late Middle Ages: A Study of Joachimism* (Oxford, 1969)

Relación de las ceremonias y ritos y población y gobierno de los Indios de la provincia de Michoacán, ed. José Tudela and José Corona Núñez (Morelia, 1977)

Ripalda, Jerónimo de, *Doctrina Christiana, con una exposición breve...* (Burgos, 1591)

Ronan, Charles E., *Francisco Javier Clavigero S. J. (1731–1787), figure of the Mexican Enlightenment: His life and works* (Rome and Chicago, 1977)

Rorty, Richard, *Contingency, Irony and Solidarity* (Cambridge, 1989)

Rubin, Miri, 'Desecration of the Host: The Birth of an Accusation', in *Christianity and Judaism*, ed. Diana Wood (Oxford and Cambridge, Mass., 1992)

Rudwin, Maximilian, *The Devil in Legend and Literature* (La Salle, Ill., 1959)

Ruiz de Alarcón, Hernando, *Tratado de las supersticiones y costumbres gentilicias que hoy viven entre los naturales de esta Nueva España*, in F. del Passo y Troncoso, *Tratado de las idolatrías*, 2 vols (Mexico City, 1953)

Russell, J. B., *The Devil: Perceptions of Evil from Late Antiquity to Primitive Christianity* (Ithaca and London, 1977)

——, *Satan: The Early Christian Tradition* (Ithaca and London, 1981)

——, *Lucifer: The Devil in the Middle Ages* (Ithaca and London, 1984)

——, *Mephistopheles: The Devil in the Modern World* (Ithaca and London, 1986)

Sahagún, Bernardino de, *Códice Florentino*, facsimile edn, 3 vols (Mexico City, 1979)

——, *Historia general de las cosas de Nueva España*, ed. Angel Ma. Garibay, 6th edn (Mexico City, 1985)

——, *Coloquios y Doctrina Cristiana*, ed. M. León Portilla (Mexico City, 1986)

Sánchez de Castro, José Jerónimo, *Vida de la V. M. Sor Antonia de la Madre de Dios, Religiosa Agustina Recolecta, y Fundadora del Convento de Santa Mónica de la Puebla de los Angeles, y después en el de Ntra. Sra. de la Soledad de la Ciudad de Antequera, Valle de Oaxaca. Escrita por su... confesor... quien la consagra a María Santíssima, señora nuestra en su dolorosíssima soledad...* (Mexico City, 1747)

Santander y Torres, Sebastián de, *Vida de la Venerable Madre María de San*

Joseph, *Religiosa Agustina Recolecta, fundadora de los conventos de Santa Mónica de la Ciudad de Puebla, y después en el de la Soledad de Oaxaca* (Mexico City, 1723)

Saugnieux, Joël, *Le Jansénisme espagnol du XVIIIe siècle* (Oviedo, 1975)

——, *Les Jansénistes et le renouveau de la prédication dans l'Espagne de la seconde moitié du XVIIIe siècle* (Lyons, 1976)

Scribner, R. W., *Popular Culture and Popular Movements in Germany* (London, 1987)

Select Documents illustrating the Four Voyages of Columbus, ed. Cecil Jane (London, 1930)

Serna, Jacinto de, *Manual de ministros de Indios para el conocimiento de sus idolatrías y extirpación de ellas*, in *Colección de documentos inéditos para la historia de España*, vol. 104

Sleigh, R. C., *Leibniz and Arnauld: A Commentary on their Correspondence* (New Haven and London, 1990)

Spink, J. S., *French Free Thought from Gassendi to Voltaire* (London, 1960)

Spinoza, Baruch de, *Tractatus Theologico-Politicus* in *Works of Spinoza*, ed. R. H. M. Elwes (New York, 1951)

Suárez, Francisco, *Opera*, 28 vols (Paris, 1856-78)

Surin, Jean-Joseph, *Les fondements de la vie spirituelle tirés du livre de l'Imitation de Jésus-Christ* (Paris, 1667)

——, *Triomphe de l'amour divin sur les puissances de l'enfer en la possession de la Mère Prieure des Ursulines de Loudun* (Avignon, 1829)

——, *La guide spirituelle pour la perfection, divisée en sept parties* (Paris, 1836)

Taussig, Michael T., *The Devil and Commodity Fetishism in South America* (North Carolina, 1980)

Taylor, Charles, *Sources of the Self: The making of the Modern Identity* (Cambridge, 1992 edn)

——, *The Ethics of Authenticity* (Cambridge, Mass., 1992)

Teresa of Avila, St, *Interior Castle ('The Mansions')* trans. E. Allison Peers (London, 1974 edn)

Thomas, Keith, *Religion and the Decline of Magic* (Harmondsworth, 1978 edn)

Torquemada, Juan de, *Monarquía Indiana*, 3 vols (Mexico City, 1969)

Trabulse, Elías, *El Círculo Roto* (Mexico City, 1982)

——, *Historia de la Ciencia en México*, 4 vols. (Mexico City, 1983-5)

——, 'Clavigero, historiador de la ilustración mexicana', in *Francisco Javier Clavigero en la Ilustración mexicana*, ed. Alfonso Martínez Rosales (Mexico City, 1988)

Tratado de las idolatrías, supersticiones, dioses, ritos, hechicerías y otras costumbres gentilicias de las razas aborígenes de México, ed. Francisco del Passo y Troncoso, 2 vols (Mexico City, 1953)

Trevor-Roper, H. R., 'The European Witch Craze of the Sixteenth and Seventeenth Centuries', in idem, *Religion, the Reformation and Social*

Change, 3rd edn (London, 1984)

———, *Princes and Artists: Patronage and Ideology at Four Habsburg Courts* (London, 1991 edn)

Trextler, R. C., 'We think they act: Clerical readings of Missionary Theatre in Sixteenth-Century New Spain', in S.L. Kaplan, *Understanding Popular Culture: Europe from the Middle Ages to the 19th Century* (Berlin, 1984)

Valdés, Joseph Eugenio, *Vida admirable y penitente de la V. M. Sor Sebastiana Josepha de la SS. Trinidad, Religiosa de Coro y velo negro en el Religiosíssimo convento de Señoras Religiosas Clarisas de San Juan de la Penitencia de esta Ciudad de México* (Mexico City, 1765)

Vaughan, Frederick, *The Political Philosophy of Giambattista Vico: An Introduction to La Scienza Nuova* (The Hague, 1972)

Vega, Garcilaso de la, *Comentarios Reales de los Incas*, 2 vols (Buenos Aires, 1943)

———, *Historia General del Perú*, 3 vols (Buenos Aires, 1944)

Vico, Giambattista, *The Autobiography of Giambattista Vico*, trans. M. H. Fisch and T. G. Bergin (Ithaca, N.Y., 1944)

———, *The New Science*, ed. and trans. T.G. Bergin and M.H. Fisch (Ithaca, N.Y., 1948)

———, *De universi juris uno principio et fine uno liber unus* [1720], in *Opere giuridiche*, ed. Paolo Cristofolini (Florence, 1974)

———, *De constantia jurisprudentis liber alter* [1721], in *Opere giurudiche* (Florence, 1974)

———, *On the Most Ancient Wisdom of the Italians* [1710], trans. L. M. Palmer (Ithaca, N.Y., 1988)

Villavicencio, Diego Jaymes Ricardo, *Luz y método de confesar idólatras*, 2 vols (Puebla, 1692)

Villoro, Luis, *Los grandes momentos del indigenismo en México* (Mexico City, 1987 edn)

Vitoria, Francisco de, *De Magia*, in *Obras: relecciones teológicas* (Madrid, 1960)

Voltaire, François Marie Arouet de, *Candide*, ed. John Butt (London, 1947)

Walker, D. P., *The Decline of Hell: Seventeenth-Century Discussions of Eternal Torment* (London, 1964)

Whitehead, A. N., *Science and the Modern World* (Cambridge, 1953 edn)

Whitmore, P. J. S., *The Order of Minims in Seventeenth-Century France* (The Hague, 1967)

Wittgenstein, Ludwig, *Philosophical Investigations*, trans. G. E. M. Anscombe (Oxford, 1953)

———, *Remarks on Frazer's Golden Bough*, ed. Rush Rhees (Retford, 1979)

Index